Navaratri

Navaratri
When Devi Comes Home

Edited by
Bibek Debroy *and* Anuradha Goyal

RUPA

Published by
Rupa Publications India Pvt. Ltd 2021
7/16, Ansari Road, Daryaganj
New Delhi 110002

Sales Centres:
Allahabad Bengaluru Chennai
Hyderabad Jaipur Kathmandu
Kolkata Mumbai

Copyright © Bibek Debroy and Anuradha Goyal 2021

The views and opinions expressed in this book are the authors' own and the facts are as reported by them which have been verified to the extent possible, and the publishers are not in any way liable for the same.

All rights reserved.

No part of this publication may be reproduced, transmitted, or stored in a retrieval system, in any form or by any means, electronic, mechanical, photocopying, recording or otherwise, without the prior permission of the publisher.

ISBN: 978-93-5520-045-7

First impression 2021

10 9 8 7 6 5 4 3 2 1

The moral right of the authors has been asserted.

Printed at Parksons Graphics Pvt. Ltd, Mumbai

This book is sold subject to the condition that it shall not, by way of trade or otherwise, be lent, resold, hired out, or otherwise circulated, without the publisher's prior consent, in any form of binding or cover other than that in which it is published.

Contents

Introduction   vii

1. Bhavani, Sharika and Sharada in Kashmir — 1
2. Devi Visits Her Home in Bengal — 13
3. Kolu and Ayudha in Tamil Nadu — 31
4. Home in the Himalayas, Shakti in Himachala — 45
5. The Flowers of Telangana — 63
6. Bali and Puja in Nepal — 79
7. Mrinmayee Murti in Odisha — 96
8. Kerala Marg in Uttar Pradesh — 112
9. Temples and Tribes in Andhra — 129
10. Satvika in Punjab and Haryana — 143
11. Vidya Dayini in Kerala — 159
12. Dandiya and Garba in Gujarat — 172
13. Shakti in the Shivaliks of Jammu — 180
14. Kamakhya of Kamarupa in Assam — 189
15. Mannami and Nave Jevan in Konkan — 195
16. Kuladevis in Rajasthan — 208

Bibliography   221
About the Contributor   227

Introduction

ANURADHA GOYAL AND BIBEK DEBROY

In some form or other, Navaratri is celebrated throughout India, and even abroad, wherever Indians and the Hindu influence have spread. Navaratri brings to mind the visual of colourful and energetic Garba from the western coast of India and, at the same time, the warm enthusiasm of Durga Puja pandals from the eastern parts. Talk to Indians from any nook and corner of the country and they will tell you their own ways of celebrating these auspicious nine days and nights. Like most things Indian, there is a common thread that runs across all Navaratri celebrations around India. The manifestations of expressions, though, are as varied as they can get. If we could zoom into the festivities, we would find a unique version of celebrations that is followed in each community or, perhaps, even each family. Most of us know our version of Navaratri, the way we celebrate it. Other popular versions of celebrations are more of trends that we sometimes follow and enjoy with people around us, and the not so popular versions remain undiscovered.

People sometimes say 'Navaratra'. Since the word is 'ratri' in Sanskrit, and of the feminine gender, the occasion should really be called Navaratri, not Navaratra. Navaratri simply means nine nights—nine nights that are special. Festivals are decided according to the lunar day (known as tithi) and lunar month, not the solar calendar. The lunar tithi does not necessarily correspond exactly to the solar day. These nine lunar tithis are known as Pratipada, Dvitiya, Tritiya, Chaturthi, Panchami, Shashthi, Saptami, Ashtami and Navami: the first lunar day to the ninth. Of course, festivities can culminate on the following Dashami, the tenth day.

Every paksha (lunar fortnight) has this cycle of nine days and nine nights. The moon waxes during shukla paksha (the bright lunar fortnight) and wanes during krishna paksha (the dark lunar fortnight). Krishna paksha is considered to be the time of the *pitris* (ancestors or manes). Therefore, typically, no worship of Devas and Devis takes place during krishna paksha.[1] That occurs during shukla paksha. Hence, though there is a Navaratri cycle in krishna paksha too, Navaratri celebrations occur in shukla paksha, in the paksha that begins with Pratipada and ends with purnima.[2] Those 12 shukla paksha Navaratris every year are therefore special. Four of these are more popular than others—(1) Sharada/Ashvina Navaratri; (2) Vasanta/Chaitra Navaratri; (3) Magha Navaratri and (4) Ashada Navaratri, named after the lunar months of Ashvina (September/October), Chaitra (March/April), Magha (January/February) and Ashada (June/July). Of these, Magha and Ashada Navaratris are known as Gupta Navaratris, the word 'gupta' meaning hidden or secret. Therefore, Devi is worshipped during these two Navaratris, respectively in winter and during the monsoon, but that worship is not openly done. That leaves Ashvina Navaratri and Chaitra Navaratri, corresponding to autumn and spring.

Sharada/Ashvina Navaratri is about the worship of Devi. There is an ancient tradition of Devi worship in India, much before what is perceived as recorded history. Popular perceptions of history often project a neat and linear timeline, with a Vedic period, followed by an Itihasa-Purana period,[3] the latter being one where Devi comes into prominence. As texts, the composition of the Itihasa-Purana corpus follows that of the Vedic samhitas, but that does not imply that

---

[1] Deva/Devata is the masculine, while Devi/Devataa is the feminine. Etymologically, Deva/Devi means the shining one, the resplendent one.
[2] Purnima is the night of the full moon. Amavasya is the night of the new moon. In some parts of India, the lunar month calculation ends with purnima. But there are also parts where the lunar month calculation ends with amavasya.
[3] Itihasa means the Ramayana and the Mahabharata. There are 18 major Puranas (known as Maha Puranas) and several minor Puranas (known as Upa Puranas).

these texts do not reflect earlier traditions and practices, regardless of whether there were formal temples or not. For example, that linear timeline of history hasn't been able to factor in excavations, old and recent, connected with the Indus-Sarasvati civilization, or the genealogy and historical timelines given in the Itihasa-Purana corpus. Among these old excavations, there is the 'Mother Goddess' sculpture, dated circa 2500 BCE, discovered in Mohenjodaro and now on display at the National Museum, Delhi. Among the newer ones, there are the sculptures found in Madhya Pradesh, such as those unearthed near the town of Baghor. The essays in this book have no intention of getting into that debate, except to point out that parallel, and not linear, traditions may have existed.

The common thread among all Navaratri celebrations is devotion to Devi, who is also the Prakriti or Nature manifested all around us, of which, we are a small part. These are the transition times, when seasons change and expect us to adjust accordingly. It is also the time to look inwards. The most popular among the four Navaratris is the Sharada Navaratri that, in a way, announces the onset of winter, celebrated during the first nine days of the bright fortnight of Ashvina month. Vasanta Navaratri, which ushers in the summer during Chaitra, is the second most celebrated. In some parts like Himachal Pradesh and Rajasthan, Vasanta Navaratri is more popular than Sharada Navaratri. It is also known as Ram Navaratri because the ninth day of this festival is also celebrated as Ram Navami—the day Shri Rama was born in Ayodhya in Treta Yuga. Sharada Navaratri, on the other hand, culminates in Dussehra, the day Ravana of Lanka was defeated by Shri Rama. Gupta Navaratris are rarely observed by the common people. In fact, most people today do not even know about these days. They are primarily observed by those who follow the Shakta or the Goddess path. Mostly, Sadhana, a prescribed spiritual routine, is undertaken by people during these times as per their own lineage and there is hardly any public celebration.

Devi Bhagavata Purana says that both the Vasanta and Sharada

Ritu or seasons are difficult for human beings as they give birth to many diseases. So, one should pray to the Goddess and observe fasts to tide over this seasonal transition. It is interesting to see that fasting is a more prevalent phenomenon in North India, where the weather changes are far starker, than in the southern parts, where the changes are at best subtle. This is how the rituals follow the rhythm of nature locally. The book reveals many such aspects of the celebrations.

Devi comes home or to the community and stays with her devotees for nine days and nine nights. She may come in the form of a Murti, a Yantra, which is a geometrical representation of the Deity, or a *Kalasha*, a floral arrangement or a collage on the wall, but she comes every Navaratri like an ardently disciplined mother. In fact, she is created by devotees the way they envision her, with whatever material is traditionally available. We could also say that Navaratri is essentially the time between Devi's arrival and departure. Bengalis treat this like the visit of a married daughter to her father's home, while in most parts of India, for women and girls, she comes just as a mother.

The whole process of the creation of Devi, worshipping her for nine days or nine nights and then immersing her in water so that she merges back with the elements she was created from in the first place, is a microcosm of how the rhythm of the universe works. Srishti (Creation), Sthiti (Sustenance) and Laya (Dissolution) is how the cosmic cycle moves. Prakriti manifests as creation; while the creation lasts, there are smaller cycles of creation, sustenance and dissolution within the larger cycle and finally there is dissolution— merging back into the same thing from which the creation sprouted. This is what is recreated, re-enacted and relived during the Navaratri festivals, time and again. It is a subtle reminder of the momentary nature of our own lives and the fact that we all are created from the same five elements and will eventually merge back into them. Observed year after year, it makes its way into our memories and our psyche, each time reinforcing that what has been created must unify with the elements of its origin after it has served its purpose. Devi's creation itself takes myriad forms, adding a style of art to the cultural map of the region. For example, the Mrinmayi or clay Murtis of Bengal or Odisha, which are skilfully carved by potters, are found in places like Kumartuli in Kolkata, but also in every village and town; or the lively floral arrangements of Bathukamma in Telangana, which are created every day during Navaratri and immersed at the end of the day; or even the decoration of pandals across the country which take on different themes.

As texts go, one should mention 'Devi Suktam'. The word 'suktam' literally means 'spoken well' and is a hymn, lauding a particular Deva or Devi. There are several such Devi Suktams from different texts—(1) 'Devi Suktam' (*Rig Veda*); (2) 'Shri Suktam' (*Rig Veda*); (3) 'Devi Suktam' (from tantra texts); (4) 'Durga Suktam' (*Taittiriya Aranyaka*); and (5) 'Ratri Suktam' or 'Devi Stotram' (from *Durga Saptashati*). The 'Devi Suktam' from the Rig Veda has Devi proclaiming her supremacy over every thing and every other divinity.[4] These Suktams are often recited at the time of Navaratri celebrations. Devi is worshipped through Mantra, Tantra and Yantra. Literally, Mantra is something that restrains the mind, Tantra is something that restrains the body and Yantra is something that restrains in general. These Suktams are nothing but Mantras.

Other than the ones from the *Rig Veda*, the others, even when they are from tantra texts, find their origin in a section of the *Markandeya Purana* known as 'Devi Mahatmya' or 'Chandi'. From the perspective of Devi's worship, the *Markandeya Purana* is the most important in the Itihasa-Purana corpus. This should not be taken to mean that stories about Shiva and Parvati do not occur elsewhere in the Itihasa-Purana corpus. For example, not only does the Mahabharata mention both, the 'Anushasana Parva' of

---

[4]Rig Veda, 10th mandala, 125th suktam. One verse states, 'यं कामये तं तमुग्रं कृणोमि तं ब्रह्माणं तमृषिं तं सुमेधाम्' 'I make whoever I wish—exalted, a brahmin, a rishi and extremely intelligent.' (English translation by editors.) 'Shri Suktam' is about Shri (Lakshmi), one of Devi's manifestations.

the Mahabharata describes an incident where Uma (another name for Parvati) tells Shiva about the dharma of women. The *Valmiki Ramayana* has several references to Shiva and Parvati stories.[5] Specific stories about Parvati tell of Sati and her father Daksha's yajna,[6] the Shakti Peethas,[7] Sati being reborn as Parvati, Parvati's tapasya to get Shiva as a husband, Shiva and Parvati's marriage, the births of their sons Skanda and Ganesha and so on. Iconography, sculptures and worship reflect these stories. Other than the *Markandeya Purana* and *Devi Bhagavata Purana*, one ought to mention the Linga and Skanda Puranas from the Itihasa-Purana corpus.[8] 'Lalita Sahasranama', which gives us 1,000 names of Lalita, a manifestation of Devi, is from the *Brahmanda Purana*. Devi is worshipped in many forms, such as Nava Durga or the nine forms of Durga—Shailaputri, Brahmacharini, Chandraghanta, Kushmanda, Skandamata, Katyayani, Kalaratri, Mahagauri and Siddhidhatri. Especially in tantra forms of worship, she is worshipped as the 10 Mahavidyas—Kali, Tara, Tripurasundari (or Shodashi), Bhuvaneshwari, Tripurabhairavi, Chhinnamasta, Dhumavati, Bagalamukhi, Matangi and Kamala. There is local worship of Devi, often specific to certain temples, at other times of the year. In Panchayatana Puja (worship of five Murtis), it is customary for Devi to be worshipped along with Shiva, Vishnu, Surya and the specific *ishta devata*.[9]

However, if it is specific to Devi's worship during Navaratri and stories connected with the asura Mahishasura, the *Markandeya Purana* is the most important. Though this major Purana has other

---

[5]The *Valmiki Ramayana* is not the only Sanskrit Ramayana. There are also the *Adhyatma Ramayana* and the *Yogavasishtha Ramayana*. In addition, there are non-Sanskrit versions of both the Mahabharata and Ramayana stories. Tulsidas's *Ramcharitmanas* is an example of this. There is also something like Kalidasa's *Kumarasambhavam*.

[6]Where Sati gave up her body.

[7]The 51 (alternatively 52) sacred places where parts of Sati's body fell.

[8]Not to forget the *Hari Vamsha*, which is not a Purana, strictly speaking.

[9]Literally, the desired divinity, cherished personally by the worshipper.

important segments, we have in mind 'Devi Mahatmya' or 'Chandi'.[10] 'Devi Mahatmya' means 'the greatness of Devi'.[11] It tells us the story of King Suratha and the vaishya Samadhi. Reduced to a miserable state, they are advised by Rishi Sumedha to worship Devi.

When the world was threatened by Madhu and Kaitabha, Brahma prayed to Devi to save creation. The prayer of Brahma is the famous 'Ratri Suktam' or 'Devi Stotram'. This beautiful prayer to Devi is often recited at the time of Navaratri. Here is the translation:[12]

> You are the supreme goddess of the universe.[13] You are the cause behind the creation, preservation and destruction of the universe. I praise the illustrious Nidra. You are Vishnu's unmatched energy. You are Svaha. You are Svadha. You are Vashatkara.[14] Sound is your atman. Your sweet form eternally exists in aksharas.[15] You are established in the three matras.[16] In particular, you are always established in the half a matra that cannot be pronounced.[17] You are Sandhya. You are Savitri. O goddess! You are the supreme mother. You are the one who sustains the universe. You are the one who creates the universe. You are the one who protects it. O

---

[10] In the nineteenth century, Haraprasad Shastri found a copy of *Devi Mahatmya*, dated 998 CE, in the Royal Library in Kathmandu.

[11] In the Markandeya Purana proper, this has 590 shlokas. Since *Durga Saptashati* implies there are 700 shlokas, some additional shlokas are added to bring the total to 700. Devi Kavacha and Argala Stotram are examples of these.

[12] Reproduced from *The Markandeya Purana*, translated by Bibek Debroy, Penguin, 2019. This begins as: त्वं स्वाहा त्वं स्वधा त्वं हि वषट्कार: स्वरात्मिका।

[13] Vishveshvari.

[14] The exclamation 'Svaha' is uttered when offering oblations to Devas and Devis. The exclamation 'Svadha' is uttered when offering oblations to pitris. Vashatkara is the general exclamation 'Vashat'.

[15] Syllables.

[16] A matra is the time required to pronounce a short vowel. The three matras refer to 'O', 'U' and 'M' of OUM. The matras of OUM are identified with Brahma, Vishnu and Shiva.

[17] The nasal sound in OUM.

goddess! At the end, you are the one who always devours. At the time of creation, you are the one who is in the form of creation. At the time of preservation, you are the one who exists in the form of protection. Like that, at the time of the destruction of the universe, you are the form of destruction. You pervade the entire universe. You are Mahavidya.[18] You are Mahamaya. You are Mahamedha.[19] You are Mahasmriti.[20] You are Mahamoha.[21] You are Bhagavati. You are Mahadevi. You are Maheshvari. You are everything in Prakriti. You are the one who creates the three gunas.[22] You are Kalaratri.[23] You are Maharatri.[24] You are the terrible Moharatri.[25] You are Shri. You are Ishvari. You are modesty. You are intelligence. You are characterized by understanding. You are shame. You are nourishment. You are contentment. You are tranquillity. You are patience. You wield a sword. You wield a trident. You wield a club. You wield a chakra. Your form is terrible. You hold a conch-shell. You hold a bow and arrows. Your weapons are a bhushundi[26] and a bludgeon. You are gentle. You are gentler than that. Your gentleness is unlimited. You are exceedingly beautiful. You are the best. You are superior to the best. Indeed, you are the supreme goddess. You are everything that exists and you are everything that does not exist. Your atman is in everything. You are the power in everything. How can I possibly extol someone like you?

---

[18] Great knowledge.
[19] Great intellect.
[20] Great memory.
[21] Great delusion.
[22] The three gunas are sattva (identified with purity), rajas (identified with passion) and tamas (identified with darkness).
[23] The night of destruction.
[24] The great night.
[25] The night of delusion.
[26] Some kind of catapult or sling.

INTRODUCTION | xv

> You are the one who creates the universe. You are the one who preserves the universe. You are the one who destroys the universe. You have brought the great lord[27] under the subjugation of sleep. Who can possibly praise you? You have made Vishnu, Isha and me assume bodies. Who possesses the capacity to extol you? O goddess! Thus praised, please use your pervasive powers to confound these two unassailable asuras, Madhu and Kaitabha. Gently bring Achyuta, the lord of the universe, back to consciousness. For the sake of killing the two giant asuras, wake him up.

Vishnu woke up and killed Madhu and Kaitabha.

The second time there was a need for Devi to manifest herself was when Mahishasura oppressed the world. For the event of Mahishasura being killed by Devi, there is yet another beautiful prayer by Indra and the gods. Parts of this are also recited during Navaratri.[28]

> We bow down to you. O goddess! Use your trident to save us. O Ambika! Use your sword to save us. Use the sound of your bell and the twang of your bow-string to save us. O Chandika! Save us in the east. Save us in the west. Save us in the south. O Ishvari! Use your whirling trident to save us in the north. Your amiable form wanders around in the three worlds. There are also extremely terrible forms. Use all these to protect the world. O Ambika! Your delicate hands hold a sword, a trident, a mace and many other weapons. Use those to protect us from every direction.

The third time Devi manifested herself was to destroy the asuras Shumbha and Nishumbha. The gods prayed to her again. This too is a beautiful prayer, recited at the time of Navaratri.

---

[27]Narayana.
[28]Debroy, *The Markandeya Purana*.

The goddess is in all beings and is spoken of as consciousness. We bow down before her. We bow down. We prostrate ourselves. The goddess is in all beings in the form of intellect. We bow down before her. We bow down. We prostrate ourselves. The goddess is in all beings in the form of sleep. We bow down before her. We bow down. We prostrate ourselves.[29]

We are, of course, more familiar with this as:

या देवी सर्वभूतेषु चेतनेत्य भिधीयते। नमस्तस्यै नमस्तस्यै नमस्तस्यै नमो नम:॥
या देवी सर्वभूतेषु बुद्धिरूपेण संस्थिता। नमस्तस्यै नमस्तस्यै नमस्तस्यै नमो नम:॥
या देवी सर्वभूतेषु निद्रारूपेण संस्थिता। नमस्तस्यै नमस्तस्यै नमस्तस्यै नमो नम:॥

The 'Devi Mahatmya' section ends by mentioning there are several manifestations of Devi, not just these three, such as Vindhyavasini (who resides in the Vindhyas), Raktadantika (with red teeth), Shatakshi (with 100 eyes), Shakambhari (who bears vegetables), Durga (slayer of the Asura Durgama), Bhima (the terrible one), Bhrahmari (the bee) and so on.

To understand Devi's worship at the time of Navaratri, one should add *Devi Bhagavata Purana*, also known as *Devi Bhagavatam*. Though one cannot conclusively establish any dates, the composition of *Devi Bhagavata Purana* was clearly after the composition of *Markandeya Purana*. This has 12 Skandhas or sections and the seventh Skandha has the famous 'Devi Gita'. Since one has mentioned 'Devi Gita', one should mention *Devi Upanishad*, composed even later, a text that repeats some shlokas from 'Devi Gita'. There are also minor Puranas like *Kalika Purana* and *Chandi Purana*. Sculpture, iconography and worship are based on these texts. This book specifically documents local customs and worship associated with Devi's worship at the time of Navaratri. Though there are regional variations, all of them are based on a common origin and legacy of Devi worship.

---

[29]Debroy, *The Markandeya Purana*.

'Devi Mahatmya', also known as 'Durga Saptashati' in North India and 'Chandi Path' in East India, is often chanted during Navaratri across the length and breadth of the country. Chandi Homam is performed in almost all temples and many homes. The text talks about the killing of various asuras like Madhu-Kaitabha, Mahishasura, Shumbha-Nishumbha and Raktabeeja by Devi in her various forms, but what it expects us to do is identify our inner asuras that resemble those that were killed by Devi. Lalita Sahasranama—the thousand names of Shri Lalita Tripurasundari who killed the asura Bhandasura—is chanted very fondly in South India. *Bhavani Sahasranama* is chanted in Kashmir. *Devi Bhagavata*, being a rather long text of 18,000 verses, remains in the realms of temples and Sadhaks. The victories of Devi, as Shakti of all the Devatas, over various asuras mentioned in these texts are recited, reminding us of the Shakti within to defeat the asuras inside and around us. Apart from these Sanskrit texts, Devi bhajan and kirtana in the local languages are fondly sung during evening Arati and night-long jagratas.

It is not just a festival dedicated to the Shakti—the divine feminine—we also see women actively taking part in its celebrations. They come together for evening worship during all nine days, with the women of the neighbourhood or extended families gathering to worship Devi. Be it the evening worship of Sanjhi Puja in Punjab, Kaan Sakhiyan in Jammu or visits to see the neighbours' Golu decorations in Tamil Nadu or Andhra Pradesh, where at times the women of the family sleep together in the room where Golu is decorated, it is the time for women to bond and revere each other. Be it the Kanya Puja of North India or the Suvasini Puja of Konkan, women around us are worshipped as swarups of Devi near us as Kanya, Lakshmi and Sarasvati. In Telangana, for celebrating the goddess Bathukamma every day during Navaratri, women create the goddess with flowers, cook for her and sing and dance to please the goddess before sitting down to eat together. There is a sense of coming together and sharing. Sharing may come by way of eating together, worshipping together or by exchanging gifts with each other. A significant part of the Navaratri celebrations belongs to Kanyas—young unmarried girls. As Kanyas, they become the Devis whom the families worship. As yet to be married girls, their future dream life takes the form of prayers to the mother divine, to marry the husband of their dreams. To us, this represents a trusting, intimate relationship between the Jagat Janani—the universal mother and her daughters, where daughters share their deepest desires with her. As a beautiful future is only possible with a suitable companion, they pray and ask for one, but not without wishing for the prosperity of their brothers. In a way, they are also following in the footsteps of Parvati, who performed intense tapasya to get Shiva as her husband. Or Sita, who prayed to Bhavani after catching a glimpse of Shri Rama in the gardens of Mithila before her svayamvara that has been well captured by Goswami Tulsidas in *Ramcharitmanas*:

गई भवानी भवन बहोरी। बंदि चरन बोली कर जोरी।।
जय जय गिरिबरराज किसोरी। जय महेश मुख चंद चकोरी।।
जय गज बदन षडानन माता। जगत जननि दामिनि दुति गाता।।
नहिं तव आदि मध्य अवसाना। अमित प्रभाउ बेदु नहिं जाना।।
भव भव बिभव पराभव कारिनि। बिश्व बिमोहनि स्वबस बिहारिनि।।

Rukmini too prayed to Girija, as she waited for Sri Krishna to come and take her away with him to Dwarka. Now, who does not want to have a husband like Shiva, Rama or Krishna!

When we visualize all the women, dressed up in their finest colourful saris and jewellery, visiting each other and praying together to that Adi Shakti, of whom they are a part, they remind us of all the manifestations of Devi like Saptamatrikas, Yoginis, Mantrinis, etc. described in Devi's stories, in a way that make these stories come alive. It is as if the inner Shakti within them has been activated and tasked with disseminating her blessings. These images also take us to the sculptures that we see on all our temples—of Mangalas or auspicious women—that are an integral part of the temple and often demarcate the visual stories on the walls, standing between the bigger sculptures of primary deities. They are nothing but the manifestation of Shakti in her blissful, auspicious form, showering happiness on anyone who looks at her, and so are all the women during Navaratri.

Like most festivals, Navaratri is also an institutionalized way of nurturing your inner creativity. Invariably the celebrations involve creating the form of the goddess symbolically—in clay or with flowers, by decorating a kalasha or arranging dolls. One is also encouraged to look at all that nature and one's surroundings have to offer and use it—be it flowers, leaves, clay, colours or decorations. Traditionally, this also teaches you to create within the constraints of what is available around you. We rarely hear of materials being brought from elsewhere for the festival. These activities are mostly undertaken by women and girls in the family, who work like a team with elders guiding them and youngsters helping out and intuitively gathering the lessons of teamwork. The tradition passed between generations, and yet no two years see the same expression of creativity. The local, temporal current affairs like elections or sporting events or anything that occupies the minds may sneak into the creation, for do the festivals not revolve around our life and times? You just have to look at the different images that come up when you type 'Navaratri' in your browser's search window.

As you read about all the nuanced ceremonies described in the different essays, you will note that many of these are done in the evening—when the day is transitioning to night. Sanjh, Sayam or Sayankala—it is called by many names. The name 'Navaratri' itself indicates that the evenings or post sunset time is more important for celebrations of Navaratri. Late evenings are the best time to go pandal hopping in Bengal and Odisha, Garba dancing in Gujarat, witness Sanjhi Puja in Punjab or see the Golu decorations in Tamil Nadu and Andhra Pradesh. In some communities, midnight Puja on the intervening nights between Ashtami and Navami or Saptami and Ashtami are performed. Jagratas, of course are night-long affairs that start after evening falls.

In any human pursuit, food can never be too far. It is not just an integral part of the festivals, but is also tied to the time and space of the festival and what our bodies need around that time. It is no wonder then that while parts of India go *satvik*—eating simple nutritious and vegetarian food only—it also means a new menu with permitted items to consume during vrata. On the other hand, people in the Himalayan valleys of Nepal feast on the animals sacrificed during the festival. Our friends from Telugu-speaking states give us a long list of items on the Navaratri menu which is followed in temples, like Kanakdurga that has a well-defined menu for Devi during Navaratri, and is replicated even at home.

Most of our food comes from agriculture. Every new crop is celebrated and offered to the deities first. In Navaratri celebrations across the regions, the harvest is seen as part of celebrations. Sprouts are a common thread across most celebrations, symbolizing fertility and prosperity. In most northern states, barley seeds are grown at the beginning of Navaratri and at the end of it worn on the ear, head or wrist, or immersed in a flowing river close by. In other regions, the newly sprouted leaves of different plants, usually nine in number, are an important part of the Navaratri rituals and ceremonies. New crops are offered to the Devi and consumed as her prasada for the rest of the year.

The Panchang that is an important part of the Navreh Thali prepared in Kashmir finds an echo in Andhra Pradesh, where the Panchang or the new year calendar is rendered publicly with the highest officials listening to what it predicts for the year, carrying forward the tradition of the kings of yesteryears. Chaitra Navaratri marks the beginning of new year for many communities across India.

Temples, especially Devi temples, celebrate Navaratri mostly through the *shringara* of the Devi in her different Svarups. Some temples have a set routine for each day, while others exercise their choice. A Chandi Homam is performed mostly on Ashtami or Navami. There are fairs organized around Devi temples, from

Teppotsavam or boat festival in Andhra to Katra Navaratri Mela at Vaishno Devi in Jammu, that are being used to showcase as well as preserve the cultural heritage of the region. The festival, though, is more popularly celebrated in the common public places, places that belong to everyone. Even the homes are opened up for the Kanyas, Suvasinis, Batuks, neighbours and sometimes even for public feasts like in the case of Himachal Pradesh.

This exploration of Navaratri reveals facets like the impact of the Vidyarambham ceremony in Kerala on its overall literacy rate, as a result of the commitment a child and the family make at the beginning of the education journey. It brings out facts like: Bathukamma flowers, when left in the waterbodies, actually help to keep them clean or that only the local Marwari breed of horses are worshipped during Ashwa Pujan in Rajasthan, promoting the preservation and conservation of local species. We rarely notice how well-woven our festivals are with our lives and how they gently guide us to live harmoniously with nature, nurture our creativity on a regular basis and with people who are an integral part of our lives.

Just like diverse manifestations of the Adi Shakti—the eternal Goddess—which Devi is worshipped as, the expression of the celebration changes as you move around the country. It may be appropriate to say that there are as many ways to celebrate Devi as there are her manifestations. There is the presence of her universal, all-permeating nature and there are nuances of her local swarups. She lets us create her as we see her, she lets us become her and enjoy the pampering, and she puts us in touch with the universe that is as much within us as it is surrounding us.

Just like the Akhand Jyoti that is kept lit throughout the nine nights and 10 days of Navaratri celebrations, may you, our readers have the eternal blessings of the Adi Shakti. May the kalasha—the symbol of prosperity—be always overflowing with *aishvarya* in your life.

1

Bhavani, Sharika and Sharada in Kashmir

SUBHASH KAK

Navaratri, the festival of 'nine-nights', marks the cosmic transitions that take place every year, especially on the nine days at the spring and the autumn equinox, but is celebrated during the lunar Chaitra and Ashvina months. At the equinox, night and day are of equal duration, but this balance, with its beginning, middle and end, must give way. The nine nights symbolize the entire cosmic drama, together with a mapping at the level of the individual's own regeneration. This is done by invoking the deities Sarasvati, Lakshmi and Durga, each for three nights. The three goddesses are the consorts of Brahma, Vishnu and Shiva, and are, therefore associated with creation, sustenance and destruction.

In the tantric perspective, there are three knots in the nervous system: Brahma-granthi is at the base of the spine, Vishnu-granthi is in front of the heart and Rudra-granthi is just above the eyebrows. In the inner world, the structure emerges out of the physical body and the information pulled in by the senses (personified by Sarasvati, the goddess of knowledge); the balance between the inner and the outer—body and mind, or heart and head—that is maintained in the breath and the beatings of the heart (Lakshmi, the goddess of prosperity) and the illusions that we create in our lives (the destructor being Durga), who removes obstacles and gives us boons.

Navaratri is, thus, a celebration of freedom. The bondage that is hardest to free oneself from is that of self-deception. The conclusion, the finale, is with the celebration of Durga destroying Mahisha, who is the falsity of life symbolized as the buffalo-asura. With the death of illusion, a new golden age can begin. The parallel celebration is, therefore, in the return to Ayodhya of King Rama, who slays the asura-king Ravana.

Kashmir has had a smarta culture—one that follows the teachings of Adi Shankaracharya. It is non-sectarian, where various Vedic deities are worshipped and both Shivaratri (as Hararatri, Herath) and Janmashtami (Krishna's birthday) are extensively celebrated. The Pancharatra's four vyuhas or manifestations, Vasudeva, Sankarsana, Aniruddha and Pradyumna, and the epic heroes Rama, Lakshmana and Yudhishthira, all appear in the Naga list of old deities in the *Nilamata Purana*, indicating that Vaishnavism had a long history in the region. The great Kashmiri Shaivite sage and scholar, Abhinavagupta (eleventh century), not only wrote the great tantric encyclopaedia, *Tantraloka*, but also penned a commentary of the Bhagavad Gita.

Goddess Worship in Kashmir

Goddess worship has long been central to Kashmiri life. To see its antecedents, the Goddess proclaims in 'Devi Suktam', *Rig Veda* 10.125: 'I am the sovereign queen of all existence… I bend the bow for Rudra; I pervade the heaven and earth.'[1] Goddess Durga is also called Ambika, Amba (Mother) and Devi Amba.

The 'Sri Suktam' (SS) gives several other names of the Goddess, including Ardra ('of the waters' in SS 13), and she is compared to the moon illumined by the sun. Indeed, it is the light (the illuminating self behind the observation) that makes her auspicious (SS 8). The image of the Goddess with the lion represents both the free-wheeling Nature which evolves by rita (natural law), as well as the control of it by a higher agency.

Nana is another name for mother and goddess (as in *Rig Veda*

---

[1] Translation mine.

9.112.3), vac (speech), and daughter in Sanskrit. Nana is attested by the name on a coin of Sapadbizes, a first-century BCE king of Bactria, and she also appears on the coins and seals of the Kushans. The Rabatak inscription of Kanishka invokes her in claiming that the kingship was obtained from Nana and from all the gods. The Sogdianas called her Nana Devi Amba.

Devi Amba has many names that emerge from the different facets of the mind. She is Sarasvati, Lakshmi and Parvati seen through the lens of learning and knowledge, fortune and prosperity and strength and devotion. As Durga, she fights the asuras of ignorance and materiality. As Goddess Lalita, she opens the doorway to the deepest understanding of the world, and is also called Sarika or Ragnya (Rajni, the Queen).

According to *Nilamata Purana*, the name 'Kashmir' is derived from Kashyapamar (the lake Satisar, which covered much of the valley before it was drained; 'mar' in Kashmiri means a body of water), and this seems to be confirmed by Kasperia, the Greek name for the region. But it came to be eventually identified with Goddess Kashmira, a form of Uma or Parvati.

The rivers of Kashmir are also personified as goddesses. Uma is the Vitasta (Jhelum), Aditi is the Trikoti, Shaci is the Harsapatha (Arapath), Diti is the Chandravati and Lakshmi is the river Vishoka.

In *Sharada Mahatmya*, Sharada is the synonym of Sarasvati and she is visualized in three colours: white, red and black, which represent the three gunas of Sankhya.[2] She is Sravani, time, and also Rudrani, the energy of consciousness. Her name is derived from 'shari', multi-hued in the form of Sarasvati that inheres Lakshmi and Durga. Indeed, the name Sharika, the presiding deity of Srinagar, may also be derived from this root and not necessarily from the common folk etymology of the Goddess in the form of the mynah bird.

The 18-armed Durga from a temple in Tengpora in Pulwama, Kashmir, is a masterpiece in stone that stresses her sovereignty in

---

[2]Sattva (purity), rajas (passion) and tamas (darkness).

18 different physical and psychological planes. This representation became the standard in Kashmir after the eighth century. The choice of 18 arms may be connected with the 36-tattva system of Kashmir Shaivism.[3] This system views Shiva as prakasha (light) and the Devi as vimarsha (reflection). When light and reflection become one, the individual finds freedom.

The liberated person—the jivanmukta—experiences the freedom of Shiva in a blissful and unitary vision of the all-pervasiveness of the Absolute. Two very interesting ideas in Kashmir Shaivism are those of recognition and vibration. In the philosophy of recognition, it is proposed that the ultimate experience of enlightenment consists of a profound and irreversible recognition that one's own true identity is Shiva. Through this recognition, the individual transcends the pashu (animal condition) by shaking off the pasha (fetters) that bind to instincts and the causal chain, and becomes the pati (master).

The doctrine of vibration speaks of the importance of experiencing the spanda (vibration or pulse of consciousness). Every activity in the universe as well as sensations, cognitions and emotions ebb and flow as part of the universal rhythm of the one reality, Shiva. This rhythm is in space, in which consciousness rests in its being, and the vibrations spread into the multiplicity of becoming. In the unfolding of time, both being and becoming come together. This also opens up many subtle practices and rituals for obtaining an understanding of the self, of which Shri Vidya is the most famous.

Goddess worship in Kashmir also provides clues to connections with western lands. For example, Rig Veda 8.21.3 calls Indra Urvarapati, 'lord of the field'. Thus, urvan–urvara are a pair just like purusha–prakrti, and urvan is the knower of urvara. Urvan appears in the Avesta, the ancient scriptures of Zoroastrianism, and from there it went into the Persian lexicon as ruh meaning 'soul'.

---

[3] The number of tattvas (principles) of Samkhya were expanded under Shaivism.

Navaratri in the *Nilamata Purana*

The *Nilamata Purana* (circa sixth or seventh century) is the source of traditional religious practices of Kashmir. It lists over 50 rituals and festivals that are still popular in Kashmir. Of these, the ones relating to the first Navaratri is the Navasaṃvatsara (Navreh), which is celebrated over nine nights in Chaitra. The second Navaratri is a celebration over the first eight days of Ashvina. It also informs us that the fourth of Ashvina and the fourth of Jyestha and Magha are also for the worship of Goddess Durga, indicating that the seasons of summer (Grishma) and winter (Shishira) were associated with lesser Navaratri celebrations.

Chaitra Navaratri. The narrative begins with how the observance should begin with a Mahashanti. The first day is the beginning of the year and is called Navasamvatsara or Navreh in Kashmiri. On the fifth day, the Shri Panchami should be worshipped. It is stressed that the worship of Lakshmi on the fifth day brings many boons; the worship of Skanda is also prescribed. On the ninth day, Bhadrakali (Durga) is worshipped with flowers, incense and grains. In addition to the named deities, Bhadrakali should be worshipped on all nine days, and in particular the ninth day. The Grihadevata is worshipped on the eleventh day and Vasudeva on the twelfth. Kamadeva, painted on a cloth and decorated with garlands, is worshipped on the thirteenth.

The Chaitra Navaratri coincides with almond blossoms in full bloom, and part of the celebration involves visiting almond orchards around the Hari Parbat for a picnic.

Ashvayuji Navaratri. On the fourth day, married women and girls are honoured, and Indra's steed Ucchaiḥshravas is worshipped. A fire ritual is performed with mantras offered to Vayu, Varuna, Surya, Shakra, Vishnu, Vishvadevas and Agni. On the eighth, the artisans should worship Bhadrakali with incense, clothes, jewels, lamps, food and drinks. A vigil is kept at night and there is dancing and singing. Books should be worshipped in the temple of Durga and the artisans should also worship their tools.

On the Ashvayuji days, houses were whitewashed and the full-moon night was observed in the name of Nikumbha, a pishacha deity, indicating that the observance included acknowledgement of the forces of the lower realm. Men and women fasted (that is, ate only the sacred feast) but the children and the sick could eat regular meals. The place of worship was decorated with leaves and fruit. Having kindled the fire at the moonrise, Rudra, Moon, Uma, Skanda, the two Nasatyas and Nandi were worshipped. Nikumbha was worshipped with *krisara* (khichri). Only vegetarian food was served at the sacred feast, and the night included drama performances and singing and dancing.

Khichri made of rice, barley, milk, curd, ghee, honey, grapes, meat, fish, bread and lentils formed part of the celebrations. Men and women of all jatis, including servants, participated in these celebrations. One was enjoined to worship Ganesha (Vinayaka) on the fourth day of the fortnight, Kumara (Skanda) on the sixth, Surya on the seventh, Shri (Lakshmi) on the fifth and Durga on the ninth.

The celebrations described in the *Nilamata Purana* offer a pleasant picture of Kashmiri women. The girls were trained in the fine arts and moved freely in society. The people were fond of music, dancing, drama and other forms of entertainment. Different types of musical instruments were played. The importance of drama as vehicle of worship is clear from the mention in the Nilamata of prekshadana, literally meaning 'the gift of a dramatic performance'. Religious observances were *yathavidhi prekshadana*, sacred theatre.

The *Nilamata* refers to images made of stone, clay, gold, silver, copper, brass, wood, sand, straw and ghee. Paintings were made on board, paper, cloth, walls and the ground. The bhumishodhana was done to prepare the ground with figures and colors to purify it for the ceremony.

A late-ninth-century image of a four-armed Sharada, the Kashmiri synonym for Sarasvati, the goddess of learning, has distinctive Kashmiri features. Her two lower hands rest on two diminutive male figures, each holding a manuscript, who embody the complementary elements of vidya (knowledge) and jnana (wisdom).

In her Mahatmya, it is said that Sharada is the same as Durga, and also the same as Sarasvati since her rajas (red) and tamas (black) aspects are hidden. As in the 'Devi Suktam', she is described as Mahamaya who has a seat above those of Brahma, Vishnu and Shiva. She controls all attachments and projects intense illusion.

The Thali at Navasamvatsara

According to custom, a thali (plate) is prepared on the eve of Navasamvatsara (Navreh). The following articles, with some substitutions, are placed on the thali: heaped rice grains, yogurt, flowers, walnuts, pen, ink pot, coin or a currency note, a new *Panchanga*, boiled rice, sugar, salt, ghee, baked rice flour bread, *wye*, a bitter herb (Sweet Flag, *Acorus calamus*), a small mirror and a picture of Vishnu–Lakshmi or Shiva–Parvati. Early in the morning of Navreh, the grandmother or the mother brings this thali for darshana by every member of the family for auspiciousness. Tahar, a rice and turmeric preparation, is cooked and served after Puja.

The uncooked rice grains and coins represent daily bread and wealth, the pen and paper a quest for learning, the mirror symbolizes introspection; the calendar signals the march of time and the deity, the Universal Spirit. The bitter herb is a reminder of life's bitter aspects. After the darshana, each person takes a walnut to throw into a stream or river. The rice is cooked to make tahar and eaten as prasada. The bitter herb is eaten with walnuts to make it palatable.

The third day after Navreh is Zanga Trayi, when women visit their parents' home—if it is close by—and return in the evening with a packet of salt, bread and a token amount of money called the athagat.

Chaitra Navami: On the ninth bright day of Chaitra, Goddess Bhadrakali is worshipped. A famous temple to Bhadrakali is located about eight kilometres to the west of Handwara in Kupwara district on a hilltop in a thick forest of Devadarus (Deodar trees). Goddess Durga is worshipped at Tulmula, Hari Parbat, Durga Nag and Akingam. On the day of Rama Navami, havanas are performed at Rama temples.

Traditionally, Kashmiris recited *Bhavani Sahasranama* instead of *Durga Saptashati*. *Lalita Sahasranama* has about 100 names common with the *Bhavani Sahasranama*.

Some devotees plant barley grains in a pot on the first day of Navaratri, water it daily and offer prayers. On the ninth day, the barley sprouts are seen as a symbol of Goddess Durga. These plants are later immersed in the river. Not all Kashmiris observe all nine days of the Navaratri, though. Some celebrate it from the fifth to the eighth day, while others do so only on Ashtami, the eighth day.

Gadabatta, a preparation of fish with rice is offered to the Grihadevata, the deity of the house, after performing Puja on the eleventh day.

In addition to chanting the 'Shri Durga Saptashloki Stotram', which is popular across India, Kashmiris also chant the 'Bhavani Ashtakam'[4] during the Navaratri days. The first three verses of the Ashtakam are as follows:[5]

न तातो न माता न बन्धुर्न दाता
न पुत्रो न पुत्री न भृत्यो न भर्ता ।
न जाया न विद्या न वृत्तिर्ममैव
गतिस्त्वं गतिस्त्वं त्वमेका भवानि ॥१॥

Neither father, nor mother, nor relative, nor benefactor,
Nor son, nor daughter, nor servant, nor husband,
Nor wife, nor knowledge, nor profession belong to me.
You are my refuge, you alone are my refuge,
O Mother Bhavani.

---

[4]Composed by Adi Shankaracharya.
[5]Translation by Subhash Kak.

भवाब्धावपारे महादु:खभीरु
पपात प्रकामी प्रलोभी प्रमत्त: ।
कुसंसारपाशप्रबद्ध: सदाहं
गतिस्त्वं गतिस्त्वं त्वमेका भवानि ॥२॥

In this endless ocean of existence, full of great sorrow, I am fearful
I have great desires and greed, am drunk and intoxicated,
I am tied in bondage to this miserable samsara.
You are my refuge, you alone are my refuge, O Mother Bhavani.

न जानामि दानं न च ध्यानयोगं
न जानामि तन्त्रं न च स्तोत्रमन्त्रम् ।
न जानामि पूजां न च न्यासयोगं
गतिस्त्वं गतिस्त्वं त्वमेका भवानि ॥३॥

I don't know charity, nor meditation, nor yoga,
I don't know tantra, nor stotras, nor mantras,
I don't know Puja, nor renunciation of yoga.
You are my refuge, you alone are my refuge,
O Mother Bhavani.

Bhajans in Kashmiri that express the same devotion are sung. As example, we have this:

Gyane data moksha data chakh Jagat Mata tsa chakh
Hey Bhavani kar me vani, sedh mukhus dim Sarasvati
Padi kamalan tal be aiseya karne chaeni astuti

You are the Mother of the Universe and bestower of knowledge and moksha
O Bhavani say the word and give wisdom to the innocent me,
I have come to your lotus feet to do your praises.

The Goddess is also worshipped by chanting 'Indraksi Stotra' and 'Panchastavi', which have been popular in Kashmir for over a thousand years. Indrakshi Durga is a manifestation of Parvati, and the 'Panchastavi' is a collection of five hymns sung in praise of Lalita Tripurasundari, the Goddess in her most expansive and subtle forms.

Shakti Peethas in Kashmir

There were many Shakti Peethas in Kashmir, but a number of them lie abandoned after the Kashmiri Hindus were driven out of Kashmir in the early 1990s. I shall speak here of the three principal ones: Kheer Bhavani, Hari Parbat and Sharada Peetha.

Kheer Bhavani

Kheer (Kahira) Bhavani is a temple dedicated to Goddess Bhavani (Maharagnya or Maharajni) at a sacred spring. The temple is at a distance of 22 kilometres east of Srinagar, near the village of Tulmula. The term 'kheer' derives from the rice pudding offered in the spring to propitiate the Goddess. The *Rajatarangini* describes Tulmula (Sanskrit: *Tulamulya*) and the spring of Maharagnya as attracting a large number of devotees from Srinagar.

A heptagonal spring flows from the west, at the head of the Goddess, to the east, at her feet. The spring is known to change its colour from time to time: red, pink, orange, green, blue and white have been noticed. A dark shade of the spring water is believed to be inauspicious.

Kheer Bhavani was visited by Swami Vivekananda and some of his followers in September 1898, who stayed there for a week. He was saddened by its ruined state (it was rebuilt by Maharaja Pratap Singh in 1912). It is said that his disciple Sister Nivedita heard Vivekananda say: 'I have been very wrong… Mother said to me, "What even if unbelievers should enter My temples, and defile My images! What is that to you? Do you protect Me? Or do I protect you?"'[6]

---

[6]Nivedita, *The Master as I Saw Him*. London: Longmans, Green and Co., 1910.

After Kheer Bhavani, Vivekananda seemed conscious of the Divine Mother everywhere and in all things. 'An overmastering love enveloped him. He believed now in nothing but love, love, love—love so intense that it would be impossible for even the vilest enemies to resist it.'[7]

Sharika Peetha

Goddess Durga is worshipped at Hari Parbat (Sharika-parvata) as Sharika or Sarika, the presiding deity of Srinagar. Another name for the hill is Pradyumna Peetha. Hari Parbat literally translates to 'mynah hill', and the story is one of the Devi who, at this spot in the form of a Mynah, drops a pebble that transforms into a rock and kills an evil asura.

The Sharika Temple of the Peetha is located in the middle part of the western slope of the hill. The Goddess is shown with 18 arms and seated on a Shri Chakra. The Chakra is engraved on a rock smeared in sindura. Because of the prominence of the Chakra, the Goddess is also locally known as Chakreshvari and the temple as Chakreshvara.

The entire hill of Hari Parbat is sacred and a number of temples dedicated to different deities are located on its parikrama path. The parikrama starts with Ganesha's shrine located on the south-western corner of the hill. From here are two parikrama routes: one along the bottom of the hill, and the other along the fortified stone wall.

The next sacred spots on the route are devoted to the Saptarshis (seven primeval rishis who are the mind-born sons to Brahma and who have given their name to the Kashmiri calendar) and to Mahakali, marked by a small temple by a Chinar tree. In front of the Kali temple is the Siddha Peetha, where devotees chant the names of the Goddess at dawn, the Brahma-muhurta; next is a stretch of open space known as Devi-Angana—the playfield of the Goddess.

Ahead on the parikrama is a rock on the north-eastern face of

---

[7]Nivedita 1910.

the hillock named after Sharika. After this come the sthapanas of Mahalakshmi, followed by that of Vamadeva, a form of Shiva, who is regarded as the consort of Goddess Ragnya. A small Hanuman temple located on the right side of the foothill is the last sacred spot on the parikrama route. Hari Parbat is surrounded by orchards of almonds (Badam-Vari) on three sides.

Sharada Peetha: The great temple to Goddess Sharada was for centuries the most famous Shakti Peetha of Kashmir. The fame of this temple as a place of learning gave Kashmir its other name, Sharada Desha. The temple is at the confluence of the rivers Kishanganga and Madhumati, but is now 10 kilometres across the Line of Control on the Pakistan side. It remains puzzling as to why the Indian Army did not attempt to take this site during the 1947–8 conflict with Pakistan.

Al-Biruni, the famed scholar who accompanied Mahmud of Ghazni on his many military campaigns into India and wrote the Tarikh al-Hind, declared Sharada to be one of the four most significant temples of north-west India, with the other three being that of Surya in Multan, Vishnu Chakrasvamin in Thanesar and Shiva in Somnath. The persistence of this influence is clear from the accounts of the travels of the great South Indian sage-philosophers Shankara and Ramanuja to Kashmir to debate and consult texts.

Kashmiri traditions have been acutely aware of the deeper meaning of the Navaratri festival due to their organization around the Trika system, which places great emphasis on the worship of the Devi, the dynamic aspect of the Absolute. No wonder Kashmir has been famous in the popular imagination as the Land of the Goddess and the Garden of the Rishis (Rishi Vatika, Reshavaer in Kashmiri).

2

Devi Visits Her Home in Bengal

BIBEK DEBROY

Mahalaya

In Bengal today, Mahalaya signifies the onset of Durga Puja season. Pitripaksha is the 16 lunar days or tithi that begin with purnima (night of the full moon) in the month of Bhadra (September–October), culminating in amavasya (night of the new moon). Mahalaya is the day of amavasya. It is the time when *tarpana* (water-oblations) and *shraadha* (ceremonies for the departed) are undertaken for *pitris* (ancestors). Specifically, tarpana is supposed to be done on the tithi on which the ancestor died. For example, if an ancestor passed away on Saptami (the seventh lunar day), the tarpana too should be conducted on Saptami. But that is rarely observed now and Mahalaya has become the general day for tarpana, regardless of the day of death. Once upon a time, people would go to Gaya (in Bihar) to perform the ceremony. Today, the nearest river that is described as 'Ganga' or a tributary of the Ganga, suffices.

Generations have grown up with the belief that Mahalaya signifies the onset of Durga Puja. In large part, this is due to the influence, rather the voice, of a gentleman named Birendra Krishna Bhadra (1905–91). He used to work for All India Radio. In 1931, All India Radio (Calcutta) broadcast a radio programme known as 'Mahishasura Mardini' at 4 a.m. on the day of Mahalaya. This had a combination of songs, vocal renditions of the story and chants of Sanskrit shlokas. The shlokas were primarily from the 'Devi

Mahatmya' section of the *Markandeya Purana*, known in Bengal as 'Chandi'. The script was written by Bani Kumar and the music director was the famous singer, Pankaj Kumar Mullick. More than the script and the songs, it was Birendra Krishna Bhadra's voice that became a roaring success. Originally a live performance, a pre-recorded version was broadcast from 1966. So successful was this, that an attempt in 1976 to replace Birendra Krishna Bhadra's voice with that of the popular actor Uttam Kumar backfired, and the Bhadra version was brought back.[1] Birendra Krishna Bhadra died in relative penury and, as an employee of All India Radio, was not entitled to royalties. But in 2006, Saregama India, which owns the copyright, made his descendants a royalty payment.

The world has moved on from radio to television and Internet-based programmes. Regardless, there will be some version of that original broadcast, spanning roughly one-and-a-half hours. Historically, Mahalaya has nothing to do with Durga Puja. At some indeterminate point in history, the two traditions merged and Mahalaya came to be regarded as the beginning of Durga Puja. Pitri paksha, which is krishna paksha, is generally regarded as inauspicious for any rites connected with devas and devis.

Mahalaya signifies the beginning of shukla paksha. This particular paksha is known as devipaksha, the fortnight that concerns the worship of Devi. The word 'alaya' means abode or residence, but in Bengali, Mahalaya is interpreted as the great journey, the journey of Devi from the Himalayas to her father's house, in Bengal. Therefore, in addition to performing rites for ancestors, it is customary to recite or read 'Chandi' or 'Devi Bhagavatam' on the day of Mahalaya.

Three Types of Pujas

Devi paksha brings us to the month of Ashvina, which is when Durga Puja is celebrated. There is an exception to this rule, which

---

[1] A 2019 Bengali film, *Mahalaya* depicts this fiasco.

occurs rarely. If there are two amavasyas in a month, that is regarded as '*mala masa*', a tainted month. No auspicious activities can be performed, and that month is skipped. This is what happened in 2020. Otherwise, the shukla paksha following Mahalaya is the period for Durga Puja, beginning specifically on Shashti (the sixth lunar tithi) and continuing through till Dashami (the tenth lunar tithi). At least, that's the impression.

Strictly speaking, the festivities end with Lakshmi Puja on the purnima that follows. Lakshmi Puja in Bengal is, therefore, celebrated at a different time from the Lakshmi Puja celebrated in other parts of the country. This particular Lakshmi Puja is known as Kojagari Lakshmi Puja. '*Kojagari*' translates to 'Who is awake?' Lakshmi travels around, checking which householders are awake, and enters those houses, avoiding houses of those that are asleep.[2]

Broadly, the Durga Puja period is thus shukla paksha in the month of Ashvina, after Mahalaya, and from Pratipada (the first lunar tithi) to purnima. This is generally true and is more or less standardized for Bengalis in West Bengal and for Bengalis residing elsewhere in India. But there are exceptions, and that has a bit to do with how Pujas developed in Bengal. There are three types of Pujas— (1) Banedi bari; (2) Math o mandir; and (3) Baroari. Today, we often identify Durga Puja with the third type, but it wasn't always so.

'Banedi bari' means a noble or aristocratic family—let's say, the zamindars. One uses the word 'banedi bari' because zamindar has a legal nuance and zamindari no longer exists. Every banedi bari was historically a zamindar family. Some of these are in Bangladesh now, like Tahirpur (associated primarily with the name of Raja Kansa Narayan, late-sixteenth and early-seventeenth century). In West

---

[2] Bengal has a variety of vratas (vows), typically practiced by women. There are stories connected with each of these vows, known as vrata kathas. There is a story about a king who brought in Alakshmi (adversity, the opposite of Lakshmi or prosperity), and all varieties of Lakshmi (Rajya Lakshmi, Bhagya Lakshmi, Kula Lakshmi, Yasha Lakshmi) deserted him and his kingdom. When the queen learnt about the vrata for Kojagari Lakshmi Puja and observed it, the Lakshmis returned.

Bengal, the earliest example of such Puja is undoubtedly that of Sabarna Roy Choudhury, started around 1610 CE. There is one that began in 1683 CE by King Rudra Roy of Krishnanagar, ancestor of the famous king, Krishna Chandra Roy. One shouldn't, of course, forget the Puja started in Shobhabajar by Nabakrishna Deb in 1757 CE, a Puja that Robert Clive was invited to.

The Banedi bari Pujas predated the British, but when some zamindars obtained wealth as a result of British rule, such Pujas received a fillip. These Banedi bari Pujas often had their own specific rites and iconography, distinct from what has become the standard in the third type. Such Pujas still retain a whiff of nostalgia, but have gone into a relative decline. Wealth is no longer what it used to be and descendants have migrated elsewhere, sometimes outside the country. The poignancy is often depicted in films and television serials.

Let's move on to the second category—Math o mandir. What's the difference between math and mandir? A math is a place where monks reside. People may go to the math because it is a sacred place, but not to worship any specific deity. A mandir is a temple, with a permanent deity instated. Regardless of whether it is time for Durga Puja or not, people go to the temple to worship the deity. Math o mandir Pujas also have their own rites and iconography. For example, Durga Puja is celebrated in Kolkata's famous Kalighat temple. But no special image of Durga is fashioned. Instead, following the rituals of *Kalika Purana*, the image of Kali is worshipped as Chamunda Durga. The district of Bankura is famous for temples, and in Bishnupur in Bankura, there is the Mrinmayi temple that goes back to 997 CE. The image in the temple is that of a 10-armed Durga, the family deity of the former king. It is this image that is worshipped during Durga Puja, but the proceedings begin on the Navami (ninth lunar day) that precedes Mahalaya, that is, during krishna paksha.[3]

---

[3] A special feature of this Puja is that Rama is worshipped on Dashami and Ravana is symbolically beheaded on Dvadashi (twelfth lunar day).

The Durga Puja that takes place in Belur Math is the most visible example of a Puja in a math. It was started by Swami Vivekananda in 1901 CE and the practices followed are those from the *Brihad-Nandikeshvara Purana*. Both Kalighat temple and Belur Math still practise Kumari Puja, a fast-dying practice and one that is connected with tantra. Without getting into finer details, a kumari is a girl who has not yet attained puberty and the story is about Devi killing a demon named Kolasura in the form of Kumari.[4]

Since I have mentioned a Puja that begins on the Navami that precedes Mahalaya, I am going to cause some confusion before I simplify. Various minor Puranas (not the major ones) mention seven different kalpas or modes for conducting Durga Puja. These are Navamyadi, Pratipadadi, Shashtyadi, Saptamyadi, Ashtamyadi, Ashtami (eighth lunar day) and Navami. Navamyadi (navami+adi) means Durga Puja that commences on the Krishna Paksha Navami that precedes Mahalaya in the month of Bhadra and concludes on the Shukla Paksha Navami in the month of Ashvina, that is for a duration of 15 days. Pratipadadi (Pratipada+adi) means Durga Puja that commences on the Shukla Paksha Pratipada in the month of Ashvina and concludes on Navami, that is, for a duration of nine days. Shashtyadi (Shasthi+adi) begins on Shukla Paksha Shashthi and concludes on navami, that is, for a period of four days. Saptamyadi (Saptami+adi) begins on Shukla Paksha Saptami and ends on Navami, that is, for a period of three days. Ashtamyadi (Ashtami+adi) begins on Shukla Paksha Ashtami and ends on Navami, that is, for a period of two days.

The Ashtami variety involves Puja only on Shukla Paksha Ashtami and the Navami variety involves Puja only on Shukla Paksha Navami. Both of these are single-day Pujas. Very few Bengalis will have heard of these seven different kalpas, sanctioned by sacred

---

[4]Kumari Puja is also performed for Pujas other than Durga Puja, such as Kali Puja. For Durga Puja, it is either performed on Asthami (eighth lunar day) or Navami (ninth lunar day). In finer taxonomies of tantra, there are different terms for a girl from the age of one to 16, with kumari interpreted as someone who is still a virgin.

texts, of conducting Durga Puja. That's because they used to be followed by Banedi bari-type and Math o mandir-type Pujas and those have declined relatively in importance. For example, in the Pratipadadi mode, Durga Puja used to be conducted for nine days, similar to 'Navaratri' in other parts of India. Accordingly, a different manifestation of Durga used to be worshipped for each of those nine days. In progressive order, they were Shailaputri, Brahmacharini, Chandraghanta, Kushmanda, Skandamata, Katyayani, Kalaratri, Mahagauri and Siddhidhatri. But as the Pratipadadi mode vanished, so did the worship of nine manifestations of Durga (Nava-Durga/Naba-Durga). The standard template now is Shashtyadi, with Puja performed on Shashti, Saptami, Ashtami (eighth lunar day) and navami. The Puja lasts for four days. There are rituals, but no Puja on dashami.

There are two words that sound similar in Bengali, but their meanings are different. The word 'sarvajanin' means a Puja that is conducted for everyone's welfare. A Banedi bari or Math o mandir Puja was also one conducted for general welfare. When a zamindar organized a Puja, it wasn't just his family members who attended the Puja and participated in it. So did all the tenants and others who resided within his zamindari. But the zamindar bore the costs. It was no different for a math or a mandir. In contrast, the word saarvajanin, a word that is grammatically incorrect, has come to mean a Puja that belongs to everyone. It is Puja that is community-funded. This is no different from Baroari (Baro + iyari) Puja, which means that 12 (baro) friends (iyar) get together and organize a Puja. Such Pujas started to gain importance during the second half of the nineteenth century, as the nationalist movement intensified and Durga came to be identified with the Mother that is the country.[5] It is fair to say Banedi bari or Math o mandir Pujas were more

---

[5] One cannot help but mention 'Vande Mataram' from Bankim Chandra Chattopadhyay's novel *Anandamath* (1882) and the 'Durga Stotra' (Hymn to Durga) composed by Sri Aurobindo in 1909.

punctilious about rituals, as compared to Baroari Pujas.

In my childhood years, growing up outside Kolkata, you identified with your local Baroari Puja and rarely went anywhere else. You remained there for all the four days, eating the bhog (prasada) and watching the cultural events in the evening. If allowed to, you even went along for the visarjana (immersion) on Dashami. Pandal-hopping wasn't the norm. By the time I was older and moved to metro Kolkata and metro Delhi, even though you paid the subscription to the local Baroari Puja, the local Puja became much more anonymous. Pandal-hopping became the norm, with admiration for magnificent and expensive pandals and tasting of all kinds of cuisine at food stalls. It is indeed a time of festivities, of buying ornaments and new garments and of Bengalis returning home, often from abroad.[6] In the process, rites and rituals have often been bypassed and simplified. There are few Bengalis who will know them now and few purohitas who can pronounce the mantras correctly.

The Purana Background

To backtrack a bit, the Durga Puja I have just described is akalabodhana, a Puja at the wrong time of the year. Bodhana means the act of awakening or arousing and akala means that which is happening at the wrong time. What do we know about the worship of Durga from the Puranas? The answer depends a bit on those sacred texts.

The first one that should be mentioned is 'Chandi' or 'Devi Mahatmya' from the Markandeya Purana. The story is a familiar one. Therefore, it can be told briefly. Betrayed and deprived of their property, King Suratha and vaishya Samadhi meet Medha

---

[6]In 2018, there was a Bengali film known as *Uma*, about a young girl named Uma, living in Switzerland and suffering from a terminal disease. Her dying wish was to see Durga Puja in Kolkata and a fake Durga Puja was organized to satisfy her dying wish.

rishi, who tells them about Mahamaya. The rishi tells them about three distinct stories that concern Devi or Mahamaya, involving the destruction of three sets of asuras—Madhu and Kaitabha, Mahishasura and Shumbha and Nishumbha. The mantras and stutis (hymns) chanted are often from 'Chandi'. What's interesting is that, in popular imagination, what really caught on was Devi as the slayer of Mahishasura. In the case of Madhu and Kaitabha, Devi's intervention was of course indirect, through Vishnu. But that argument doesn't hold for Shumbha and Nishumbha.

Perhaps the Mahishasura account captured the imagination because it was one-on-one, not two against one. Perhaps it was the form Mahishasura took, half-asura, half-buffalo. When the mass of energy generated from the bodies of various devas gathered together, it took Devi's form in the ashrama of Rishi Katyayana. That's the reason Devi is known as Katyayani. She manifested herself on Chaturdashi (fourteenth lunar tithi) in krishna paksha in Ashvina. Rishi Katyayana worshipped her on Saptami, Ashtami and Navami, and Katyayani killed Mahishasura on Dashami. This tells us why these dates are important for Durga Puja. What's interesting is that in 'Chandi', the name Durga doesn't figure when Devi kills Mahishasura. It figures in the context of Shumbha and Nishumbha.

The word Durga can be interpreted in different ways— someone who is difficult to reach, someone who enables you to cross something that is difficult to cross. In 'Chandi', Devi herself says that she is known as Durga because she killed an asura named Durgama. There are more esoteric interpretations too. In Durga, 'D' signifies the destruction of asuras, 'u' indicates she is the remover of impediments, 'g' is her attribute as the destroyer of sins and 'a' indicates that she is the one who removes fear.

Devi isn't born. She isn't created. She is always there. Whenever people face difficulties, she manifests herself. Accordingly, there have been repeated manifestations after she has been repeatedly worshipped. For example, the *Brahmavaivarta Purana* tells us she was first worshipped by Krishna in Vrindavana and Goloka. To destroy

Madhu and Kaitabha, she was next worshipped by Brahma. And so the list goes on. There are more detailed stories in the *Devi Bhagavata Purana*.[7] The *Devi Bhagavata Purana* is important to understand the worship of Devi and also includes 'Devi Gita' and a retelling of the Mahishasura story. But accounts from such Puranas do not add much, beyond what 'Chandi' states, to understand Durga Puja in Bengal.

There is a story in the *Kalika Purana*, not regarded as a major Purana, about Rama worshipping Durga. This is not an account that occurs in *Valmiki Ramayana* or any other important Ramayana versions. The Kalika Purana is not a major Purana. Therefore, it has no standardized Sanskrit text one can refer to. It is a brief Purana and has around 90 chapters. The chapter that I am going to quote from is Chapter 60 in my version of the text and the chapter is titled, 'The Story of Mahishasura'. When I say quote, I mean that I will selectively translate some verses from the Sanskrit.

> On great Navami in autumn, using mantras from tantra texts about Durga, the great festival of Durga must be organized. Kings and others must offer bali.[8] Ashtami tithi in shukla paksha in the month of Ashvina is spoken of as great Ashtami and brings great delight to Devi. The Navami that follows is known as great Navami. On that tithi, everyone must worship Shiva's beloved... On shashthi, the branches of a bilva[9] tree must be used to wake up Devi... An excellent devotee will perform visarjana[10] on Dashami...To show a favour to Rama and to ensure the destruction of Ravana, in ancient times, Brahma woke up Mahadevi in the night. On the first day of shukla paksha in Ashvina, she gave up her sleep and went to

---
[7]The third skandha of Devi Bhagavata Purana has sections on Navaratri vrata and Kumari Puja.
[8]Bali is a sacrificial offering, but is not necessarily an animal sacrifice.
[9]Wood-apple.
[10]Avahana is the act of invoking a deity. Visarjana is the act of releasing the deity. We loosely equate visarjana with the immersion of a Durga idol on Dashami.

the city of Lanka, where Raghava had already reached. Having gone there, Mahadevi engaged Rama and Ravana in a battle, though Ambika herself remained hidden... Mahamaya, who pervades the universe, made Rama kill Ravana on Navami... Devi was released on Dashami.

Earlier, I have mentioned the notion of akalabodhana, waking up at the wrong time. The traditional worship of Durga has always been in vasanta (spring), in shukla paksha in the month of Chaitra. This is the Puja that King Suratha initiated and is known as Vasanti Durga Puja. In rare cases, meaning Banedi bari or Math o mandir, Vasanti Durga Puja is still performed, with Devi worshipped as Annapurna.[11] Baroari Puja is invariably akalabodhana. The incident concerning Rama shifted the focus from Vasanti Durga Puja, which used to be the norm earlier, to akalabodhana. Why is there a reference in the translation to Devi giving up her sleep? Dakshinayana is when Devas and Devis sleep, uttarayana is when they are awake.[12] Vasanti Durga Puja occurs during uttarayana, but the fight between Rama and Ravana occurred during dakshinayana.

Hence, Devi had to be woken up at the wrong time. In fairness, the *Kalika Purana* doesn't quite say Rama worshipped Durga, at least not explicitly. Brahma did it for him, which is also what the *Brihaddharma Purana* says Brahma did for the sake of Rama's victory. There are stray mentions (*Devi Bhagavata Purana*,

---

[11]The story goes that when Shiva and Parvati resided in Kailasa, there was an argument between the husband and wife because of lack of affluence in the family. As a result, Parvati (who is Annapurna, goddess of harvests) left Kailasa and there was famine and drought everywhere. To save devotees, Shiva assumed the role of a beggar. But there were no alms available anywhere. Shiva heard of a lady in Kashi who was distributing alms. Having gone there, he got alms from the lady, whom he naturally recognized as Annapurna. He built a temple to Devi and she manifested herself there on Panchami (fifth lunar tithi) in shukla paksha in the month of Chaitra.

[12]Uttarayana is the movement of the sun to the north of the equator, the period from the winter to the summer solstice. Dakshinayana is the movement of the sun to the south of the equator, the period from the summer to the winter solstice.

Brahmanda Purana) of Rama worshipping Devi, but those don't help to pin down akalabodhana.

In Bengal, perceptions about the Ramayana aren't primarily based on the *Valmiki Ramayana*, but on the *Krittivasi Ramayana*, composed in the fifteenth century by Krittibas Ojha. It retells the Rama story, but with its own embellishments. Building on the bits from the Purana stories I have cited, Krittibas Ojha created his akalabodhana narration, one that most people in Bengal are familiar with. Or perhaps not the younger generation so much. The incidents occur in Lanka Kanda. When asked by Indra and the other gods, Brahma narrates that because of Shiva's boon, Mahamaya resides in Ravana's house. Nevertheless, Ravana will be killed. In the course of the final encounter between Rama and Ravana, when Ravana prays to Ambika, Ambika comes and offers him protection. At this, Brahma advises Rama to worship Devi, undertaking akalabodhana.

There is a discussion between Brahma and Rama about whether Devi can be worshipped at the wrong time of the year. Brahma replies that the Puja initiated by King Suratha started on Pratipada. If Rama starts the Puja on Shashthi, no norm will be violated. Along the shores of the ocean, Rama reads from 'Chandi' and performs the Puja. On Navami, he offers 108 blue lotuses, gathered by Hanuman. To test Rama, Devi steals one of these lotuses and Rama is about to offer one of his eyes as replacement, when Devi stops him and promises him that she will leave Ravana. The visarjana is performed on Dashami. Meanwhile, just before the eventual clash, Brihaspati is reading 'Chandi' in front of Ravana. Making himself as small as a fly, Hanuman blurs one of the letters, so that the recital of 'Chandi' is also not done perfectly. That ensures Ravana's destruction.

Raghunandana, Mangal Kavya and Agamani

In Bengal, one often comes across the term *smarta brahmana*—or at least one did, once upon a time. Smarta brahmana simply means a brahmana who has authored a smriti text or is proficient in the smriti texts. From the eighth century to the eleventh and twelfth centuries, Bengal was part of the Pala Empire. The Pala kings were Buddhists and Buddhism flourished. The Sen dynasty followed in the eleventh and twelfth centuries and led to a revival of Hinduism and learned brahmanas. Though the Sen dynasty did not last, there were several prominent smarta brahmanas, for several centuries. For our purposes, the most important was Raghunandana Bhattacharya, in the sixteenth century. He was known as Smarta Raghunandana and wrote copiously on several topics. For our purposes, the relevant texts are *Durgotsav Tattva*, *Durgapuja Tattva* and *Kritya Tattva*.

In any Puja, there are rituals and practices that go beyond mantras. Drawing on Puranas and tantra texts, Raghunandana laid out the rituals for Durga Puja, for example, the kalpas (modes of worship) mentioned earlier.[13] The current Shashtyadi Puja practices are in accordance with Raghunandana's writings—bodhana under a bilva tree and Puja of a pot on Shashthi, and worship of the mrinmayi pratima[14] on Saptami, Ashtami and Navami. Raghunandan Bhattacharya wasn't the only smarta brahmana who wrote about worshipping Durga. For example, before him, there was Acharya Shulapani. But Raghunandana was the most influential and left a lasting legacy. These writings led to rituals that go beyond mantras—

---

[13] In Volume 7 of the *Collected Works of Swami Vivekanananda*, there is the following. In May or June, 1901, seeing the disciple at the Math Swamiji said, 'Bring me a copy of *Ashtavimshati-Tattva* (Twenty-Eight Categories) of Raghunandan at an early date.' Disciple: 'Yes, sir, but what will you do with the Raghunandan Smriti, which the present educated India calls a heap of superstition?' Swamiji: 'Why? Raghunandan was a wonderful scholar of his time... This time I have a desire to celebrate the Durga Puja (worship of Goddess Durga). If the expenses are forthcoming, I shall worship the Mahamaya. Therefore I have a mind to read the ceremonial forms of that worship.' In his 1901 Puja, when Swami Vivekananda performed Durga Puja according to *Brihad-Nandikeshvara Purana*, he followed the principles set out by Smarta Raghunandana. This collection, *Ashtavimshati-Tattva*, had 28 essays on assorted topics and included *Durgotsav Tattva*.

[14] Image made of clay.

bathing, offering bali, homa (oblations into the fire), offering panchamrita[15] and panchagavya,[16] bathing/smearing the image with different kinds of clay[17] and finally bathing the image with water from eight different pots.[18] Unfortunately, with the prevalence of Baroari Puja, these traditional practices, which preceded the main Puja, have all but died out and no one even remembers them.

Mahishasuramardini (the crusher of Mahishasura) is a fierce goddess. She resides in hills and valleys, not in urban settlements. She is Vindhyavasini (one who lives in the Vindhyas). There are sculptures that depict Mahishasuramardini. She is alone astride her mount, the lion, piercing Mahishasura in the chest. There are no family members with her. That domestication of Mahishasuramardini occurred through a corpus of texts known as *Mangal Kavya*, loosely translated as poetical compositions for benediction and ensuring auspiciousness. These were composed between the thirteenth and eighteenth centuries and each kavya was specific to a specific deity, often female. Manasa (the goddess of snakes) and Shitala (the goddess of diseases) are examples. For our purposes, one should mention *Annada Mangala*, authored by the poet Bharatchandra Ray in 1752–3. *Annada Mangala* was about Devi Annapurna, depicted like a Bengali housewife. There were also a series of texts, authored by different poets, under the rubric of *Chandi Mangala*.

The agamani songs also contributed to this understanding of the Devi. Agamana means arrival and agamani songs are folk songs

---

[15]Five kinds of amrita—milk, curds, ghee, honey and sugar.

[16]Five products obtained from a cow—milk, ghee, curds, cow's urine and cow-dung.

[17]Clay, as in *mrittika*. Mrittika had to be collected from different places, the two most important ones being rajadvara (a king's threshold) and veshyadvara (a brothel's threshold).

[18]The number eight is auspicious. This bathing was to be done to the playing of musical instruments, according to a specific raga. In progressive order, the ragas mentioned are malava, lalita, vibhasa, bhairava, kedara, indrabhisheka, varati, vasanta and dhaneshri. This is a list of nine, not eight. Dhaneshri seems to have been more of a concluding raga. Unfortunately, some of these ragas have been lost and no one seems to remember what malava, varati and dhaneshri actually were.

that celebrate the return of Uma for three days to the home of her parents. More specifically, they are about both her arrival, when she is greeted with joy, and about her departure back to Kailasa, with the songs tinged with sadness. Among famous poets who composed such songs, one should mention Ramaprasad Sen, Kamalakanta Bhattacharya, Ram Basu and Dasharathi Ray. The time period spans the first half of the eighteenth century to the first half of the nineteenth century.

All of these strands led to Durga being depicted as a daughter and as a wife. When she returns to the house of her parents, her entire family has to be with her. Therefore, she is not only accompanied by her obvious sons, Kartikeya and Ganesha, but also by two daughters, Sarasvati and Lakshmi, who were superimposed. There is no satisfactory answer as to when and how Sarasvati and Lakshmi came to be added as daughters, to complete the portrayal of a happy family. The iconography also evolved, such as in pattachitra (patachitra), traditional folk art. All pattachitra is not about Durga. Those that are specific to Durga are sometimes known as chalachitra. So far as the actual worship of an image is concerned, the one started by Sabarna Roy Choudhury became a template, at least initially, despite occasional differences. Lakshmi and Ganesha are to Durga's right, Lakshmi a little above Ganesha. Sarasvati and Kartikeya are to Durga's left, Sarasvati a little above Kartikeya. Kartikeya, instead of being shown as a god of war, came to resemble a zamindar's son. The images were meant to be ekachala, that is, in a single frame, signifying the united family returning home together.

These days, Baroari Pujas have often moved away from that ekachala concept, and Durga, Lakshmi, Sarasvati, Ganesha and Kartika can be in different frames. Texts like *Agni Purana* have clear principles on how the image of a Deva or Devi must be fashioned. Needless to say, these principles are often violated now. In Banedi bari Pujas, images were fashioned in-house. They are naturally outsourced now and Kumortuli/Kumartuli ('kumor' meaning potter) is a major source of images, not just for Durga Puja. In line with the changing times, images have become environment friendly in terms of the material used.

As a background is necessary to understand Bengal's observance of Durga Puja, one should remember that the region has a strong tradition of Shakti worship[19] and tantra. There is no unambiguous and consensual identification of Shakti Peethas in India, with several claiming that honour. Subject to that, no one will dispute the claims of Kalighat and Nalhati. Kankalitala, Sainthia and Murshidabad are a bit more speculative. Especially in the districts of Bardhaman and Birbhum, there was a strong tradition of such worship. Though not quite a Shakti Peetha, Tarapith (in Birbhum) is famous.

The Rituals

In conclusion, one should mention the rituals followed for a Durga Puja, though we have already alluded to them in passing. These rituals are for a Shashtyadi and Baroari Puja, the norm now.

Shashthi[20]

Bodhana—Worship of bilva tree.

Actually, this is a worship of navapatrika (nabapatrika), nine leaves. The original nine plants were plantain, turmeric, jayanti (sesbania), bilva, pomegranate, arum, paddy, colacassia and ashoka, identified with nine forms of Durga—Brahmani, Raktadantika, Shakrohita, Kalika, Durga, Kartiki, Shivaa, Chamunda and Lakshmi. The word 'kala' means plantain/banana in Bengali and the word 'bou' means wife. Throughout the four days of the Puja, navapatrika stands next to Ganesha and is incorrectly assumed by many to be Ganesha's wife. In popular parlance, it is referred to as Kalabou.

---

[19] And worship of local goddesses like Manasa and Shitala.
[20] All these are lunar tithis. Though this point has been made earlier, one should stress that a lunar tithi can straddle more than one solar day. The intervening period between two tithis is known as sandhi and on some days, sandhi Puja has special significance.

Adhivasa and baran—Upchara (Offering cosmetics and various articles) to Durga to welcome her.

The barandala (plate of offerings) will typically include a lamp, clay from Ganga, sandalwood, a small stone, paddy, a flower, a fruit, a betel-nut, a leaf with a svastika mark drawn on it, a case for collyrium (known as kajal-lata), a conch-shell, sindura (vermilion), curds, ghee, gold, silver, white mustard and turmeric.

Sankalpa—The resolution for the Puja.

Saptami

Avahana—Reception of Durga.
This includes the bathing and worship of the navapatrika. For the bathing of Durga, a mirror is placed in a bowl and the bathing is symbolically done of the reflection in the mirror. This includes the use of water from eight pots.
Sthapana—Instating the image.
Chakshurdana—Infusing activity into the eyes of the image.
This is first done for the left eye and then for the right eye.
Prana-pratishtha—Infusing life into the image.
The Puja for this is done with 16 kinds of upachara.
The family members who have accompanied Durga are worshipped, and so are the mounts and Mahishasura.[21]
Pushpanjali—The offering of flowers.

Maha Ashtami[22]

The pattern of Puja during Maha Ashtami follows that on Saptami, except that 64 yoginis who accompany Durga are also worshipped on Ashtami. There is also a worship of Nava-Durga. A special feature of worship on this day is the worship of Durga's weapons (astra Puja). When Kumari Puja is done, it is also done on Maha Ashtami.

---

[21] Durga gave Mahishasura a boon that he would also be worshipped along with her.
[22] Strictly speaking, the prefix 'Maha' is only used for Ashtami and Navami.

The sandhi Puja between Ashtami and Navami is particularly important, as is the arddha-ratri Puja (Puja at midnight). In the course of sandhi Puja, 108 lamps are offered, Arati takes place and selected parts of 'Chandi' are recited.

Maha Navami

The pattern of Puja during Maha Navami follows that of Maha Ashtami. The Kumari Puja is sometimes done on Navami and if there is a proper bali, that is often done on Navami, though it can also be done on Ashtami. A havan on Navami is also quite common.

Dashami

This is the concluding day of the celebrations and there is no actual Puja. It is the day for visarjana. Married women sprinkle sindura on the parting of Durga's hair, followed by doing this to each other. This is known as *sindura khela*, portrayed in the 2012 Hindi film *Kahaani*. An offering made of ordinary rice, puffed rice, curds, sugar and bananas known as dadhikarma is given to Durga for her return journey. The immersion ceremony takes place.

After this, there are benedictions for peace and the associated sprinkling of *shanti jala* (water), people greet each other and offer each other sweets. In some cases, Aparajita Puja is held in conclusion.

But as I have said earlier, Durga Puja doesn't really end without the Lakshmi Puja on the succeeding Purnima.

Lakshmi Puja

For a Baroari Puja, there is nothing special that needs to be said about Lakshmi Puja. It concludes the festivities and the principles follow the standard ones of any Puja. Except for Banedi baris, Durga Puja will not typically be performed by a household. That's not the case with Lakshmi Puja. There is a tradition in Bengal known as vrata katha. 'Vrata' means observance of vow and 'katha' means narration of the account connected with the vow, explaining why the vow on that particular day is important. The vrata katha is also known as panchali, written in verse form. Hence, there are vrata kathas and panchalis connected with various divinities. Lakshmi is one of the most important of these and typically, Thursday is the day on which Lakshmi's vrata katha or panchali will be read. But Lakshmi is also worshipped on other important days, such as major sankrantis.[23] For our purposes, we draw our attention to the worship of Lakshmi in households at the time of Kojagari Lakshmi Puja. Reciting the panchali is an important part of this, as is the drawing of alpana (what is elsewhere called rangoli) on the floor of the house, using rice flour. Usually, the alpana will depict an ear of paddy, a lotus, Lakshmi's feet and an owl (Lakshmi's mount). The alpana must extend till the door of the house. On seeing the alpana, Lakshmi will know which house is worshipping her and which house she should enter.[24] Some houses will arrange for the navapatrika to be placed near the entrance. The night of Kojagari Lakshmi Puja is also believed to be an important night for thieves. A thief who manages to steal from a household on the night of Kojagari Lakshmi Puja is regarded as an excellent thief and is honoured by his peers.

Many traditions have been forgotten, some have been lost. Those that remain are often not understood. It is important to document and disseminate what has not already been lost, so that one understands there is so much more to Durga Puja than regarding it merely as an occasion for a social gathering, especially for the younger generation.

---

[23]Sankranti is the movement of the sun from one sign of the zodiac (rashi) to another. Thus, there are 12 of these, but some are more important than others. The entry of Surya into Capricorn, with the movement from dakshinayana to uttarayana, is known as makara sankranti, while its entry into Cancer, with the movement from uttarayana to dakshinayana, is known as *Karka Sankranti*.

[24]White flowers and tulasi (holy basil) must never be used to worship Lakshmi. Nor should one use jasmine or bilva. Many households offer Lakshmi a pair of hilsa fish.

3

Kolu and Ayudha in Tamil Nadu

LAKSHMI ANAND

Navaratri, specifically Sharada Navaratri, is a festival that is eagerly looked forward to in Tamil Nadu. The first day follows the Amavasya (the day of New Moon) of the Tamil month of Puratasi, usually October/November. The temperature then is often at its most pleasant. Given that this is a state which, with very few exceptions, is hot through much of the year, even the weather seemingly facilitates the gaiety.

Adi Shankara mentions *Shanmata Sthapanam*, referring to the worshipping of the same imminent truth in six different forms—Shiva (Shaivam), Vishnu (Vaishnavam), Ganesha (Gananatham), Skanda (Kaumaram), Surya (Sauram) and Shakti (Shaktam). The basis of Navaratri is generally accepted as the glorification and celebration of the female form of divinity—the Goddess. The *Shrimad Bhagavatam* says that propitiating the female Goddess makes for a good family life, so much so that if there is family trouble, invoking the Devi is strongly suggested to resolve the matter. As can be expected, Navaratri is of particular importance to Shaktam worshippers.

While all the nine days of Navaratri are celebrated by most brahmins and some members of other communities such as Chettiars, Nadars and Pillais, all Hindus throughout the state celebrate the last day of Navaratri, which is called Ayudha Puja or Sarasvati Puja, with much pomp.

The word 'Ayudham', literally meaning weapon, refers here to 'tools of the trade'. Artisans and others clean up and perform ritual ablutions to worship the implements and equipment they use to earn a living. The brahmins, seen as keepers of knowledge, pay obeisance to books, musical instruments, stationery and so on—observing the day for Sarasvati Puja. On Sarasvati Puja, after the prayers have been offered, no academic or intellectual activities are permitted since the assemblage is awaiting Goddess Sarasvati's blessings. The following day, Vijaya Dashami, is a day to embark on and vociferously continue academic activities after the Puja has been completed.

The eponymous nine days are said to be devoted as three days apiece to Durga, Lakshmi and Sarasvati, in that order. While elders speak of this triad of goddesses in terms of practical observance of the rituals, there is little difference among the days, except for the ninth day—Sarasvati Puja or Ayudha Puja, as the case may be.

In Tamil Nadu, Navaratri is synonymous with kolu—an arrangement of several dolls stacked in tiers, akin to a narrowing staircase, and displayed undisturbed for all nine days. In many neighbourhoods, several weeks before Navaratri, dolls of all types, sizes and varieties are displayed in an eye-catching fashion in street markets and stores, inviting even casual passers-by to steal a look and purchase a doll or two. Tradition dictates that at least one new doll be added each year to the display.

It is important to know that the keeping of kolu is neither compulsory nor all-pervasive in families that observe the entire nine days. There is a deep-rooted belief, though, that if the tradition exists in the family, one should sustain it uninterrupted (except in the cases of ritual pollution surrounding death). Many families would start the tradition of kolu when a girl child is born. A one-off kolu is frowned upon as being capable of imminent negative repercussions. Therefore, once begun, the keeping of kolu is a lifetime, multi-generational commitment.

In families that keep the kolu, the preamble for the preparation begins on Amavasya, with a *Ganga snanam* or a bath that includes washing of the hair by all those handling any of the ritualistic/Puja items. In brahmin homes, traditionally, a 9-yard saree is prescribed for married women of the house at the time of handling these items. (It is to be noted that until some 70 years ago or so, all married brahmin women wore only the 9-yard saree daily after marriage. Now, it has become more of ceremonial wear, though there are still a few who wear it every day.) On that day, the festival is generally inaugurated by the preparation of and ushering in of the 'kalasham' (not every family has the kalasham tradition either). The kalasham is prepared by the lady or other females of the house; anyone who is not a widow can participate in the rituals.

A Kalasha Puja accompanies the setting up of the kalasham. The first two shlokas below explain the significance of the kalasham:[1]

कला कला हि देवानां दानवानां कला कला:।
संगृह्य निर्मितो यस्मात्कलशस्तेन कथ्यते ॥

Collecting each kala (portion) from devas and collecting each kala from danavas, what is devised is spoken of as kalasha.

कलशस्य मुखे विष्णु: कण्ठे रुद्र: समाश्रित: ।
मूले त्वस्य स्थितो ब्रह्मा मध्ये मातृगणा: स्मृता: ॥

Vishnu resides in the mouth of the kalasha, Rudra on its neck. Brahma is established in its base and the Matrikas[2] are said to be in the middle.

The subsequent shlokas of Kalasha Puja indicate that the items used for the kalasham symbolize the seas, rivers, earth and all the Vedas too.

The preparing of the kalasham is as follows: on a 'palagai' (low sitting stool—essentially a rectangular piece of wood with trivets on them), a 'kolam' (rangoli) is drawn. On that kolam, a fresh banana leaf is laid; if that is is unavailable, a ceremonial plate or tray (it should be something that has not been eaten from or used

---

[1] Translations by editors. Kalasha sthapana (establishment of the kalasha) mantras figure in all compilations of mantras connected with rituals.
[2] Divine mothers.

in daily household activities) can be used. Some rice or a rice-and-dal combination is laid on the base. On this bed of grain, a 'sombu' (small pot) or a 'kudam' (large pot of the type used to carry water) is placed. The sombu or kudam is typically made of brass or silver, which has been painstakingly cleaned and polished to remove any tarnish from previous Pujas.

The vessel is then decorated all around with hand-applied turmeric powder and *kumkumaa 'pottus'* (bindis). Water is poured into it, and turmeric powder, a coin or two, a piece or two of cardamom, some raw camphor (the edible variety used as flavouring for South Indian sweets), cloves, etc. are added. Into the rim of this sombu/kudam is laid a cluster of mango leaves, spread out to be as decorative as possible. Now, a whole coconut is decorated usually by smearing a thick layer of turmeric powder accented by red kumkuma for colour contrast. This decorated coconut is placed atop the vessel, ensuring that the mango leaves are spread out evenly and prettily below it—akin to the appearance of a large bud with sepals underneath. The vessel is then decorated with a colourful piece of cloth, usually a new, unstitched saree blouse piece, draped and tied around with a thread to make it look like a frilled skirt. Then the coconut and the vessel are covered with flower garlands. Jewellery, colourful bangles and other adornments are used for further embellishments.

In terms of flowers, hibiscus, oleander, rose (the local, non-hybrid magenta variety) and fragrant jasmine are preponderantly employed. With the exception of hibiscus and oleander, only fragrant flowers are recommended.

Once the preparations are done, the kalasham is brought in by the lady or ladies of the home, usually to the accompaniment of auspicious songs or shlokas, and is installed on the highest step of the kolu display. This should be the first installation, to be left undisturbed for all nine days of the festival.

The next installation is typically the *marapachi bommai*, a pair of tall, thin wooden dolls (incidentally, thin people are sometimes derisively referred to as looking like marapachi bommais!). The wood for these dolls is typically redwood, red sandalwood or wood of the silk-cotton tree. The marapachi is ubiquitous in all families that keep the kolu. The dolls symbolize the first human couple from whom the rest of humanity sprouted. Both dolls in the pair are practically identical in appearance but are usually dressed in a dhoti and a saree, respectively, to indicate the gender.

The significance of this pair of dolls can be understood from Verse 2290 from the eighth tantra of a seminal work in Saiva Siddhanta, the *Tirumandiram* by Tirumoolar. It was one of the 18 Siddhars (a perfected individual as per Tamil tradition) and one of the 63 Nayanmars—Shaivite mystics believed to have lived between the third and the eighth centuries CE.

மரத்தை மறைத்தது மாமத யானை
மரத்தில் மறைந்தது மாமத யானை
பரத்தை மறைத்தன பார்முதல் பூதம்
பரத்தில் மறைந்தன பார்முதல் பூதமே

Maraththai maraiththadhu maamadha yaanai
Maraththil maraindhadhu maamadha yaanai
Paraththai maraiththana paarmudhal boodham
Paraththil maraindhana paarmudhal boodhamae

The first line states that the 'imaginary elephant conceals the wood,' while the second says that the 'wood conceals the imaginary elephant'. If one looks at it as an elephant, one does not notice that it is just a piece of wood. But if one looks at it as a piece of wood, one does not notice the carved elephant. Thus, the first line refers to how the form—an elephant here—masks the material it is made of. The second line says the material eclipses the form entirely. The third and fourth lines state that, when we see the universe, we forget ourselves (the atman) and when we discover the atman, we forget the universe.

In certain Nadar families, there is one marapachi pair installed in the kolu per patrilineal couple in the household. So, if there are two sons in the family, there will be three pairs of marapachi dolls—one for each son and one for the parents.

The kolu dolls are arranged in steps—one gets metal or wooden foldable steps at stores expressly for this purpose, or families employ available odd bits of furniture and set them up at different levels innovatively to give the appearance of steps. While tradition suggests that the length of the steps increase symmetrically from the top to the bottom, practically, this does not occur always.

The steps are then decorated colourfully, often using sarees or dhotis. Modern innovations include colourful electrical lighting and even strobe lighting to highlight what the creator wishes to. Regardless of any decorative lighting, a traditional lamp—known as a 'kuthuvilakku' is always kept lit (on the floor at the base of the display) during dawn and dusk. During Navaratri, it is ensured that the lamp stays lighted throughout the evening hours in particular.

While there are no strictures on the exact type of dolls to be installed (except for the marapachi, which is pretty much a standard all over), the arrangement in steps is considered compulsory. There is also a prescribed minimum of three steps, with no upper limit other than that the total number of steps should be an odd number. An explanation given for this stipulation stems from the ubiquitous belief in Tamil society that, when going anywhere with an auspicious or good portent (a place one would like to return to), one places one's right foot over the threshold first. With an odd number of steps, one would also end on the right foot—literally and figuratively!

Generally, the dolls are arranged, with the statues of gods (including their manifestations, representing entire episodes of their lives) on a higher pedestal, and then come the others. Humans, animals, plants, vegetables, fruits and other objects, more or less in that order, are arranged on the lower ones (again, this is convention—one is unable to find any rules laid out). There are two explanations for the steps and the general order practised. Looking at the overall display, one sees the gods atop as one's goal—to become one with the divine. The order symbolizes the evolution that the Bhagavad Gita talks about—one accumulates 'punyam' (merits) or 'paapam' (sins) in each birth according to which one either ascends up those steps to a more evolved form or descends into a lower life form. The second explanation is akin to Abraham Maslow's famous Hierarchy of Needs (physiological, safety, belonging, self-esteem and self-actualization). If one looks at the steps starting from the bottom, one frequently sees display of food, shelter, etc. gradually moving on to displays of family, more affluence and eventually the gods and goddesses—the need for self-actualization.

From the following evening, the first day of Navaratri, 'suvasinis' (ladies) and 'kanya' (girls and other children) are invited to view the kolu, partake of the prasada and take a goodie bag home. A suvasini is defined as a married woman whose husband is still alive. Kanya girls are also considered very auspicious and, ideally, at least one kanya should visit the kolu each day. The generally understood definition of kanya girls is any pre-pubescent girl; however, the scriptures define a kanya as a girl eight years old or under.[3] That the nomenclature includes only kanya and suvasini, and nothing in between, probably results from the tradition having originated when girls were married very early, the transition from kanya to suvasini thus being seamless. There is also a prescription of a particular age of kanya girl being most auspicious for each day of Navaratri with this age increasing gradually—the awareness of this tradition or exactly what the prescribed ages are is practically nonexistent currently, with no one following it.

Suvasini archana preetha: The phrase itself can be interpreted in two ways—Suvasinis doing archana or worship has beneficial effects, or that doing archana to suvasinis has beneficial effect. By keeping a kolu, the first tenet is met. The second interpretation is

---

[3]Texts have different definitions of kanya. In some cases, kanya is defined as a girl who is under 10 years of age. Suvasini (Su + vasini) has different meanings. One of these is that of a married woman whose husband is alive.

met when women and children are invited home in the evening. The most desirable time for the suvasinis and kanyas to visit is sayam sandhya—the interval of time when day becomes night, and soon after.[4]

The visiting ladies are asked to render a song on the Goddess—this probably stems from the days when practically every brahmin girl learned the rudiments of Carnatic music which, historically, has been religious and spiritual in nature. A prasada is given which, regardless of what else it might constitute, always includes cooked lentils or pulses. The pulses are either boiled or roasted and prepared fresh each day. The significance of the preparation probably originates from the fact that such prepared pulses can never sprout again. By cooking these unsproutable lentils as prasada, one is entreating the Goddess to ensure no more janmas or rebirth—sprouting being synonymous with rebirth, effectively.

The cooked pulses are seasoned simply with salt, a tempering of mustard and dried red chilli, coconut and, frequently, asafoetida as well. In Tamil, it is called sundal. Many families try to offer a different lentil for sundal each day. This, experts say, is not required—it seems to be more of a case of satisfying our own palate's need for variety whilst keeping up the required tradition. As is the case with most Pujas, a dessert of some kind is also usually given—often a variety of kheer.

Since all nine days are auspicious, having an open home during Navaratri with admittance at any time is considered ideal for the families keeping kolu. This was a matter of routine and not at all cumbersome back in the days when large joint families were the rule. Having many ladies present meant someone was always home. Anyone could come in any evening to see the kolu and receive the customary accoutrements. Similarly, ladies of the host family too could step out unhindered since there would always be others at

---

[4]Sandhya means the time that joins night and day. Sayam (evening) pins it down to the evening sandhya.

home to welcome any visitors. This has, however, become unfeasible now, due to the preponderance of nuclear families. As a result, hosts now specify certain days and times for visitors to come. This allows the host to go out on other days and to also curate the guest list for each day based on common connections. Hosts have frequently taken to keeping the prasada packed in a ready-to-go format to be given part-and-parcel with the haldi kumkuma. This allows the visitors to move on to the next home on their list in quick succession. While having some ladies and children visiting every evening is considered auspicious, it has ceased to be possible in modern times.

Along with the compulsory haldi and kumkuma, given with betel leaves, betel nuts, a fruit, some strung flowers and, often, a coconut too, most hosts add on some other gifts but these are not required. An unstitched saree blouse piece used to be the standard addition. Nowadays, between the combination of sarees being less in vogue and individuals preferring designer blouses, many are resorting to other gifts, something they envision will make the visit to their home more memorable—it could be a bag, a storage container, a decorative knick-knack, a gift certificate or even something off-the-wall. In Tamil Nadu, in almost all brahmin families and in some families from other communities, any visiting suvasini or kanya is frequently given haldi and kumkuma when they are about to leave, regardless of whether it is a festival or not. During Navaratri, this is done without fail even in homes that do not keep kolu.

Dietarily, there are some practices that are still observed as a matter of routine and others that small sections of the kolu-keeping legion do. Onion and garlic are eschewed across the board on all nine days. Some people avoid eating rice, the staple food in Tamil Nadu, and items containing rice. The logic behind it being that when one takes food that is not one's normal staple, one will automatically eat less. Some sacrosanct observers maintain a salt-free diet for all nine days. The removal of salt is considered equivalent to fasting rather than feasting since one will eat such unseasoned food only minimally. A heavy meal often leads to torpor, thus the idea behind fasting and/or a lighter diet—to allow the mind to focus more easily on the divine—one could equate it to the working lunch concept.

It should be noted here that even if the host and her family maintain a salt-free diet, the prasada should be made with salt. If guests are invited for a meal, a sumptuous, properly seasoned meal is to be prepared and served. The dietary stipulations are intended for those observing the tradition and not for the visitors.

Spouses are advised to abstain from conjugal relations during the entire period of the Puja. This is recommended for all religious ceremonies and holy days, in keeping with the spirit of maintaining self-discipline to direct one's thoughts towards the divine. In some Nadar families, all the daughters-in-law and the matriarch will sleep in the room where the kolu arrangements are set up—this practice facilitating the abstinence.

The decorating of the Goddess or the divine form, in general, is strongly encouraged as it is considered necessary to reduce ego vs. our bedecking ourselves which can breed and foster narcissism. This is the explanation given for the immense effort put into the decorative aspects in religious traditions. This extends to the often-elaborate kolams drawn outside the home for festivals. The act of thinking through how to produce this large piece of art and the effort taken to draw it are all aspects of the effort put in for the festival—that concentration takes our mind away from the otherwise care-ridden days. The scriptures say this is a very legitimate form of worship. The festival often includes the offering of a garment to the Goddess as well—*vastram samarpayami*[5]—traditionally a saree or a pavadai (traditional skirt worn by young girls) is offered. On Vijayadashami day, which signals the conclusion of Navaratri, that garment can be worn by suitable denizens of the household.

---

[5] 'I offer you a garment.'

Another interesting tradition is the making of an offering to, and the feeding of, a brahmachari on each of the days of Navaratri—Batuka Bhairava Puja, as it is called. This is rarely done these days and few are even aware of it. On the other hand, it often happens involuntarily in a modified way as some of the ladies who come on kolu visits frequently bring their young male progeny too and hosts keep some extra knick-knacks around to give these children for such occasions.

If one were to look at the prescribed, recommended tradition, one kanya girl, one brahmachari and at least one suvasini are to be fed and made offerings to each day. The current lifestyle entails that it is rare for these standards to be met on a daily basis. However, collectively, over the nine days, they often are. Certain Nadar families begin their Navaratri by inviting nine brahmin ladies either to their home or a temple, giving them a saree (or any other offering) each and serving them a ceremonial meal.

Kolus now range from the fairly basic to the highly elaborate. Themed displays, with custom made dolls for the occasion are spread out all over the home, in addition to the steps, with cricket, other games, village scenes, etc., frequently depicted.

Some will spread out dirt on a mat and plant mustard seeds a few days earlier so the sprouts can mimic fresh grass for these displays. Strictly speaking though, all the prep work for the kolu, from the planting of any seeds to arranging of dolls right from the kalasham to the marapachi has to be done no earlier than on Amavasya day. Nowadays, the dolls are often arranged earlier due to practical constraints since most adults are working or studying. The shelves, arrangements, etc. often require help from others and hosts often try to outdo themselves in decoration which again requires assistance. There is also, frequently, the desire to impress visitors from the very first evening of Navaratri with a lovely display and well-oiled logistics.

On Vijaya Dashami, one doll is usually turned to a prone position in place on the rack, as though sleeping. This symbolizes the end of that year's Navaratri. Some Nadar families have a more elaborate ritual. On the evening of Vijaya Dashami, one pair of the marapachi dolls is laid on a cot in a separate room, and basic offerings like a banana, milk, etc. are placed next to it (the standard refreshments laid out for a newly married couple's first night together). The room is closed and left undisturbed. The following day, the dolls are given a ceremonial bath and laid aside. Traditionally, only married women are allowed to participate in this ritual—nowadays, however, all in the vicinity participate with gusto.

Examining the festival from the standpoint of the ladies, it seems ritualistic rather than religious in nature. This is, in large part because, in Tamil Nadu, for any Puja, most of the religious aspects—the recitation of shlokas and mantras—is done by the men. The ladies typically handle all the ancillary aspects of a Puja—getting all the necessary items ready, preparing prasada, the festive meal, the on-hand assistance during the Puja, etc. The benefits from the Pujas are said to accrue in equal measure to the spouse reciting the mantras (typically the husband) and the spouse who does the associated tasks for and around it (typically the wife).

Ladies do read certain scriptures and shlokas, but not in a Puja format. For Navaratri, the 'Lalita Sahasranamam' and 'Durga Saptashati' are of particular significance. The 'Lalita Sahasranamam', from the Brahmanda Purana, is a series of shlokas listing 1,000 names of the Mother Goddess—Shakti. Many women routinely recite these periodically throughout the year and, during Navaratri, might recite it each day of the festival. The 'Devi Mahatmyam', also called 'Durga Saptashati', is a set of 700 shlokas from Chapters 81–93 of the Markandeya Purana. This too is a central text read particularly during Navaratri. For Shaktam worship, the 'Durga Saptashati' is as central as the Bhagavad Gita is to Vedanta. Other shlokas that can be recited on all nine days are 'Durga Ashtottaram', 'Shyamala Dandakam', 'Lakshmi Sahasranamam', 'Lakshmi Ashtottaram', 'Sarasvati Stotram' and 'Sarasvati Ashtottaram'.

In fact, there is nothing actually prescribed for men during

Navaratri, except on the ninth day of Sarasvati or Ayudha Puja. Those who are religious by nature often use this time to read more shlokas devoted to the Goddess. In certain Maths, a Chandi Homam (havan) is performed, typically on the ninth day, whereby several priests collectively recite 'Devi Mahatmyam' while making offerings to the fire. This can be done at home as well, individually. At home, any of these Devi shlokas, such as 'Lalita Sahasranamam', 'Devi Mahatmyam' or others, can be recited as an archana with flowers by the men. Again, this is not obligatory.

On the ninth day, men from all communities, as already mentioned, clean and decorate their tools and instruments and observe Ayudha Puja with flowers and some recitation of mantras. In offices, computers, typewriters and cupboards are smeared with sandal paste and kumkuma. In factories, this is done for the plant and equipment. The Ayudha Puja is also done for bigger 'instruments', including cars, motorcycles and bicycles. A lamp (kuthuvilakku) is lit and an offering of lighted camphor is made in front of the tools. Cars and cycles are circumambulated with the lighted camphor. A pumpkin and limes are place in front of the tools on the day of Ayudha Puja. The Puja is observed in almost all homes and offices across Tamil Nadu, and in offices, it is common for non-Hindus to participate in the festivities. On Vijaya Dashami, the pumpkin and limes are broken after lighting camphor, and with them the 'evil eye' is dispersed.

On the ninth day, in many brahmin families, men do Sarasvati Puja with flowers, the deck of books and stationery covered in a silk cloth placed in front of images of Goddess Sarasvati and a recitation of 'Sarasvati Ashtottaram', which lists the 108 names of Sarasvati. For those who do Sarasvati Puja, Vijaya Dashami is marked by a small (abbreviated) version of the Sarasvati Puja, followed by distribution of books and stationery to the family by the person performing the Puja (usually eldest male relative). These are in addition to the Ayudha Puja and post-Ayudha Puja rituals for things other than books.

In terms of Shakti Peethams,[6] there is only one in the state—the hallowed Kamakshi Temple in Kanchipuram. Unlike some other states, Tamil Nadu has practically no concept of a community Navaratri Puja.

The fervour of Navaratri is felt throughout the state of Tamil Nadu, viscerally by some, mildly by others, but between the street vendors, the women and children dressed in traditional garments and much more, the festive atmosphere is all pervasive. The weather being at its most conducive further accentuates the atmosphere of a festival that fosters social interaction and where the anticipation of that social interaction itself changes the course of daily life in that period.

Note

This chapter could not have been written without the assistance of Smt. Anusha Ramesh, Brahmashri Sri B. Sundarkumar, Smt. Prema Krishnamurthy and Sri R. Ramesh who spent significant time and effort at short notice to provide authentic detail. I am sincerely thankful to them. Further, I would like to express my gratitude to those who lent further perspective or pointed me towards good sources of information: Smt. Sharmilee Yogasaravanan, Smt. Parvathy Nagappan, Smt. Sathyabama Shyam Sunder, Sri N. Vijay Siva, Sikkil Sri B. Balasubramanian, Prof. Arunkumar Sridharan and Sri R.K. Shriramkumar.

---

[6]One of the 51 or 52 sacred places where a piece of Sati's body fell.

4

Home in the Himalayas, Shakti in Himachala

DIVYA PRASAD

हिमाचलसुतानाथसंस्तुते परमेश्वरि ।
रूपं देहि जयं देहि यशो देहि द्विषो जहि।।[1]

'Argala Strotram': *Devi Mahatmayam*

In Himachal Pradesh, the legendary birthplace of Parvati, Shakti worship echoes in the highest and remotest corners. Shakti worship is deep-rooted in the agricultural ecosystem, a part of life in the hills. Shakti represents the cycle of the universe—its root, source, creation and order. In mountain culture, Shakti is worshipped in her infinite forms. Folklores have been passed on orally from one generation to another, along with rituals, beliefs, folk dances, music, arts and crafts.

The Devis here communicate, guide, assist and instruct the locals on day-to-day life through their 'chosen man' called Gur—a shaman or a medium. Births, marriages and victory days of Devis are celebrated through various festivals and fairs throughout the year. Navaratri is just one small part of that. After all, Shakti worship is intrinsic to the culture and lives here.

Devi in her Vedic and Puranic forms, is celebrated as the feminine half of Shiva; her infinite manifestations can be seen everywhere in the

---

[1] One who is praised by the lord of the daughter of Himachal, that Parmeshwari, May you give us form, victory, glory, and vanquish our enemies. Translation by the editors.

state. She is the great divine mother, worshipped as Saptamatrikas—Brahmani, Vaishnavi, Indrani, Maheshvari, Kaumari, Varahi and Chamunda. In Himachal, though, Devi is celebrated as Prakriti or Nature.

Traditions of Living Devi-Devata

There are terrestrial goddesses like Prithvi (Earth), Ratri (Night), Usha (Dawn), fertility, forests and rivers. Dakinis, Apsaras, Yoginis—the mystic goddesses are worshipped too. Some of these goddesses reside high up the mountain peaks and passes called Jyot—meaning light.[2] In some parts of the Kangra and Kullu valleys, the goddess of the household stove, Chulha Devi, is honoured with an offering of the first morsel of the meal cooked on fire.

The Yoginis reside in Devbans or the remote sacred forests or sacred water bodies as divine spirits cleansing, protecting and energizing them with their 'shakti'. They are the accompanying and empowering shaktis of not just Devi-Devatas and rishis, but also their rathas and paalkis (chariots and palanquins). The Jogini Falls, high up in Vashishta Village near Manali, is revered as one such abode of Yoginis, marked by a sacred stone where a temple stands today.

Devis are territorial entities in Himachal. As the presiding deity of their land, they are the sole authority governing the culture and lives of their respective villages. Every few kilometres, the traditions, culture and language of villages differ along with the deities. People honour deities from other villages but they must fulfil the duties of their principal village deity, failing which can invoke the wrath of the deity.

Devi has also been worshipped as snake goddesses since the times of Rigveda. For example, the highly revered Naga Devi, Budhi Nagin, is the mother of all Naga Devatas in the state. Sitting atop

---

[2] From jyoti.

Serlosar lake above Jihi, she is believed to be an incarnation of Durga, creator of the Naga Devatas and Naga Lokas, guarding the universe of serpents. She is the Kuladevi of Naga Kulas spread across the state. During the Budhi Nagin Devi Mela, her paalki is carried to the sacred Serlosar lake, for a ritualistic royal bath. Similarly, Bhaandal Nag Mata of Goshal village near Manali is the Naga Mata to 18 Nag Devatas of Kullu valley. These Devis are sometimes depicted as snakes coiled over the Devi, her breasts or her left hand.

Gur, Paalkis and Moharas

The Gur hums the prayers,
Sacredness rises
In Juniper's wisps
The Gur voices Devata's call

The other-worldly eyes
Guide the spirit back home
The Devatas dance
To their heart's beat

The lost parts within
Find their home
The Gur sings
Stories of the heart

Swaying Devi–Devatas
Tap into rhythms of cosmos
The divine light opens
Heart's infinite flower.

Despite these multiple forms, Devi lives as one amongst her people. She is the mother, a counsellor and a metaphysical healer for her people. She manifests and communicates through her 'Gur'. All grievances as well as the deity's love towards an individual or community as a whole is expressed through the Gur. A Gur is the medium or channel representing the Devatas—a kind of bridge between Devatas and people. A male Gur is chosen by the deity, irrespective of age or caste and put through a rigorous test. A novice is called a Bathar and after years of rigorous trials and tribulations, he graduates to a Gur. Sometimes, he is required to go on a pious journey alone in the mountains for Sadhana or to procure sacred herbs as a part of their rituals.

The Gur leads a life of seclusion, away from worldly activities. He is expected to follow a prescribed diet, hygiene and lifestyle including growing his hair to channelize energy. His sole purpose is to serve the deity and community. Every village deity has its own set of rituals and ceremonies performed to initiate the Gur according to the deity's innate nature. These Devatas have their own constitution—unwritten and passed through oral traditions, based on concepts known as 'Kar' and 'Antar'[3] in Deo Bhasha.

The deities communicate in Deo Bhasha[4] that only the Gur understands after his ritualistic initiation. This ritual of channelling is called Deo Khela, when the Gur wears his traditional white robes called Chola. Every Devi–Devata has an autobiography—an oral narrative called 'Bhartha', narrating who they are, which forest they originated from, their important life events, birth and death details and legends. This too is narrated through the Gur in Deo Bhasha. In Kullu valley, these mediums are known as Gur and in Kangra valley, as Cheli or Chela.

Devatas are represented through a unique paalki or ratha and moharas (masks in specific numbers). The paalki or ratha is built with wood procured from the forest or Devban associated with the deity. The moharas are carved in Ashtadhatu, an alloy of eight metals, or Panchaloha, an alloy of five metals, or gold or silver, depending on the deity's preferences and directives. During festivals,

---

[3] Kar and antar are like body of action and the atma.
[4] Literally, language of gods/goddesses.

when the paalki is led naturally by the spirit of deities, expressing themselves through movements, the emotions vary from anger to joy and everything in between. You feel the Prana Shakti—the life force—flowing through it as it moves. This year on the Shashti (sixth lunar day) of Chaitra Navaratri, I witnessed Devi Hidimba dance in joy at a ritualistic Dev Milan[5] in Goshal for Chautthi Bhandara[6].

Chaitra Navaratri

The month of Chaitra celebrates Devi in her myriad forms as per the traditions of her region, differently across Himachal. It is important to note that the traditions pertaining to Devi are not merely limited to Navaratri. Due to its common history with Punjab, Himachal shares most of its culture with its neighbour. The Shakti Peethas worship Devi throughout nine days, while the locals worship as per their family traditions and beliefs. Bhandaras or feasts are hosted by Shakti Peetha temples for nine days. Most Devi shrines perform 'havan', a ritual involving a sacrificial fire, and paath, chanting of Vedic and Puranic texts such as 'Durga Saptashati'. Jagraatas—the tradition of celebrating Devi with singing and dancing—can be seen across Himachal. Most villages hold melas or fairs for their presiding Devis during this time. In Kullu valley, the Chachauhali Mela and Karjan Mela happen in the first week of Chaitra Maas.[7]

Chaitti Ralli Pooja for Devi

In parts of Kullu, Kangra, Mandi, Chamba and Sirmaur districts, Chaitti Ralli Puja is celebrated by women to find a desired husband. This is more common and intrinsic to the culture of Kangra valley.

---

[5] A meeting of the deities through their paalkis.
[6] A bhandara held on the fourth day of the month as well as during the festival.
[7] The month of Chaitra, which is from mid-March to mid-April according to the Gregorian calendar.

This festival begins on Mesha Sankranti—the first day of Chaitra Maas—also known as Chaitti mostly but Chaitrali in Kullu and Dholru in Chamba. An edifice is made with a variety of grass for worship. In a corner of the house facing east, jaun (barley) seeds are sown with soil, cow dung and coconut. This plant is worshipped as Devi Bhagwati with ritual Pujas and offerings for nine days. On Dashami, the sprouted shoots of jaun, called riholi, is shared as blessings of Devi with everyone.

Folklore has it that a girl named Ralli was forcibly married off to a younger boy by her family. When her doli[8] was being led to her husband's home, she stopped by a river on the way. Ralli jumped into the river, after telling her brother, 'I couldn't change my fate but any woman who worships Shiva–Parvati for a month and performs their wedding ceremony will find her desired partner.' At the sight of this, even her husband jumped into the river. This led to the tradition of Ralli Puja. Since then, young unmarried girls create and worship Murtis of Shiva and Parvati throughout Chaitra. The girls go to a nearby lake for a ritual bath, singing folk songs of the divine couple. They fill pots with water to bathe the Murtis. At the end of Chaitra Maas, a ritual wedding of Ralli as Parvati and Shiva is performed, followed by a wedding feast of Bhath. On the day of Baisakh, the Ralli Murtis are placed on a palanquin and immersed in the river.

In Sirmaur district, it is celebrated as Chaitraul. Homes are painted with male animals and crops symbolizing abundance of life. A traditional feast is hosted. The family deities are taken to the fields where a special wheat flour dish, poltu, is cooked for them. Some families break earthen pots to ward off evil spirits and bless their homes.

And in Chamba, the Sui Mata Mela honours the goddess Sui Devi from the fifteenth day of Chaitra Maas to the first day of Baishakh Maas. Only women and children are allowed to be a

---

[8] Palanquin

part of her mela. However, with changing times the mela is now celebrated for three days and is open to all.

Sharada Navaratri

The first nine days of Sharada Navaratri are not as important in most upper regions of Himachal Pradesh. In Kullu valley, the tenth day— the Vijaya Dashami or Dussehra—is culturally significant. It was the day when Shri Rama gained victory over Ravana, symbolizing the victory of good over evil. When Dussehra ends in other parts of India, celebrations begin across Kullu valley for the next 10 days. The paalkis of all deities in the valley gather to honour Raghunathji of Ayodhya at Dhalpur grounds in Kullu. This gathering is known as Dev Milan.

The paalkis of Devi-Devatas come together, dance, feast and celebrate. Natti dance is performed to greet the deities. The ritual of Deo Khela is performed—where individual deities are invoked by Gurs. On the last day, Raghunathji's ratha is taken on a yatra around the town to bless devotees. Eventually, the ratha is stationed along the banks of the Beas river, where an effigy of grass and wood known as 'Lanka' is set on fire. Lanka Dahan symbolizes the destruction of Ravana and his clan, and also of evil in the collective consciousness.

In parallel, Vijaya Dashami is revered as the divine intervention of Mahadevi to vanquish Mahishasura.

On the Ashtami of Sharada Navaratri, a special mela is held at Tara Devi's shrine located about 11 kilometres from Shimla.

In Ladbharol tehsil of Mandi district, a special festival locally known as Salindara[9] is held during both Chaitra and Sharada Navaratris. It's when Sharada Simsa Devi—also known as Santan Datri[10]—blesses childless women with a child. An ancient ritual worship, Dharna, by women is a tradition at her shrine. After a

---

[9]Dream
[10]Bestower of children

ritual bath at a holy water source by the shrine, women sleep on her temple floor, observing a fast. Devi answers their prayers for a child through a dream while they are asleep. She also gives symbolic signs such as fruits, vegetables, metal, wood, stone or other objects, clearly indicating its manifestation—whether they will be blessed with a child or not.

During Chaitra and Ashwin Navaratris, from Shukla Ashtami to Chaudas,[11] two major melas honour Devi Bala Tripura Sundari of Trilokpur.

Gupta Navaratri

Most Devi temples in Himachal celebrate Gupta Navaratri as per the swarups or manifestations and gunas[12] of their presiding goddess. At Sharvari Devi temple in Shuru village of Kullu valley, Gupta Navaratri in Baisakh Maas is a significant celebration.

Households also have their ways to celebrate the festival. Across Himachal, every village, valley and their community honours the Devi through their own set of unique indigenous traditions and rituals. In Kullu valley, Chaitra Navaratri is celebrated in a simple but subtle way, compared to Kangra valley, the lower mountain belts home to the Shakti Peethas. Gurs follow their respective indigenous rituals during Navaratri. In most communities and tribes, an upavasa—a fasting ritual for nine days is common amongst the female folk. On Ashtami, kanyas (young unmarried girls) are worshipped as Devi Swarups. Some families also host Jaatars and Jagraatas—a feast along with folk music and dance to honour their ancestral and chieftain village Devis. Let us look at some of these rituals.

Sowing the Jaunraa: On the eve of Navaratri, jaun seeds are sown in a mixture of cow dung and soil. The pot is kept at the altar of Devi

---

[11]Chaturdashi or fourteenth day

[12]Three gunas being sattva, rajas and tamas. Each manifestation of the Goddess has one dominant guna.

and watered for nine days. This symbolizes fertility—an essence of Jagat Mata herself and harvest in our lives. As they sprout into saplings, a tiny bunch of the harvest is offered to Devi with an intent of inviting fertility and abundance into their lives. On the ninth day, it is distributed amongst the folk as blessings. The Himachali men would often pin it on their colourful woven topi.

Lighting the Akhanda Jyot: On the first day of Navaratri, an oil lamp or akhanda jyot is lit at Devi's altar. This symbolizes divine light that lends enlightenment, knowledge and wisdom. It is also the Agni Chetana—the first step in any Hindu ritual. The women of the household ensure that the lamp remains lit throughout all nine days.

The Ghatasthapana: A copper pot is filled with water with a blend of sindura, haldi, a piece of gold, a coin and supari. A coconut with a red thread tied around it is set over the pot to cover it. This forms the kalasha, which symbolizes abundance and prosperity. In this form, Devi is adorned with a red cloth and offerings for nine days. On the ninth day, the coconut is either planted in soil or immersed in the river.

The Betthhar Smudge: At the beginning of prayers to the set-up altar, dried strands of betthhar—Juniper shrub—is burnt to invoke Devi. Sacred betthhar grows high up in the mountains. It's a tradition in every Himachali home to smudge it before commencing auspicious rituals.

The Kanjika Puja: All through the nine days of Navaratri, families welcome kanyas as Devi Swarups. Girls are welcomed by the members of the house, who wash their feet and worship them with oil lamp. Grains of rice and flowers are showered on them and a tikaa is applied on their forehead. The girls are worshipped in groups of nine—as nine forms of Devi. In most valleys, these rituals happen on Ashtami and Navami. Women come together to prepare sooji halwa or vrat ki kheer as prasada. They are fed a lavish bhog—a sattvik meal cooked for Devi—the common spread being bhaturo and kaale chane. They are honoured with gifts such as bangles, henna, clothes, money, etc. After this ritual, the bhog is served to everyone.

Jaatar—A Feast for Devi: Some families, especially in Kangra valley host a feast to honour their ancestral goddess. The Jaatar is an open invitation for all to pay their obeisance to Devi. In Kangra as well as Kullu valleys, a traditional dham—a ritualistic feast for Devi is served, which is cooked by designated priests known as Botti. Invited or uninvited, a dham is open to all, irrespective of caste, creed or religion. Traditionally, it's served on a pattal—a plate made of big dried leaves. Everyone sits on the ground and savours it together, irrespective of their social or economic status.

Jagraata—The Night of Devi: Most households host a celebratory night for Devi on one of the nine days. Keertans, Bhajans and folk songs, praising the Devi, are sung all night until morning. The women also perform their folk dance 'Natti'.

The Folk Devi Melas

Each Devi has a unique identity and traditions associated with her worship. They have their own mela held as per their own calendar.

The Chaitra Maas ushers in the spirit of the Devi. My heart springs in joy as Docha Mocha Devis, revered in the Kullu region, bring everyone together at Karjan, marking the first mela of the year in the valley. A few days later, Devi Sandhya Gayatri lights up Jagatsukh village during her Chachauhali Mela. Decked up beautifully, she dances and sways to the rhythm of Bazzantari (the sacred orchestra), greeting Devata Takshak Nag, Fai Nag and Devi Sharvari. In Jyeshtha Maas,[13] Devi Hidimba comes out to bless everyone at Manali's grandest—Dhungri Mela. A glimpse of Maa's

---

[13] The month of Jyeshtha, from mid-May to mid-June according to the Gregorian calendar

paalki swaying in trance and coming alive into her Gur is an intense experience that my words can't express logically. It's as if Devi's aura wraps all living beings in motherly protective love. Around the same time, her Guru also hosts a mela at Shuru village.

In the beginning of Bhadron Maas[14]—on Krishna Pratipadia, Chrewal celebrations honour Devi Prithvi for her blessings of abundance. Known as Badranjo in Kullu and Pathroru in Chamba, this is a time when Prithvi Devi is given complete rest. Hence, agricultural activities such as farming, ploughing fields, yoking with oxen, etc. are paused. Donning vibrant traditional attires—Pattu and Luanchari—the women dance to hymns on nature's fertility and abundance.

Prominent Shakti Peethas and Shakti Sthalas

Jwala Mukhi, Kangra: Situated south of Kangra valley, at the spot where Sati's tongue fell, Devi lives in the form of Ambika or Siddhida. She sits in the form of flames, which miraculously keep burning, even under layers of rocks, hence worshipped as Jwala Devi—the goddess of nine flames. It's a divine mystery that the flame is eternally lit without any human intervention.

Chintpurni Devi, Una: The Chintpurni or Chinnamastika Shakti Peetha is located in Una district. Devi Sati's feet fell here and a holy shrine was later built around it.

Chamunda Devi, Kangra: Chamunda Devi Temple in Kangra depicts scenes from 'Devi Mahatmyam', the Ramayana and Mahabharata. Sati's skull fell on the spot. Devi's Murti is flanked by Hanuman and Bhairava. According to the legends, Chamunda, the tamasic incarnation of Kali, was the chief deity Rudra Chamunda in the battle between Asura Jalandhara and Shiva. The locals say that every single day, there is at least one corpse burning at the cremation

---

[14] Also called Bhadrapada, from mid-August to mid-September.

grounds by her shrine. Bali, or animal sacrifices, are an accepted practice at her shrine.

Brajeshwari Devi, Kangra: The Brajeshwari or Vajreshwari Devi Shakti Peetha is located where the left breast of Sati fell. Legend has it that Devi assisted Maha Durga in defeating Mahishasura and injured her chest. She healed her wound by applying butter, which became a tradition at her shrine. Every year during Makar Sankranti, a pindi—an edifice of butter is made at the temple, symbolizing Devi. This butter is known for miraculously healing varied skin diseases.

Naina Devi Shakti Peetha, Bilaspur: This is where the eyes of Sati fell. A lake here is believed to be Sati's beautiful blue eyes. The temple is known as Mahishapitha due to its association with the legend of Shakti defeating Mahisasura. She was incarnated on a nearby hill known as Mahishapitha and plucked out Mahisasura's eyes, giving his skull to Brahma. Hence, the gods referred to her as Naina Devi. Devotees flock to honour her at the hilly abode— Naina Dhar—during Navaratri. The Chaitra and Shravana melas are also considered auspicious here. As per Hindu panchang, Dasa Mahavidya jayantis are celebrated around the year to honour each of the 10 goddesses.

Besides the well-known Shakti Peethas, Himachal has its own territorial Goddesses where the community comes together to celebrate her festivals as well as Navaratri. Allow me to introduce you to some of them.

Devi Sandhya Gayatri, Jagatsukh: An incarnation of Sarasvati, she is the presiding goddess of Jagatsukh village—earlier known as Nasth—the ancient capital of Kullu. Legend has it that the Pandavas worshipped her during their exile at Jagatsukh. Devi Sandhya Gayatri is the union of day and night at dusk and dawn. She embodies a three-fold form as Brahma Gayatri, Vishnu Gayatri and Shiva Gayatri. The temple houses a white Pancha Mukhi Murti—her five faces symbolizing *pancha tattvas*—Agni, Vayu, Akasha, Prithvi and Jala.

In the beginning of Chaitra Maas, a havan is performed. She is channelled to provide guidance about the appropriate time for sowing the first seeds after winters. The most fertile days are determined by Devi and the whole of Kullu valley follows her word. During her Chachauhali Mela in Chaitra Maas, she greets a territorial circle of Devatas from nearby villages. Invoking herself within the Gur, she guides all. Tuning into the traditional Natti, she dances with the Devatas and people. The Ashtami of Chaitra and Sharada Navaratris are auspicious at her shrine, celebrated with indigenous rituals and bhandaras.

Sharvari Devi, Shuru: High in the forests of Shuru sits Goddess Sharvari as the adolescent Kanjika Parvati. Here burns an infinite dhuna—a mysterious occurrence which creates vibhuti (sacred ash)—since ancient times, without ever spilling out or needing any cleaning. Devi is known for her healing powers, breaking evil magical spells and curing metaphysical illnesses.

According to folklore, this village was once inhabited by the Shavar hunter tribe that hosted Pandavas during their exile. Arjuna performed tapasya at nearby Arjuna Gufa (cave) to receive Pashupati Astra.[15] Shiva and Parvati appeared as Shavars or hunters to test his devotion before granting him the boon. Since then, Devi has been worshipped as Sharvari by the hunter tribes and presided over Shuru village. Devi Hidimba worshipped Sharvari Devi as her Guru for over 12 years to tap into her own powers. Even today, Hidimba Devi's paalki stops by her shrine to seek blessings on the way to Kullu Dushhera Mela. Hidimba Devi sweeps her Guru's temple floor as Seva, followed by banters over chai.

Both these Devis are ancestrally connected to Kullu's royal family. By happenstance, I once attended a ritualistic 'Mata ki Raat' on the occasion of her conception, a day before Shivaratri. It is believed

---

[15] Pashupati (Shiva's) weapon.

that Devi fasts for Shiva. Hence, a night-long jagraata celebrates her. Only on this night, Devi's Mohara Darshan and Garbha Griha is opened for all and it was sheer luck that I had been there to experience it. The Gupta Navaratris are highly auspicious at her shrine, apart from her own Sharvari Mela falling in Jyeshtha Maas.

Devi Tripura Sundari, Naggar: Devi Tripura Sundari is the presiding deity of Naggar, Kulaj or Kuladevi of Kullu's royal family. Folklore has it that Naggar was conceived with her divine will. She transformed into a makari—spider—and spun a web of light. Her temple roof resembles a web and is a one-of-a-kind Kath-Khuni structure in Kullu valley.

Devi Hidimba—Dhungri, Manali: Up in the Deodar forests of Dhungri, sits Hidimba—the presiding Devi of Manali, ruling over the Rohtang Pass. The legend is that the forests here were ruled by an Asura, Hidimb—Hidimba's brother. The Pandavas on exile defeated him with Hidimba's guidance. Bhima married Hidimba and their son Ghatotkacha was born. Krishna blessed Hidimba and said that she will be a Devi in Kaliyuga. Devi Sharvari is her Guru. She is also the main Kulaj Devi to Kullu's royal family. Today, she is revered as Maha Kali and bali is an ancient sacrificial ritual practised at her shrine.

The Kullu Dussehra begins only after Devi Hidimba and the royal family welcome Raghunathji. Five species of animals representing each of the pancha tattvas are sacrificed for her during Dussehra. Her paalki blesses devotees on the three days of Dhungri Mela in May on the occasion of her jayanti. During a recent Deo Khela, Devi channelled herself through her Gur, assuring protection and support to residents during the Pandemic. During Chaitra and Sharada Navaratri, Chandipath is chanted and havans are performed. However, her Bhandara is hosted at the Durga temple in Manu market, Manali.

Devi Mrikula Devi, Udaipur (Lahaul-Spiti): The shrine houses the Murti of Mahishasura Mardini. The temple walls bear carvings of three-headed Vishnu and episodes of Samudra Manthana, the great churning of the ocean, and scenes from the epics Ramayana and Mahabharata. This entire temple is believed to have been built from the wood of just one Deodar tree. She is revered both as Markula, a form of Maha Kali, by the Hindus, and Vajravarahi or Dor-je-phag-mo by the Buddhists of Lahaul valley. It is also one of the 24 Buddhist Tantric Peethas. Every year in July, the Markula Devi fair is held.

Maa Docha Mocha, Karjan: The Goddesses Docha Mocha from Karjan village are the conjoined twin sisters—an incarnation of Tripura Sundari and Mahakali. One sister is known for her peaceful nature, while the other is known for her vikraal (harsh nature). They are also one of the Kulaj—ancestral goddesses of Kullu's royal family. They have one unified form for their mohara and paalki. Their Karjan Mela is the first Devi Mela in Chaitra Maas, wherein Devatas from nearby villages gather. During one such mela, I saw Devis Docha-Mocha channelling through their Gur during Deo Khela, voicing their guidance and concerns. Both Devis tapped to Natti dances and folk songs with people. I witnessed some ancient folk rituals unique to these Devis like the burning of mashala (a sacred fire on a log of wood) and a folk skit performance called Horan. The Chaitra and Sharada Navaratri are celebrated at the shrine. A havan and paath are performed followed by a feast—Bhandara on Ashtami. Every year, these Devis attend Kullu Dussehra to honour Raghunathji.

Devi Bhimakali, Sarahan, Kinnaur: Sarahan was the ancient city of Shonitpura of the Bushahr Dynasty on the ancient Hindustan–Tibet Silk Route. Legend is that the Devi Bhimakali defeated the asura Banasura who once ruled over Shonitpura and buried his head at a spot, which is now the entrance of her shrine. It is also said that Sati's left ear fell here. A local legend tells us that Bhimakali came from the stick of Sage Bhimgiri. It's a tradition that no one can build a house as ornate and grand as the Mother's temple. But Masoi, a man from the town Rohru, dared to do so and the King's army brought down his house.

A massive stone from his roof was placed at her shrine's entrance steps, serving as a reminder that those who attempt to rise above the Mother would be trod upon by all. The ego's head shall rest at her feet, just as Banasura's head, buried at her shrine. Once in every hundred years, the festival of Udyaapan Jag is celebrated to honour Devi. During Chaitra and Sharada Navaratris, Durga Shaptashati Path, havans, and Bhandaras are hosted. Animal sacrifices and tantric rituals are performed at her shrine. There is a dried-up well at her temple complex where human sacrifices were made in the ancient times only upon her approval and acceptance.

Mathi Devi, Chitkul: As an incarnation of Maha Durga, she sits in one of the oldest Kath-Khuni shrines with intricate carvings that depict scenes from folklore. As per legends, Devi Mathi, the consort of Badrinatha, blessed the Garhwal regions and journeyed to Tibet before settling down in Chitkul. She arrived at Chitkul after an arduous journey from Brindavan. The locals believe that abundance and prosperity flowed into Chitkul due to Mathi Devi.

Devi Hatkoti, Jubbal in Shimla: Hatkeshwari Devi is the consort of Shiva, her Ashtadhatu Murti with 10 hands shows her riding her vahana—the lion. The locals believe that her Murti changes expressions—from a smiling face to a wrathful one—from time to time. They regard her as Prakriti, nature personified, with her varied moods. Her shrine (believed to exist from the Mahabharata era) has five stones locally known as Deouls representing the five Pandavas. She is also worshipped as Vaishnavi, tracing her connection to the Saptamaatrikas.[16] The Chaitra and Sharada Navaratris are considered auspicious here.

Devi Kunzum, Kunzum La Pass: As an incarnation of Durga she protects the treacherous Kunzum La Pass—the gateway to Spiti from

---

[16]Seven manifestions of the Devi as Brahmi, Maheshwari, Kaumari, Aindri, Vaishnavi, Varahi, Narsimhi or Chamunda that appear in 'Durga Saptashati' to kill Asuras Shumbha and Nishumbha.

Lahaul and Kullu valleys. On my journey to Kunzum La, I recall the Himachal Roadways bus making a parikrama around Devi as I stuck my wish to her on a coin. People stick coins on her pindi and it is said that if it sticks, their journey is blessed.

Devi Aadi Parashakti, Chhatrari in Chamba: The local lore is that king Meru Vermana once had a dream and he ordered the royal architect Gugga from Medhi village to build the temple. The walls of her shrine are decorated with vegetable-dye paintings. According to folklore, Gugga sculpted the Murti of the goddess taking inspiration from his beautiful daughter. Since his daughter had squinted eyes, Devi's Murti too features squinted eyes. Gugga's Murti can be seen beside the Devi's Murti. By her shrine flows a natural spring of a Naga Devata which heals illnesses.

The Chhatrari Jaatar Mela is celebrated every year by the Gaddi shepherd tribes. They sacrifice a part of their dhan (wealth) or cattle to appease Devi. Four men perform a folk dance while wearing wooden masks. One of the men wears the mask of Parashakti and defeats the other three men donning masks of rakshasas. Another ritual involves people of the lower castes wearing masks of Khappar Buddhe and roaming around the town on a chariot decorated with bicchu buti (stinging nettle leaf plant) for protection. During the Chaitra and Sharada Navaratris, havans, paaths and jaatars are hosted.

In conclusion, Devi is the source, means and end of life. As Himalaya Putri—a living force, the daughter of the mountains—she is humane, connected and accessible to all. My journey towards her is only the beginning, for she lives within all. Shakti runs deep within the Himachali women too, who hold their universes together in the spirit of purest love.

Note

I would like to thank Pundit Budhram Sharma of Dev Rishi Trust, Jagatsukh, Late Pundit Jeevanan of Haripur, Pundit Gopal Sharma of Gayatri Devi temple at Jagatsukh, Pundits Rajiv Sharma and Amit Sharma of Hidimba Devi Temple, Manali, Pundit Sharma of Shravani Maa Temple, Shuru and Pundit Subhash Sharma and his daughter—the medium for goddess Tripura Sundari, Gauri Shankar Temple, Naggar for their valuable inputs for this essay. I also take this opportunity to thank the staff at the District Library at Kullu.

5

The Flowers of Telangana

JAYA RAO DAYAL

Telangana is situated on the Deccan plateau. The terrain is mostly hilly, with rocky mountain ranges and thick forests. Centuries ago, it was a landscape conducive to the pastoral nomadic life. One dynasty with vision took it upon itself to make irrigation its focus and that changed the future of the region, making it an agrarian society. The Kakatiyas, who ruled from the eleventh century to nearly the first half of the fourteenth century, are known to have made a lasting impact on the history and civilization of the state.

So why would I be talking about this, when we are here to discuss Navaratri as celebrated in different parts of India? In all my reading about the Bathukamma—its ethos, the prevalent practices, the philosophy behind it, the interpretation, linguistic implications, metaphors and the language—what emerges is that it all echoes a collective memory that stems from a certain fear of scarcity, disease and infertility. The celebration of Bathukamma marks a celebration of a wish for abundance, progeny, good health and camaraderie.

Each year, after a very harsh summer, with the rainy season comes the relief of ponds filling up with water, replenishment of the water table, trees blooming, the flora and fauna alive in their symbiotic best. The festival is about hailing the mother Goddess in thanksgiving. Bathukamma literally means, 'Mother, come alive' ('brathuku' meaning life and 'amma' meaning mother.)

Cultural practices are a reflection of the geographical locale.

For states that are dependent on rain water, the sowing of seeds in usually done during the advent of the south-west monsoon, which generally lasts from June to November, with minor variations in across regions. Close to the period of reaping season is the period of kharif, which corresponds to the time of Navaratri. The kharif crops, which are the monsoon crops, are ready to be harvested during this time.

The Telugu calendar, also called the Shalivahana Shakh calendar, considers the Ashvayuja masam, or the lunar month of Ashvina, as an important month for people to worship the Devi. This corresponds to the months of September or October in the Gregorian calendar. Telangana has one of the most unique celebrations of Navaratri, which commences on the day of the Mahalaya Amavasya, during the period of pitri paksha.

The Bathukamma is clearly a family and community festival. Daughters return to their mothers' home and what follows are splendid nine days full of merry making, dancing, singing, storytelling and regaling childhood memories, accompanied by festivities and prayers while savouring good, healthy food. The naivedyam (food offering) offered each day is different for each of the nine days.

Legends Associated with Bathukamma

Reading about all the legends associated with Navaratri made me realize that they are fodder for all the songs of Navaratri, which the women sing and dance to for the nine days.

The first one is the story of King Dharmangudu and his wife Satyavati, who are believed to have lost their children in war and had prayed to the Goddess for progeny. They were assured by the Goddess that she would be born to Satyavati as their daughter. The girl, who was born to them, was named Bathukamma, which translated then as 'Live, o child'.

The second story revolves around the Rajarajeswara Temple built by the Chalukya kings of Vemulavaada (present day Karimnagar district), which is a much-visited temple by the people of the state. The heir of Raja Raja Chola, who ruled between 985 and 1014 CE, was Rajendra Chola, who reigned 1014–1044 CE. He is said to have attacked Vemulavaada and destroyed the famous temple. It is believed that he took away the Brihat (huge) Shivalinga from here and gifted it to his father. The Shivalinga was subsequently placed in the Brihadeshvara temple that he built.

The loss of the Linga dejected the locals. In symbolism, to comfort Goddess Parvati, also called Bruhadamma, who is known to love flowers, an array of flowers was arranged like the mountain Meru. A Murti of Gauramma, Mother Parvati, made from turmeric paste was then placed on top of the flowers. The loss of the Shivalinga and the pain the locals felt were recounted in their songs and dance. Finally, immersing the flowers, which symbolize Parvati, in the water, the people begged her to return to them again. Over time, this ritual took the shape of a festival that has been observed since.

Another story in the 'Devi Mahatmayam' recounts the death of Mahishasura at the hands of Goddess Gauri following a fierce fight. After this serious act, she is said to have gone into deep sleep due to fatigue on Ashvayuja Padyami day. All the devotees prayed for her to wake up, using medicinal flowers. It is believed that she woke up on Dashami, the tenth day.

What sets the Bathukamma festival apart is that the Goddess who is being revered is not really enshrined in a temple. She is visualized as being present in a very unique creation. Each day, she is made in the form of an array of flowers, where she is made to sit right at the summit. Come evening, she is set out in the local water body, be it a pond, a lake or even a well. This is called nimmanjanam, which literally means to submerge. It is also believed that the flowers used have medicinal properties and they purify the water by tackling water contamination. The interconnectedness of women and water is symbolic of the notion of fecundity, which has implications of being fruitful in offspring or vegetation.

In the villages, during Navaratri, each day, the men folk head out to the nearby groves and meadows and bring back lots of flowers and leaves. The women of the household use them to form the Bathukamma. Tradition has it that once the family begins this ritual, they must continue it for posterity. There could be several units, the first being the individual home, where it is placed in the vakili or the courtyard of the house. Traditionally, the vakili is cleaned and cow-dung smeared on the floor, after which the *mangala aakara* or *muggu*[1] is made with rice flour.

These are geometrical patterns and are considered auspicious. It is also done as a collective activity, where a cluster of homes (called the veedhi or a lane, implying here people living in the lane will make one Bathukamma together and congregate every evening around it). It may also be placed in common places like the village temple, the place where the panchayat congregates or even a school. Bigger ones are found at the angadi bazaar (a place where weekly markets are held) or even the everyday marketplace. In towns and bigger cities, Bathukammas in common areas are more prevalent, where different communities host and organize it.

Creating Bathukamma

The Bathukamma is a conical formation of flowers placed in layers on a thambalam, typically a large brass plate. The 'sibbi reku' could also be used. A sibbi reku is a brass plate used as a cover for the large vessel in which rice is cooked. I think about how certain words may become obsolete given that bigger utensils may not be in use in urban nuclear homes! The bigger formations are made on wooden or bamboo plate-like structures which resemble the yantra[2] in Shakti worship.

The first layer on the brass plate is that of the *gummadi aaku* or the field pumpkin leaves. From there on begin the various flowers.

---

[1] A geometrical pattern drawn with lines of flour or coloured flour.
[2] A geometrical diagram used in meditation and prayer.

A list of over 15 kinds have been enumerated—all of these are native to Telangana. The flowers are carefully strung or tied with thread to keep them in place. The main flower used is the Thangedu puvvu,[3] which grows on trees and is found in abundance. In order to give it a conical shape, the leaves are carefully trimmed. The turmeric form of Devi Gauramma or the Mother Goddess is placed right at the summit of this structure. These rituals are all followed through oral tradition and do not mark a presence in scriptures. Wisdom can be seen permeating through the practices. Placing Gauramma on top of the pyramid structure takes me back to the *Lalita Sahasranama*,[4] which mentions the Devi as being *sumeru srunga madhayasta* or 'one who dwells on the mid most peak of Mount Meru'.

While each layer is of a different colour with different flowers, sometimes the gunugu puvvu (celosia) is dropped into colour to dye it as required in the pattern. The final product is a work of art in itself. It requires a sense of colour composition and subtle aesthetics. The art of arranging flowers for Bathukamma is a specialized one, an art, where skills are honed and carried over through generations from mother to daughter. What is interesting is that the 64 kalas or performing arts, include flower arrangement as one of them. Vatsyayana has been credited with enumerating the Chatushashti or the chausath kalas in the Kamasutra which dates back to 400 BCE–200 CE. This also finds mention in the *Srimad Bhagavatam, Devi Bhagavatam* and the *Shukra Niti*.

The kalas that correspond to the making of the Bathukamma floral pyramid are as follows. Tandula-Kusuma-Bali Vikara, the seventh among the 64 kalas or the art of preparing offerings from rice and flowers. It is the art of arraying and adorning a Murti. Here, of course the Murti too is made in the process of arranging flowers using turmeric. Next is Malaya-Granthana Vikalpa, which is

---

[3]Telangana's state flower Cassia auriculate.
[4]From Brahmanda Purana.

the fifteenth kala. This corresponds to making garlands and wreaths, in this context designing a preparation of wreaths.

The flowers are all native to the land. Each one of them is known to be used in traditional and folk medicines. They have a host of medicinal properties, some are anti-microbial, anti-inflammatory, anti-helminthic and anti-bacterial, and some are immunomodulators. As many as 50 chemical compounds have been found in the humble ridge gourd or Luffa or Curcubita acytangula. The Chandrakantha flower (*Mirabilis jalapa*) plant is known to have a potential for bioremediation of soils which are polluted with moderate concentrations of metals such as cadmium. The katla puvvu or the sky-blue cluster-vine is used for pollination purposes and for bee keeping.

Three categories of flowers have been listed here. The first section consists of flowers which grow on trees, shrubs, etc. The second consists of flowers and leaves of local vegetables and condiments, which are again seasonal and abundantly available at this time of the year. For the third, I make note of those flowers which are used as hair accessory—an integral aspect of women's attires for the festive season. The names of flowers in Telugu are followed by the common name and then the botanical name. It would be helpful in knowing two Telugu words which constitute an important part of this festival of flowers: puvvu or puvvulu (plural) are the Telugu words for 'flower' and 'flowers' respectively and aaku for 'leaf'.

Common Flowers of the Region Used for Bathukamma

1. Thangedu puvvu: *Tanners cassia* or *Senna auriculata*. Yellow in colour, this is one of the main flowers in the making of the Bathukamma.
2. Gunugu puvvu/pattu kuchhu puvvu: Silver cock's comb or Red cock's comb, both from the *Celosia Agrentea* family. The one that is white in colour is often dyed in different colours depending on the design and sequencing of the pyramid.
3. Ganneru puvvu: *Oleander nerium* or Oleander.

4. Tamara puvvu: Also called the *Erra Tamara, Lotus nelumbo* or *Nucifera Gaertn*. This is one of the important flowers used in worshipping the Goddess.
5. Chamanti puvvu: Chrysanthemum or *Tarquina Bianco*.
6. Chitti chamanti puvvu: Button pom of the Chrysanthemum family.
7. Banthi puvvu: Marigold or *Calendula officinalis*.
8. Gaddi chamanti puvvu: Tridax Daisy or *Tridax procumbens*. It is a weed and pest plant typically found in fields and meadows. These flowers are white and yellow in colour.
9. Katla puvvu: Sky blue cluster-vine or *Jacquemontia/pentemontia ipomea*.
10. Rudraksha/chandrakantha puvvu: 4 o'clock flower or *Mirabilis jalapa*.
11. Gilledu puvvu: Madar/Crown flower or *Calatropis gigantea*.
12. Challagutti puvvu: Stick bush or *Cleodendrum Chineuse*.
13. Kasiratnam: Scarlet morning glory or *Ipomea hederifolia*.
14. Nandivardhanam: Butterfly gardenia or *Tabernaemontena divaricata*.
15. Mandara/Dasana: Hibiscus or *Hibiscus Rosa-Sinesis*.
16. Gaddi puvvulu: Sedge or *Rhychospora wightiana*.
17. Teku puvvu: Teak flower or *Tectona grandis*.

Flowers and Leaves of Seasonal Vegetables and Spices

1. Gummadi puvvu and aaku: Flowers and leaves of field pumpkin or *Curcubita Pepo*. The leaves form the first layer of the Bathukamma pyramid.
2. Beerakaya puvvu: Flower of ridge gourd, Luffa or *Curcubita Actangula*.
3. Dosakaya puvvu: Flower of the cucumber vine or *Cucumus Melo*.
4. Vama puvvu: Carom seed flowers (popularly called ajwain) or *Trachyspermum ammi*.

Flowers and Leaves Used as Hair Accessories

Particularly during the festive season, these flowers are strung as either a separate flower sequence or in combination of all three, which is called kadambam, meaning assortment.

1. Malli puvvu: Jasmine or *Jasminum fluminense*.
2. Kanakambaralu: Fire cracker or *Crossandra infudibuliformis*.
3. Maruvamu: Marjoram or *Marjorana hortensis*.

Nine Nights and 10 Days of Navaratri

The first day of Navaratri coincides with what in Telangana is called the Pethara Amavasya. On this day, people pay homage to the deceased in the family. Offering food is an important part of the ritual. Festive days have always meant special cuisine. Even the simplest of fare has the best of taste. This could be attributed to the ambience around, the improved weather, onset of the Sharada ritu (autumn months). Each day, a different Naivedyam or offering is made for the goddess. The culinary varieties are season specific, they are all very simple preparations made from locally grown/sourced ingredients. Each day of the Navaratri is classified by the name of the offering made.

1. Engili Pulu (puvvala) Bathukamma: Commences on the Mahalaya Amavasya. The naivedyam is prepared with nuvvulu (sesame seeds), biyam pindi (rice flour) and nookalu (coarsely ground wet rice).
2. Atkula Bathukamma: The day is called Padyami and is the first day of the Ashvajuja masam. The naivedyam is prepared with sapidi pappu (bland boiled lentils), bellam (jaggery) and atukulu (flattened rice/ rice flakes)
3. Muddapappu Bathukamma: Vidiya (from Dvitiya) is the second day of Ashvayuja masam. The naivedyam for the day is muddapappu (cooked lentils), paalu (milk) and bellam.

4. Nanabiyam Bathukamma: Tridiya (Tritiya) is the third day of the Ashvayuja masam. The naivedyam for the day is relish made with nanesina biyam (soaked rice), paalu and bellam.
5. Atla Bathukamma: Chaturdi (Chaturthi) is the fourth day of Ashvayuja masam. Atla means a pancake. This pancake is made with uppidi pindi (coarsely ground rice flour).
6. Aligina Bathukamma: Panchami or the fifth day of the Ashvayuja masam. This day no naivedyam is prepared as it is believed that the goddess is sulking. It probably corresponds to a break, halfway through the nine days.
7. Vepakaya Bathukamma: Shashti or the sixth day of the Ashvayuja masam. The offering for the day is small deep-fried balls made out of rice flour, which are shaped like the fruit of the neem tree.
8. Venna mudda Bathukamma: Saptami or the seventh day. Venna means butter. The offering for the day is made with nuvvulu (sesame seeds), naiyi (clarified butter or ghee) and bellam.
9. Saddula Bathukamma: The ninth day of Bathukamma is celebrated on Ashtami or the eighth day of *Ashvayuja* masam and coincides with Durga Ashtami. Five types of cooked rice dishes—perguannam saddi (curd rice), chintapandu pulihora saddi (tamarind rice), nimmakaya saddi (lemon rice), kobbara saddi (coconut rice) and nuvvula saddi (sesame seeds rice)—are offered as naivedyam.

It would be worthwhile to know another Telugu word of the region, 'saddula', which refers to cooked food that is carried to be consumed elsewhere. After the hectic afternoon of making the array of flowers, cooking food, dressing up and then stepping out to sing and dance and finally immerse the flowers, everyone is hungry. Finally, the sheer joy of sharing the food!

Song and Dance

Music and dance are an integral part of the Navaratri celebrations in Telangana. The songs are called *janapada geethalu*, meaning the songs of the people. While some are songs that hail the goddesses, other are Itihasa-Purana stories, legends related to Bathukamma or some that simply describe the quotidian, sharing as they sing the woes of life. The phrases are short and epichoric, in that, one word, 'uyyalo', is repeated at the end of every phrase. 'Uyyala' means a swing. Presumably it has been changed to uyyalo and repeated to mimic the swinging movement in song. The refrain remains constant.

> Bathukamma Bathukamma uyyalo,
> Bangara Bathukamma uyyalo.

> (Come alive O Mother,
> Golden Mother, come alive.)

I have chosen to translate a song 'Kalavari kodallu uyyalo',[5] which depicts the typical setting in a village where the brother comes to take his sister home for the festive period. Each phrase usually ends in 'uyyalo', which has been done away with in the translation to understand simply the context without the distraction of the epistrophe.

> Daughter-in-law of a wealthy family,
> Charming lady with an auspicious gaze
> Was washing lentils.
> Just then arrived
> Her older brother.
> She gave him water to wash his feet
> As her eyes welled up with tears.
> 'Why my little sister?
> What difficulties (bother you)?

---

[5]Translation mine

> Come dear, let's go!
> Ask your mother-in-law (for permission).'
> On a wooden chair
> Is seated the mother-in-law.
> 'My older brother has come,
> Will you permit me to go (home)?'
> 'Where are your brothers?
> Where are their horses?'
> 'In the street,
> The horses are outside.
> They are here alright.'
> 'But what all have they brought?'
> 'A silk shirt for the toddler,
> A milk bowl,
> A water jug,
> A black saree for me,
> A blouse of the colour of the peacock feather.'
> 'Well, then this is all we want.
> (Nevertheless) do ask your father-in-law.'

With this, the lady goes puttintiki (literally 'the home where she was born') from her attagari illu (her in-laws' home). Navaratri is also the much-needed break from domesticities. In the week to follow, there are festivities galore. Each day, women of the household get together to create the Bathukamma, cook delicacies, dress up in their fineries, head to the pond to go singing and dancing and finally immerse the goddess into the waters. They share the cooked food after tiring themselves from dancing and share their stories.

The festival of the mother goddess is indeed a festival of flowers, water bodies, thanksgiving, of sisterhood and, most importantly, a festival of replenishment and regeneration.

On Vijaya Dashami day, or as it is called, Dasara, people in Telangana offer prayers to the Jammi tree, which grows in villages, in the countryside and is also found in temple complexes. In Sanskrit, it is called the Shami tree and holds an important place in Vedic practices. The twig of the tree is used for a yagna or the sacrificial fire. It is one of the 27 nakshatra vriksha, where each constellation is known to have an associated tree. The Shami tree is associated with the Dhanisthta nakshatra.

It has also been conferred the status of a Deva vriksha, because Agni or the fire god is known to have concealed himself in the Shami wood. The tree *Prosopis Cineraria* also happens to be state tree of Telangana and Rajasthan. Apart from the villagers and farmers, environmentalists too have campaigned for the cause of using it actively for afforestation in arid regions. It is one tree that can grow in extremely harsh weather, practically without any water. The roots are known to grow as deep as 35 feet. A full-grown tree can yield up to 50 kilograms of fodder a day for cattle. Hence, while being a symbol of firmness, perseverance and persistence, the notion of sufficiency and abundance also seems to be built into the ritual. The leaves are guarded and stored in rice bins as a symbol of replenishment.

After circumambulating around the tree, people carry back leaves which are offered to elders in the family. The members of the family take blessings from them by touching their feet. It is called by other names such as Jambhi, and in the north it is called the Khejri or the Ker Sangri tree. The prayer chanted goes as follows:

शमी शमयते पापं शमी शत्रु विनाशिनी ।
अर्जुनस्य धनुर्धारी रामस्य प्रियदर्शिनी ॥

Shami cleanses sins. Shami destroys rivals.
The bearer of Arjuna's bow (Gandiva) and the favourite tree of
Shri Rama.

There is mention of the Shami tree in both the important epics, the Mahabharata and the Ramayana. In 'Virata Parva', which is also called the 'Samaya Palana Parva', the Pandavas after losing the game of dice had to exile themselves for 12 years and then spend the thirteenth year incognito. At the beginning of the *ajnata vasa* or the period of living incognito, the Pandavas were said to have left their weapons on the Shami tree. At the end of the year, when they went back to collect them, the weapons were supposedly intact. They prayed to the tree before getting back to war with the Kauravas, which they eventually won. Their victorious return is also celebrated as Vijaya Dashami. On this day, people venerate their tools and weapons (ayudha or astra) as a thanksgiving to the divine force. It is hence called the Ayudha Puja or the Astra Puja. This day is also considered auspicious to embark on new ventures.

In the *Valmiki Ramayana*, there is a mention of the Shami tree in the 'Aranya Kanda', in the eighteenth shloka of the fifteenth sarga.[6] This is more an enumeration of the varied trees of Panchavati—sandalwood, spandan, dhava, asvakarna parnasha, khadira, sami, kimsuka and patala trees.

चन्दनैस्पन्दनैनींपै: पर्णासैर्लिंकुचौरपि।
धवाश्वकर्णखदिरै: शमीकिंशुकपाटलै:॥

Rajputs, originally from the warrior clan, venerate the tree during Dussehera as they believe that lord Rama prayed to Aparajita Devi under this tree.

Shakti Peetha in Telangana

Goddess worship is known to have been thriving in the region of Telangana for several centuries. Various rulers of different dynasties have been the followers of the Shakta tradition and commissioned the construction of some beautiful temples. The Nava Brahma temple complex, which as the name implies, consists of nine temples dedicated to Brahmeshvara and Goddess Yogulamba or the mother of all yogis. Herein, is housed one of the 18 Shakti Peetha temples

---

[6]The numbering of both the shloka and the sarga can depend on the edition of the text.

or the ashtadasha shaktipeetha—the Jogulamba. This is situated in Alampur by the bank of the river Tungabhadra, in Gadwal district. I consider myself fortunate to have visited all the Shakti Peethas with the exception of the Sarasvati Peetha and the Pradyumna Shrinkhla Devi.

The 'Ashtadasha Shakti Peetha Strotram' by Adi Sankara is an intriguing written map of all the sacred places where parts of the Devi's body were supposed to have fallen when she consigned herself to flames because of the insult meted out by her father Daksha to Lord Shiva. The parts of the Devi's body which fell to earth are considered the sacred Shakti peethas.

लङ्कायां शाङ्करी देवी कामाक्षी काञ्चिकापुरे ।
प्रद्युम्ने शृङ्खलादेवी चामुण्डी क्रौञ्चपट्टणे ॥
अलम्पुरे जोगुलाम्बा श्रीशैले भ्रमराम्बिका ।
कोल्हापुरे महालक्ष्मी माहूर्ये एकवीरिका ॥
उज्जयिन्यां महाकाली पीठिक्यां पुरुहूतिका ।
ओढ्यायां गिरिजादेवी माणिक्या दक्षवाटके ॥
हरिक्षेत्रे कामरूपा प्रयागे माधवेश्वरी ।
ज्वालायां वैष्णवी देवी गया माङ्गल्यगौरिका ॥
वाराणस्यां विशालाक्षी काश्मीरेषु सरस्वती ।
अष्टादश सुपीठानि योगिनामपि दुर्लभम् ॥
सायङ्काले पठेन्नित्यं सर्वशत्रुविनाशनम् ।
सर्वरोगहरं दिव्यं सर्वसम्पत्करं शुभम् ॥

Shankari in Lanka, Devi Kamakshi in Kanchipuram,
Shrinkhala Devi in Pradyumna, Chamunda in Kraunchpattan (Mysore)
Jogulamba in Alampur, Bhamarambika in Shri Sailam,
Mahalakshmi in Kolhapur, Ekaveera in Mahur
Mahakali in Ujjain, Purhuthika in Peethika,
Girija in Odhyana and Manikya in the garden of Daksha
Kamarupi in the kshetra of Vishnu, Madhevaswari in Prayag,
Vaishanavi Devi in Jwala [mukhi], Mangala Gauri in Gaya
Visalakshi in Varanasi, Sarasvati in Kashmir,

Eighteen Peetha of Shakti, which are difficult even for the yogis.
One who reads this every evening, all his enemies are destroyed,
All diseases are cured and one gets all types of divine auspicious wealth.

Another important temple where Navaratri is celebrated for 10 days is the Jnana Sarasvati temple in Basara in Adilabad. It is called the Devi Navathrulu, which literally means the nine nights of the Devi. The temple, which is situated on the banks of the river Godavari, is one of the two famous temples of Sarasvati in the Indian subcontinent, the other one being the Sharada Peetha in Kashmir (POK).

Bathukamma—Then and Now

I was all of six when our family relocated from Secunderabad. My earliest memories of Bathukamma at Bowenpally, a scantily populated sleepy cantonment, are still vivid in my mind. The house was an erstwhile army officers mess of the British Era, with huge gardens and a long drive from the main gate and a mini forest therein. Each evening, the women from the nearby bastis (slums or hutments of the people from lower socio-economic status), other local women would congregate at the Prakash Reddy household, the owners of the house, who would graciously host the gathering. The swaying to and singing of 'Bathukamma bathukamma uyyalo', the fragrance of the flowers and the nip in the air are images I continue to carry with me even five decades later.

Today, Bathukamma is the state festival of Telangana. It is celebrated on a scale where there are not enough water bodies to send away the Mother Goddess, without inundating the ponds beyond recognition. Fish have been introduced into ponds to feed on the flowers. There is a common folk saying: '*Parasparam upakaraka bhave phalitamaaha*', meaning 'the earth and all living beings are mutually dependent, just as the bees and honey are'. Devi who is revered as Prakriti, not only gives birth to all life forms; she also nourishes them.

Note

Bathukamma is a tradition of storytelling. As I embarked upon writing this piece, I took a decision to transcribe aural memory into writing. I am grateful for a conversation I had with Sri Mamidi Hari Krishna, director, Department of Language and Culture, Government of Telangana. I would like to acknowledge Srilatha, Varalakshmi and Anita, who, by virtue of hailing from different parts of Telangana, regaled me with interesting anecdotes of their Bathukamma stories.

6

Bali and Puja in Nepal

RUPA JOSHI

A mixture of fragrances and feels: That is what Dashain used to be. Cool, white mist that tickled your nose along with the fragrance of crushed sayapatri (marigold) and piping hot sel roti.[1] Then the early morning plaintive notes of the malsiri[2] on flute, interspersed with the bleating of the goat tied up and waiting for its time to come under the khukuri (Nepali curved knife). These are the 'flavours' of Dashain that take me right back to my childhood, growing up in a meat-eating brahmin household in Kathmandu valley. These are sights and sounds predominantly found in the hilly areas of the country. But over the decades, with creeping 'development', mainly in the form of transportation, globalization and migration to the cities or to the plains, some of these flavours have diluted, while others have been coloured with new exposures and experiences. Also, there are more and more voices being raised against animal cruelty and animal sacrifice during Dashain, and urging people to focus on nonviolent celebrations.

Dashain has always been the most awaited festival, especially for children. It meant a long school holiday, getting—in those days rare—new clothes, soaring on the bamboo swing or letting the westerlies waft your kites high up in the air. A time when dakshina (monetary gift) from elders would fatten our piggy banks. And a

---

[1] Home-made sweet rice-bread.
[2] The malashri raga.

time when there were feasts, with a lot of meat, in our homes and neighbourhoods.

We, the children, didn't care about the significance of Dashain—the red tika on our foreheads made of rice, yogurt and vermillion powder, the jamara (barley shoots) on our hair or the worshipping of goddesses, machinery, weapons, girls. Nor did we delve into the mystery of why the nine-day rituals of Nauratha happened in a darkened Puja room, conducted only by adult males of the family. As children, we never wondered why Dashain was celebrated or of its importance in the socio-cultural fabric of the country. It was a fun-filled, responsibility-less period for us, which continued on to Tihar a fortnight later.

Depending on the lunar calendar, Dashain can be in September or October. The biggest and longest festival for Nepalis, celebrated from at least half a millennia ago, starts on Ashvina Shukla Pratipada with Ghatasthapana (placement of the water pot) and ends with the full moon on Kojagrat Purnima. It is said that earlier, people used to celebrate Dashain in the month of Chaitra, until for some reason, possibly a more favourable post-harvest climate, it got shifted to autumn. So, people still celebrate a shorter Chaitey Dashain, and a longer, more elaborate Bada Dashain (greater Dashain).

Dashain in Nepal is like a salad of rituals—one celebration with distinct ethnic and regional variations and influences. A result of harmonious living as well as diversity brought about by the country's unique topography crisscrossed by mountains and rivers. Rituals vary amongst those with Hindu and Buddhist leanings, with those living in east or west, in the mountains or plains. There are borrowed rituals, modified customs. The rituals of animal sacrifice and non-vegetarianism, for instance, is practised mainly by the Shakta sect of Hindus who worship Devi, the supreme goddess, in all her various manifestations.

But all over, it is a time for celebration, a time for spiritual reflection, of purification of the soul, and a time for catching up with extended family, elders and friends. Till a few decades ago, when transportation was not that developed, family members thought the worst of their loved ones if they did not come back home for Dashain.

Like in the rest of South Asia, here too Dashain or Vijaya Dashami, depending on whether one resides in the hills or plains, celebrates the victory of good over evil, of Rama over Ravana, of Shakti over the asuras Mahishasura, Chanda–Munda and Shumbha–Nishumbha. The terms may differ, from the more prevalent Dashain to the more localized Mohani of the Newars, Dashahara for the residents in the southern Mithila plains, to Dasya for the Tharus in the western plains. Amongst the Newars too, it is mainly the followers of the Vajrayana sect of Buddhism who celebrate Mohani.

While Dashain is celebrated in a mainly non-vegetarian way in the hills, those celebrating Dussehra in the plains or amongst the Marwari communities actually fast and eat only fruits and dairy products during the 10 days. The Tharu settlements during Dasya resound with the beat of the madal (two-faced Nepali drum) accompanying the sakhya and paiyan dances throughout the Dasya nights. The madals played by the men are in fact blessed and 'empowered' a month earlier by the guruwa (village elder). Sakhya is a circular dance accompanied by a song that sings praises of Sri Krishna.

Preparations for Dashain

A ditty regarding Dashain reflects the socio-cultural-economic impact of the festival. It is recited by children using their fingers. I remember doing this myself and then with my children. The little finger exclaims, '*Dashain ayo!*' ('Dashain is coming!'), the ring finger says, '*Khaunla piunla!*' ('We will eat and drink!'), the middle finger asks, '*Kahan paunla?*' ('Where can we get that?'), the index finger says, '*Chori lyaunla!*' ('We will steal!') and the thumb in disgust says '*Dhatta papi ma ta chhuttai basaunla!*' ('You sinner, I'll stay away from you all'). And that is why, we were told, the thumb lives away from the other four digits!

The economic burden of Dashain is probably what makes many

with less means wonder whether Dashain is a dasha (curse). There is a popular saying: '*Ayo Dashain dhol bajayi, Gayo Dashain rin bokayi!*' ('Dashain arrived with a lot of fanfare, and departed leaving a burden of debt!') Dashain does become a festival that drains the pocket, due to its length and the various rituals it entails. It involves a lot of preparation, starting over a month before the festival.

Preparing for Dashain

Since it is a time for renewal, first of all, homes, offices, neighbourhoods need to spruced up. Neighbours get together to clean pathways, wells and water-spouts. It is time to give that yearly fresh coat of paint to homes. Although modern homes do not need to be painted often, the mud mortar homes in the villages are splashed with a coat of white and ochre clay annually. It is often the women who go and dig for these coloured soils and the male members who do the painting. The women in the eastern Terai decorate their homes with Mithila artwork, and the Tharus[3] living in the western Terai go the extra mile by adding beautiful motifs of pairs of elephants, deer, horses, fishes or peacocks fashioned out of clay and rice husk on the walls next to the main door of their homes.

But renewal is not limited to homes and neighbourhoods. Dashain is the time to buy new clothes. In earlier days, when readymade garment shops were a rarity, even in the capital Kathmandu, all clothes had to be stitched by local tailors. The more adventurous ones in the hills talk about trekking several days into neighbouring Indian towns to buy clothes and shoes. Of course, it was easier in the Terai plains bordering Bihar and Uttar Pradesh. People dress up in their best attire when receiving tika, either in their homes or visiting relatives. Nowadays in the cities and towns, it might mean a trip or two to the shops for readymade clothes. But for us as children, it meant a trip to the much-in-demand tailors.

---

[3]Residents of the Tarai region in southern Nepal.

I fondly remember the tailor who used to visit our home with a measuring tape hanging around his neck, a pencil stuck behind his ear, clutching a dog-eared Sears catalogue under his armpit. Measurements would be mumbled and jotted down, and a design for a frock tick-marked, the page bookmarked with a fold. 'Remember to leave enough room in the hemline. It has to fit her till next year!' would be mother's parting remarks to him. When the clothes came back from the tailor's, they would be treasured for the tika ceremony starting from the tenth day of Dashain.

Dashain is a busy time for adults loaded with responsibilities to prepare for the festivities. In the city, menfolk set out in search of crisp bank notes or shiny new coins to be distributed as dakshina (gift of money) later. They also busy themselves buying goats or fowl to be sacrificed and eaten on Ashtami (eighth day of Dashain). Goats being dragged on a leash, taking a ride on top of buses, riding pillion in motorbikes are common sights.

Women, meanwhile are fretting about preparations for the bhoj (feasts) and snacks to feed visitors who come for tika. Where it is not readily available in the market, rice flour needs to be pounded to make the ubiquitous sel roti or chiura (beaten rice) needs to be de-husked. Masala needs to be pounded for meat. And the giant, foot-long ripe cucumbers must be cut and pickled, for what is masubhat (mutton curry and rice) without the crunchy tangy khalpi achar on the side.

While the adults are tied up in Dashain preparation, the youngsters have a field day, with their eyes to the skies. Except for the occasional hiley (muddy) Dashain, the post-monsoon sky is blue with white cumulus clouds blown by the westerly winds—perfect for kite-flying. People say that kites are flown at this time of the year to send a message to Indra to stop the rains, as it is harvest time. This is also why kites aren't flown at other times of the year when rain is needed. Some believe that kites are messengers to our dead ancestors in heaven to tell them we are okay.

With the youngsters nowadays glued to their screens, kite-flying seems to have taken a backseat during Dashain. When we were young, preparations for kite-flying would begin as soon as my brothers and cousins returned home from boarding school. They would start preparing majha for the 'splice-on-contact' kite thread. The recipe for the majha could include anything slippery from slug slime to glue, aloe or arrowroot gruel to be mixed with pounded glass (mainly from old light bulbs). This concoction would be applied on thread with corn husk. These were days before the imported pre-treated-to-cut kite threads from India. They bought few kites, the sluggish Nepali rice paper ones as well as the swift 'Lucknow' kites that made' jhir jhir' noise when they dived upon their prey! The rest of the kites had to be collected when chet (cut) kites landed in our compound. Although kites would be flown before Nauratha too, they peaked from Saptami to Navami. Families would meet on rooftops to support or hoot at the kite fliers!

Around the same time, people would put up lingey ping (bamboo and twine swing) in neighbourhoods. These tall swings would attract not just the young, but even adults. It is said that for at least once a year everyone should leave the ground, fly and in a way, detach oneself from the Earth and worldliness.

The day before Ghatasthapana, the Dashain kotha (room) or any secluded corner in the house is readied, floor cleaned with a paste of cow-dung and clay, if it is an adobe house, and the area darkened with thick curtains, to worship the goddess in a secretive, almost tantrik manner. All the rituals for the nine days would be done by male elders of the family or a hired priest. For Newars, these rituals take place in their household shrine called Agam Chhen.

Ghatasthapana

The first day of Dashain is when a ghata or kalasha (water vessel) is set up in the Dashain kotha. I remember my mother decorating the kalasha with strips of firm cow-dung and planting long-eared barley seeds into them. By Dashami, these would have sprouted too.

Many people get fresh sand from rivers to plant barley seeds for jamara (barely shoots), while others make do with sand mixed with soil in leaf plates, pots or boxes. The Puja rituals on the auspicious hour invoke the Tri Shakti—Goddesses Mahakali, Mahalakshmi and Maha Sarasvati—to reside in the kalasha for the entire 10 days. According to the *Kalika Purana*, however, it is not just the goddess trio, all other gods, all rivers, the seven seas and continents and all pilgrimages are said to settle into the *kalasha* during Dashain.

Once the kalasha is established, barley seeds are then sprinkled on the sand and kept covered so that the jamara shoots remain yellow. Some, like the Tharus, sprinkle corn too. The kalasha is worshipped daily in the mornings and evenings by reciting 'Chandi', 'Stotra Ratnavali', 'Kalika Stotra', 'Durga Kavacha', 'Srimad Devi Bhagvata' and 'Durga Saptashati'. The jamara is watered every day too.

According to Mithila tradition, young girls go to the local ponds or rivers, fill the kalasha with water and go around the village before setting them down in the place of worship, usually temples. The Tharus in western Nepal refer to Ghatasthapana as Jyura dharna and they worship their ancestors, their home deity Rajaji and village deity Dihibar Baba.

For both the Mithilabasi and Tharus, Dashahara or Dasya is also a time when they believe evil eyes are on the roam and thus, they need special rituals to ward them off. For instance, in the eastern plains on the day of Ghatasthapana there is a tradition of painting black circles on doors of homes, which would be painted over with vermilion paste on Saptami. Similarly, the Tharus in western plains paint dain jogin (evil eyes) on their doors as well as granaries on the fifth day of Dasya which they paint over with vermilion on Saptami. In Mithila, they also apply black marks on children's belly buttons and eyes, hang a pod of garlic round their necks and do not allow them to venture out of the house too much. They even have a special dance—Jhijhiya—to ward off the eyes of witches. Groups of women balancing perforated clay lanterns on their heads go from door to door in the village. They dance shaking their heads vigorously so that witches, who are after their lives, are unable to count the number of holes in their pots.

For the Newars celebrating Mohani, family members are discouraged from spending nights away from home for nine days following Ghatasthapana, or Nalaswane, the first day of Mohani.

From Ghatasthapana to Saptami

After the gods have been invoked to the kalasha on the first day, various forms of Goddess Durga are worshipped in nine days leading to Dashami. It starts with Shailaputri, Brahmacharini, Chandraghanta, Kushmanda, Skandamata, Katyayani, Kalaratri, Mahagauri and ends with Siddhidatri. It is said that while worshipping the goddesses and praising their prowess in vanquishing asuras, we are actually supposed to defeat the asuras in all of us—our greed, hatred, lust, pride and envy.

In the Terai plains, people raise contributions to set up pandals (stages) with the clay sculptures of Goddess Durga in neighbourhoods, which function as temporary temples for worshippers throughout Dashahara. Nowadays, even in the capital Kathmandu and other towns in the hills, people set up such places of worship decorated with Murtis prepared by artisans from the plains. Ramlila is staged in various places in the plains, more so in the Awadhi speaking areas of western Terai. In Mithila, people also organize Mahabiri Jhanda Mela (fair), where a big tower made with bamboo and coloured paper honouring Hanuman is raised and people throng around singing songs. They perform tricks with sticks and organize wrestling competitions too.

Till Saptami, there are no special rituals. During these days, tailors work hard to stitch all those clothes in time. Shopping centres are teeming with people, as are the *khasi bajars* (goat markets). Children wait on rooftops for a good breeze to set their kites aloft, while their mothers are most likely busy in the kitchen, preparing delicacies to feed their Dashain guests.

Saptami: The seventh day of Dashain, also known as Phulpati, starts building up the crescendo of the final three important days of the festival. The Newars, for instance, have family feasts everyday starting on Saptami and households have no need to cook meals at home.

Phulpati literally means flowers and leaves. With the summer and monsoon gone, it is believed bringing a potpourri of vegetation with medicinal values cleanses the air of bugs and creepy crawlies. And that is what people do, bringing a bouquet combination of nine plants—including belpatra, pomegranate, paddy, turmeric, banana, ashoka, manabrikshya, jayanti and ginger—into the Dashain shrine with a fanfare of conch shells, bells and damaru. The Phulpati is then worshipped along with the kalasha and jamara for the rest of Dashain. As children, it was fascinating to watch this noisy mini-parade in the house, only to see the Phulpati disappearing behind those thick curtains of the Dashain kotha. It always left us wondering about what was happening in there!

Kathmandu sees a different sort of celebration on Saptami. Following the trail of the Shah kings from Gorkha, Phulpati from the Dashain shrine in Gorkha Palace is brought to Hanuman Dhoka Durbar (former palace of the kings). In Kathmandu, it is taken in a parade through the traditional route through alleys in a special silver palanquin. Meanwhile in the centre of the valley, at the Tundikhel parade ground, the Army puts a special *feu de joie* ceremony firing muskets and ancient cannons.

Phulpati is also a day when farmers worship paddy and take a paddy plant into their homes. The Tharus, meanwhile, on this day, make their popular dish—dhikri or steamed rice cake—that will later be offered to their deities on the ninth day.

Ashtami: The eighth day of Dashain is very busy one. Pujas are offered to Bhadrakali and people visit shrines of Goddess Kali, as well as their *kul deuta* (clan deity). They also sacrifice goats, chickens, ducks or buffaloes at these shrines. Meanwhile, there is a growing trend of people opting for the vegetarian offerings of coconut, sugarcane, ash gourd, banana or other fruits to the deities. This offering of animal sacrifice in the temples during Dashain is mainly present in the hills. Those celebrating Mohani, Dashahara or even Dasya do not offer sacrifices in this manner in temples. Animal sacrifice, where their heads are just slit and not severed so as to bathe the Murtis in blood, is increasingly being protested by activists of non-violence to animals. Scholars too chip in to say that the essence of Dashain should be to slay and sacrifice the animals residing inside humans and not killing innocent animals or birds. They say that these sacrifices were meant to give up our 10 vices—lust, anger, greed, attachment, vanity, prejudice, envy, malice, deceit and pretence. Instead, in order to attain happiness, prosperity and peace, people switched to sacrificing animals—goats for lust, buffaloes for anger, sheep for greed, chicken for vanity and ducks for prejudice!

The Newars have a story about the dasha (curse) for animals during Mohani. In the story the roosters crow out, '*Mohani wala*' ('Mohani is here'), while the blue headed ducks quack, '*Kanhey Kenney*' ('It's tomorrow'). Then the sheep bleat, '*Aa gahtye yaya?*' ('What to do?'), the goats give a resigned reply, '*Mya mya*' and the poor buffaloes say a prayer '*Narayan!*' ('God help us!')

In the mountains of Rasuwa district, north of Kathmandu, Buddhist monks and their followers visit the gumba (monastery), to offer special chhyama (forgiveness) prayers during the whole of Dashain. They have taken the burden on themselves to rid the sins of all citizens involved in slaughtering animals. They ask for forgiveness for those who sacrificed animals during Dashain, for the lasting peace of those dead animals and also to forgive those who unintentionally killed innocent animals or birds at other times. For three days, the Lamas perform the strict Kukpa tiba rite by taking a vow of silence and fasting, without even drinking water.

Historians say that the practice of animal sacrifice and worshipping of arms in Dashain is a remnant of the martial past in the history of the country. Rulers of the principalities before Nepal was annexed as a nation used to consider Dashami as an auspicious day for Simolanghan or setting forth to battle across borders. The red tika worn during Dashain is also supposed to reflect the custom of applying tika with blood of the vanquished, which, with time, got transferred into wearing tika that was a mixture of blood of sacrificed animals and rice, and finally ended up using crimson powder for colour.

Meat eaters, like me, have developed the convenient skill to disassociate animal cruelty while being served a non-vegetarian spread. Guilt gets masked by gluttony when Dashain mutton comes swimming in piping hot suruwa (curried coup), cooked to the bone dark kabab, fried bhitri haans (innards) or spongy deep-friend ragti (coagulated blood)! And then all of these items cooked with mother's loving hands, on open log fire, in big vessels before pressure cookers, became the norm, adding extra flavour to our meals.

Newari cuisine is even more elaborate, maybe because they have more meat and organs from larger animals like buffaloes to experiment with. The Mohani revellers have a special clan feast called Kuchhibhwyae on Ashtami. On this day all their tools, from agricultural to martial ones, are kept in the Agam chhen (courtyard shrine) to be 'recharged' through divine power overnight.

Meanwhile in the western plains, the Tharus on this day celebrate Dhikrahwa when the houses are cleaned and purified, and the shrine decorated with rice flour paste hand prints. The head of the household performs rituals at the shrine that go on through the night and culminate in wrapping their deity, created in the image of a clay horse, with thread to invoke the gods. Outside in the village, sakhya and paiyan dancers sway rhythmically to the beat of the blessed madals.

The Marwaris, who are vegetarians and worship Devi as Shakti, the better half of Shiva, during Dashahara offer the deity vegetarian prasada of halwa and puri on Ashtami.

Navami: The night between Ashtami and Navami, known as

Kalaratri (the dark night) is a busy one. Secret rituals are performed in the shrines and weapons are worshipped for their sacrificial duty on Navami. In the courtyard of Hanuman Dhoka, a total of 108 animals (54 buffaloes and 54 goats) end up under the khukuri as part of appeasing what some refer to as a bloodthirsty goddess.

This is the final day of Navaratri when Durga's avatara Siddhidhatri is worshipped. On Navami, people perform Puja to their machines, including vehicles and planes, and invoke blessings of Vishwakarma to protect them from mishaps in the year ahead. That day, one can find cars plying with their wheels and hoods adorned with marigold garlands, tika and red and white cloths.

The Newars refer to this day as Syakutyaku. The tools that had been put inside the Agam chhen on the day before are worshipped with offerings of sacrifices of animals, birds or eggs. That day they also worship any machinery, or instrument from which people make a living, including automobiles.

Navami is the most important day in Dasya for the Tharus in the west. On this day, the family head starts by cleaning the entrance of the house with cow-dung and clay paste. He then paints a circle in the middle with rice flour paste and a lamp in placed in the centre of the circle. Their deity is worshipped with flowers of the kubhindo (ash gourd) and a kubhindo is also duly sacrificed and its stem portion is kept on the roof of the entrance. They worship their ancestors, and sacrifice a chicken at the shrine. At midday, they assemble at the chieftain's house and sing sholkas from the *Tharu Mahabharata*.

Hanuman Dhoka in Kathmandu opens its doors to devotees just for one day in a year on Navami as does the tall and majestic Taleju temple that dwarfs other temples and homes around it.

Many households on this day also worship kanyas (pre-puberty girls). Some worship all nine kanyas representing the nine avataras of Goddess Durga, while others settle for one. Many many moons ago, a major attraction for me during Dashain was Kanya Puja. Getting up early (when you can still see three stars in the sky, as mother used to say), taking a cold bath, wearing a red dress and waiting for my aunt to arrive with goodies for the Puja. The kanya at that time is looked upon as a manifestation of the goddess and is given the full Puja ritual of one. The lamps, bells, garland, tika and offerings of sweetmeats, fruits, dried fruits, dakshina (money) and best of all, clothes and related accessories! It feels almost trance-like when everybody—elders and youngsters—start bowing down at your feet. And as a little goddess, you give them prasada of tika and flowers. I saw the same fascination in my daughters' eyes, and now I see them in my granddaughters'!

The night of Navami is when final preparations are made for the Dashami tika the next day. Food readied, carpets in homes covered up to protect them from tika droppings. New clothes laid out. Exciting!

Dashami: This is the day when the mystery is revealed. The door and curtains of the Dashain kotha are opened to 'lesser mortals'! I still remember the eagerness with we used to troop to the Puja room, dressed in our best, taking in all that we had been missing the last nine days—the kalasha with green jamara sprouting from the cow-dung, heaps of flowers on top and around the kalasha, the Phulpati leaning on the wall in the corner and the heady aroma of gokul dhoop (gum incense). The jamara patch is also opened up temporarily to reveal lemony yellow shoots 6 to 7 inches tall.

With the final Puja rituals, comes the dreaded abhisheka (sprinkling of holy water) accompanying the shanti path (prayer for peace). With experience we had learnt to dodge the sprinkling of the 10-day-old water flavoured with putrefied flower offerings. After the prasada from the Puja, it is time to take tika from the elders.

The tika we make at home is a mixture of rice, vermillion powder and yogurt. Some add sugar to make it stick to the forehead. But not everyone uses red tika. It is said that the sticking of rice to your foreheads (without colour) probably reveals the practice as arising from nature and agriculture worship. Earlier, before synthetic red colours entered the market, people either just wore rice and yogurt, thus, the white tika. Then came the practice of red tika. The Limbu people in the eastern hills, for example, who look upon Dashain not as a religious festival but as a time to make merry and visit family and friends, used to wear white tika. They slowly converted to red but are now once again going back to their old custom.

The Newars also wear black *Mohani Sinha* (Mohani Tika). The tika is prepared from the soot collected overnight on Navami over an oil lamp in the Agam chhen. This tika is supposed to energize the wearer of the tika with shakti (power). Many people who used to put white tika, now opt for the more common red one, including the Tharus who traditionally wore tika made of rice flour.

The tika is put on the forehead just above where the eyebrows come together. They say this is what opens up the third eye, the one that looks inwards, and not outwards. It is the spot of the Agnyachakra—the confluence of the Ida, Pingala and Sushumna chakras.[4] It is when the elders put the tika on you and recite a mantra of blessings in the process that one can feel the energy flowing from their fingertips and entering our system, into our veins. The Sanskrit mantra most elders use is:[5]

आयुर्द्रोणसुते श्रीयं दशरथे शत्रुक्षयं राघवे ।
ऐश्वर्यं नहुषे गतिश्च पवने मानञ्च दुर्योधने ॥
शौर्य शान्तनवे बलं हलधरे सत्यञ्च कुन्तीसुते ।
विज्ञान बिदुरे भवति भवतां कीर्तिश्चनारायण ॥

It wishes for your life to be as long as Ashvatthama's was, vanquish

---

[4] Three nadis or energy channels connect our chakras and run, vertically, from the base of the spine to the head. Ida is situated on the left, Sushumna in the center and Pingala on the right.

[5] This is for males. In a variant, Karna is mentioned instead of Bhishma. Women use:

जयन्ती मङ्गला काली भद्रकाली कपालिनी।
दुर्गा क्षमा शिवा धात्री स्वाहा स्वधा नमोऽस्तु ते॥

जय त्वं देवी चामुण्डे जय भूतार्तिहारिणी।
जय सर्वगते देवि कालरात्रि नमोऽस्तु ते॥

enemies like Shri Rama did, have the aura of King Dasharatha, glory like King Nahusha, speed like Hanuman, honour like Duryodhana, valour like Bhishma, strength like Balarama, honesty like Yudhishthira, wisdom like Vidura and repute like Narayana. Those who do not recite the blessings in Sanskrit improvise as per what they want the person to be or to achieve. After the tika, a bunch of jamara is put on the head, either stuck behind the ears, topi or clasped with clips. It is said that these barley shoots, loved by the Goddess Durga, possess medicinal properties and people these days drink jamara juice as immunity booster.

Along with the tika and jamara, the head of the household also gives other family members strips or strands from the red and white cloths that had adorned the kalasha during Navaratri. These doros (threads, called kokha by the Newars) are meant to carry the power of rejuvenation and all-round protection for the wearer. The elders also give dakshina as per their means to those junior to them in age or relation.

Once all the elders in the family have applied tika on younger family members and the family rituals are over, they visit their closest relatives and elders to receive tika. They move from house to house, their foreheads filling up with tika, jamara covering their hair and their tummies filling up with snacks offered in each house. This trend continues for three to four more days (depending upon the lunar calendar dates) until the full-moon day. The Newars, however, do not need to go visiting relatives in this way. For them, unlike the other, Mohanis celebrations are very much limited to their closest family members. They only go to *nakhatiya sategu* gatherings where they are invited for tika and food. No dakshina is exchanged either in that process. Also, in the western hills of the country, people only apply tika on Dashami, a custom probably necessitated by the need for the migrant menfolk in a hurry to rush back across the border to work, to attend to pressing harvest duties at home.

The Tharus in western Nepal go to the Mahaton (chieftain) to receive tika. Then throughout the day, like others days of

Dasya, young girls and boys go from house to house of the elders performing the sakhya dance. On this day, they also worship clay Murtis of Durga, Kali, Lakshmi, Sarasvati, Ganesha and Kartika. They consider this day to be very auspicious and open all doors and windows of their homes to let in the positive energy.

For the Newars, Dashami is the culmination of their concentration during Mohani on imbibing and renewing power in oneself, in one's tools. The Paya procession of khadga (straight sword) taken out in various parts of Kathmandu neighbourhoods, as well as in other Newar settlements, is a display of this new imbibed power—the power to destroy evil elements. People take out the khadgas from their shrine, the Agam chhen, and go around the city. The Paya procession ends in crossroads when the khadga is used to chop down kubhindo (ash gourd) as the final act of slaying evil outside and within us.

Kojagrat Purnima: This is the final day of Dashain, culminating in worshipping Goddess Lakshmi. It is like a mini form of Lakshmi Puja (Diwali), which follows a fortnight later. The rituals are all the same, although the fanfare is less—no deepawali or patakas (fireworks) in this one. People worship Lakshmi in the evening, brighten up their homes and make them as welcoming as possible for the goddess of wealth. The offerings in the Puja include sel roti, malpuwa, haluwa, coconut kheer, radish and fruits. Young girls are assigned to make *Lakshmi ko paila* (Lakshmi's footsteps) with rice flour paste coming inwards from the main door to the place of worship. The soles of the steps are made using the side of the closed fist and then fingertips for toes. I remember my mother telling me that one of my aunts once made the footprints the wrong way, heading out to the door, and grandmother feared the worst about the family's fortunes that year!

Many stay awake the whole night praying and singing bhajans to the goddess on Kojagrat. They do so because they believe that on that night, Goddess Lakshmi goes around the world to check 'who is awake' (thus Kojagrat) and who is asleep, and blesses those who remain awake to welcome her with prosperity.

After the worship, all the jamara and the kalasha are dutifully disposed in rivers, ponds or safe areas, thus wrapping up Dashain celebrations.

Next Up—Tihar: Dashain over, now all eyes are set on Nepal's next big festival, Tihar, which is a personal favourite of mine too! Dashain used to be fun as a child but not much fun as an adult loaded with responsibility to ensure everybody is provided for, fed, clothed and entertained! And yet, living in the midst of a now congested city, when I close my eyes, I can in a wink get transported back to those Dashain days. I can hear the melodious malsiri, feel that cool misty air in my nose along with the aroma of sel roti and sayapatri. I can see myself running to catch a chet kite, feel the cool touch of water and other offerings on my feet during Kanya Puja and hear myself playing with my fingers saying, '*Dashain Ayo!*'

7

Mrinmayee Murti in Odisha

NIVEDITA PANDA GANAPATHI

The state of Odisha celebrates the Sharadiya Navaratri festival in the month of Ashvina (September/October), with its own unique practices to honour and revere Ma Durga, the ultimate manifestation of the Mother Goddess. According to scriptures, Durga emerged with the combined energies of the Trinity and other devatas to vanquish the asura Mahishasura (the evil force) who dethroned Indra and created panic amongst the gods and demigods. She is thus known as Mahishasura-Mardini (the destroyer of Mahishasura). 'Durga Saptashati' (consisting of 13 chapters in 700 shlokas) from *Markandeya Purana* depicts Goddess Bhagavati (Durga) as the Universal Mother who inspires awe, fear, reverence, devotion, love and affection. During the nine nights of Navaratri, her Shakti is invoked to surmount obstacles and propel humanity forward.

The Durga Puja festival in Odisha embraces duality. On the one hand, Durga Devi is prematurely awakened to destroy evil on earth, and so the festival is marked by animal sacrifice and the worship of weapons. On the other hand, the Devi visits her home, thus, the festival is celebrated as a family event marked by feasting, family reunion, shopping and entertainment. The Devi, therefore, is simultaneously invoked and worshipped both in her ruthless manifestation as a destroyer of evil, as well as her peaceful and prosperous manifestation that symbolizes creativity, prosperity and wisdom.

The uninterrupted celebration of Durga Puja in Odisha, from antiquity to modernity, is a testament to the integral nature of Shakti worship in Odisha's socio-religious tapestry. All the complexities, dualities and multidimensional aspects of the Great Goddess are lovingly worshipped and celebrated across the length and breadth of the state, cutting across barriers of caste, sect, hierarchy and geography.

Durga Puja and Navaratri

While Durga Puja, as it is currently celebrated in Odisha, largely resembles the festivities in Bengal, Odisha has centuries-old traditions and rituals that vary greatly across the state itself. Moreover, unlike the Navaratri festival in north India, which is marked by fasting and austerities, Durga Puja in Odisha—barring Maha Ashtami—is a time of feasting and merry-making. Another difference is that in north India, Navaratri is uniformly celebrated as a nine-day festival from Prathama (Pratipada) to Navami, while Durga Puja in Odisha can vary anywhere from three to 16 days—depending on whether the Puja is done at home, at the peetha (temple), or at a community pandal. *Mata ka Jagarana* and Kumari Puja, which are followed in north India, are not commonly observed in Odisha.

However, another north Indian celebration called Ravana Dahana (burning the effigy of Ravana) has become quite popular in Odisha in the last few decades at community celebrations. Even within the state, there are significant variations in the worship and celebrations of Ma (as the Goddess is popularly referred to in Odisha). These intra-state variations are reflective of the ancient Shakti tradition in Odisha, combined with the prominent subcultures which have assimilated practices from the neighbouring states. Public celebrations of Durga Puja are a relatively modern cultural affair in Odisha, but beneath the current pomp and grandeur of

Bollywood-style community celebrations, Durga Puja has deep roots in Vedic, tantric, tribal and Buddhist traditions.

Types of Pujas

Durga Puja is magnificently celebrated in Odisha in three ways: Most popularly in community pandals (temporary stages) referred to as Mrinmayi Devi Puja, at home and in temples (Shakti Peethas).

Originally, Durga Puja was celebrated as the Shodasha-Dinatmaka Puja, a millennia-old ritual of Odisha which starts from Mulashtami, seven days prior to Mahalaya, and continues for 16 days till Maha Ashtami, with a celebratory completion on Bijaya (Vijaya) Dashami. The Shodasha Puja is now only followed in peethas/temples and in some brahmin families with Durga as the Adhishtatri Devi (established deity). Purity and sanctity are critical because 'it is believed that any departure from the rituals will incur the wrath of the Goddess.'[1]

In recent decades, due to a dearth of qualified priests and the overwhelming nature of the rituals, Durga Puja has been increasingly celebrated as a community festival rather than at home or in peethas. While the community Pujas usually celebrate Pancha-dinatmaka (five days from Shashti to Dashami), many households still observe the nine-day festival (from Dvitiya to Dashami). There is also a unique, fourth type of celebration, which is conducted by royal families, which follow both the Odisha style of 16 days temple worship at their Kuladevi (presiding deity of the clan) temples and the nine days for the home Pujas.

Durga Puja usually starts after the Mahalaya rituals. Mahalaya is on Amavasya (day of the new moon) and is the last day of the Pitri Paksha, which is the period when offerings are made to

---

[1] Abhisek Kumar Panda, 'The New and the Old of Durga Puja,' *The Daily Guardian*, 26 October 2020, thedailyguardian.com/the-new-and-the-old-of-durga-puja/. Accessed on 10 June 2021.

one's ancestors. Mahalaya marks the beginning of Devi Pada (Devi Paksha), a time of the year considered auspicious to get the blessings of the Devi for ultimate liberation through pindadaana (offering of food) to the pitris (ancestors). Thousands offer tarpana (prayers to their ancestors) at the river banks, lakes and ponds.

Mrinmayi Devi Celebration

It is believed that the Bengali community brought the tradition of Mrinmayi Puja (clay Murtis) of Goddess Durga to Odisha around five centuries ago. However, these community Pujas have now become the most popular way of celebrating Durga Puja in Odisha today. The Mrinmayi Puja is a public event representing the community aspect of Durga Puja. Hundreds of temporary stages called Pandals are built in community squares and Sahis (colonies). Various market committees or youth clubs organize this Puja with money collected from local residents called Chaanda and donations from many groups. The community Puja usually starts on Maha Shashti where the local community welcomes the Goddess and festive celebrations are inaugurated. Maha Saptami, Maha Ashtami, Maha Navami constitute the main Puja. Dasahara marks the end of the festival.

Large clay Murtis of Durga, along with Lakshmi, Sarasvati, Kartikeya and Ganesha on their respective vahanas (vehicles), are worshipped in beautifully decorated stages. The preparations for making the Murtis start on an auspicious day after Janmashtami with collection of clay from the river bed. After the prescribed rituals, the clay is transported to the location where the Murtis will be made. There is a tradition of adding a little Punya-Mati (soil from the doorsteps of prostitutes or 'besyas'). It is said that when a person visits a prostitute, Lakshmi gets off at the doorstep. Thus, the soil at the door steps of a besya is sanctified with the Padadhuli (dust from the feet) of Lakshmi. After collecting clay, the kumbharas (clay artisans) start making the Murtis.

The Goddess is depicted in her semi-fearsome mood with soothing eyes and 10 arms, each holding different weapons. The kumbharas have a time-bound programme to complete the Murtis by Mahalaya Amavasya, which is also known as Khadi-lagi Amavasya, as on this day, khadi (chalk paste) is applied as a primer coat on the Murtis. Thereafter, regular colours are applied and the Murtis are made ready for the Puja. Traditionally, all these are carried out behind a screen and nobody other than the kumbharas or chitrakaras (painters) are allowed inside. During these periods they maintain austerity and do not eat meat, drink alcohol or even smoke.[2]

On Maha Shashti (the sixth day), it is said that Goddess Durga arrives on earth from her heavenly abode, accompanied by Kartikeya, Ganesha, Ma Lakshmi and Ma Sarasvati. The celebration and worship start with the Kalashi Jatra (Yatra) to the closest waterbody, from where three to 108 kalashas (pitchers) of water are brought to the Puja area with a ceremonial procession, accompanied by traditional drums and bells. At the midway point, the Kshetrapala Puja is done to get the blessings of the presiding deity of that area. Then the Kalashas are brought to the stage where the Bela Barana Puja is done. The branch which has two Bela fruits[3] is indicative of the Devi's presence and is used to invite the Devi in. She is welcomed with much fanfare.

On Maha Saptami (the seventh day), the nine forms of the Devi are worshipped with Nabapatrika Puja. The saplings or leaves of nine types of plants—representing the nine manifestations of the Goddess—are worshipped. Chandi Patha starts on this day. A stem of the banana sapling is draped in a new sari. The banana sapling and other leaves tied in a white Aparajita creeper are brought back in a procession and are placed on the stage. Then, Chakshu Daana

---

[2]'Account of Durga Puja,' *Odisha Tourism*, odishatourism.gov.in/content/tourism/en/blog-details.html?url=an-account-of-durga-puja-in-odisha. Accessed on 10 June 2021.

[3]Bela is the Bengal quince, *Aegle marmelos*.

(eye opening) and Praana Pratisthaa (invoking life into the Murtis) are performed amidst the chanting of shlokas, mantras and homa (fire ritual). These are important rituals performed by the priest behind a screen and the public is not allowed to view it till after the ritual is completed.

The Maha Ashtami (eighth day) is the most important day of the entire festival. Chandi Patha and homas continue in community Puja pandals as devotees offer Pushpanjali (flower offerings) to the Goddess. Most people maintain a day-long fast and break it with Bhoga (food offering) after the evening Puja. In western Odisha, this fast is called Bhai Jiuntia—which is a Rakshabandhan-like festival when sisters pray for the brother, while in Brahmapura, it is called Phala Badhaa, where all kinds of fruits are offered to the Devi and mothers fast for their children.

Sandhi Puja is the most important ritual on the cusp of Maha Ashtami and Maha Navami, and is performed near midnight, between 24 minutes before expiry of Maha Ashtami and 24 minutes after the start of Maha Navami.[4] Worshippers believe that during this period, the Goddess assumes her most fearsome form and vanquishes the asuras. It was customary to sacrifice a buffalo to appease the Goddess. With the ban on animal sacrifices by the government, it is substituted with a fish sacrifice, a Boiti Kakharu (pumpkin) or a Lau (gourd) at many places. The smoke from the homa, sounds of traditional instruments, chanting of mantras and the jostling crowds charge the atmosphere with religious fervour. Though late in the night, devotees come in hordes to witness this spectacle.

On Maha Navami (ninth day), the main Navami Puja begins after the end of Sandhi Puja. Since the Goddess is believed to be in a ferocious form, Shanti Pujas are performed to bring her back to her benevolent self. Elaborate Navami Bhoga is offered to the Goddess, which is later distributed as prasada (sanctified food) to

---

[4]A muhurta is a span of 48 minutes and an auspicious muhurta also lasts for 48 minutes.

the devotees. There are many local traditions, such as Cuttack's pokhala bhoga (rice fermented in water), followed on Navami to calm down the ferocious form of the Goddess. Thereafter, the Devi rests on Navami.

On Bijaya Dashami or Dussehra (tenth day), after the Aparajita Puja (a ritual to receive the Shakti invoked in the Murtis), the clay Murtis are taken in a big procession around town and finally immersed in a local waterbody to bid the Goddess goodbye. The Bisarjan Jatra (Visarjana Yatra) or immersion procession is as grand as the Puja itself, with truckloads of people accompanying the Murtis amidst singing, dancing, chanting; even loud popular film music blares on the loudspeakers in a climactic finish to the festival.

It represents the impermanence of life—after weeks of tireless efforts to create the Murtis and Medhas, they are immersed into a body of running water to spread the blessings of the Goddess. This ritual is a symbolic reflection of the cycle of life—the Murtis merge back with the river clay they were made from just as the atman (soul) merges with the panchabhootas (five elements) it is created from. Mixed emotions, ranging from relief from exhaustion to sadness of farewell to implorations for a quick return, find many people crying as if they are giving a farewell to a family member. After the immersion of the Murtis, people celebrate Ravana Poda (burning effigies of Ravana filled with fire crackers).

Medhas

Medhas (tableaus of the Murtis on temporary stages) are a major attraction across cities during Durga Puja. Exorbitant amounts of money are spent to create breathtakingly beautiful structures. Local artisans and craftsmen get an opportunity to show off their handiwork. There is a friendly competition to earn the recognition of being the biggest and the best Medha in town. Most of the

Medhas of Goddess Durga are often accompanied by Ganesha, Kartikeya, Lakhmi, Sarasvati and in some places even Shiva. The names of the Medhas in Puri (Kakudikhai, Dahikhai, Sunya Gosani, Barabati and Kanta Kadhi) are descriptive of the sacrifices made to the Devi, while in Cuttack and Bhubaneswar, the Medhas (Choudhury Bazaar, Binod Bihari Khan Nagar, Bomikhal and Chauliaganj) are named after the Sahis.

The pandals vary in size, themes and decorations. Over the years, they have gone from simple bamboo structures to extravagant productions involving enormous budgets. Food stalls selling local delicacies and a variety of ethnic cuisines and bazaars are a part of these community celebrations—pandal hopping is a popular activity during the festival. Theatre forms like Daskathia and Pala where actors artistically blend singing, dancing and knowledge of the Puranas with poetry, wit and humour were the traditional forms of entertainment. 'Sword fighting was prevalent in villages within the Paika community. Bullock cart races are also organized and are still alive in the coastal village of Chandrapur.'[5]

Unfortunately, these performing arts are disappearing, as people prefer Bollywood-style entertainment. The bigger Medhas even get local film and TV celebrities to entertain the huge crowds. Cuttack has a more than 200-year-long history of pandal celebration. It is famous for the Chandi Tarakasi Medha, where silver filigree work (native to Cuttack) is used for the deities' ornaments. More than 250 kilograms of silver are used to create the intricate masterpieces that take numerous skilled silver filigree craftsmen almost a year to make. Imposing gates, with bright LED lights, up to 5 kilometers long, are erected to suffuse the whole ambience with a celebratory mood.

---

[5] Abhisek Kumar Panda, 'The New and the Old of Durga Puja,' *The Daily Guardian*, 26 October 2020, thedailyguardian.com/the-new-and-the-old-of-durga-puja/. Accessed on 10 June 2021.

Pujas at Odia Homes

Private home worship varies according to the traditions of different Jatis. Generally, in the brahmin sasans (exclusive brahmin habitations), Durga Puja is performed with strict observation of the Vedic principles. These families have a Murti of Goddess Durga set up in the north-east side of the house known as Dian Ghar (Puja room). The Goddess is worshipped with Shodasha Upachara or 16 offerings. The rituals start with Shuddhikarana (sacred purificatory ritual), where the male members have to consume Panchagavya (a mixture of cow dung, cow urine, milk, curds and ghee) and then change their sacred thread to begin the rituals. The rituals follow the temple style of worship with the exception of the animal sacrifice. During the entire duration of the Puja, sexual intimacy, shaving, haircuts, cutting of nails and outside laundry service are prohibited, as these acts are believed to deplete the Shakti invoked within oneself.

Each day, the Goddess is worshipped thrice with offering of Bala Bhoga (in the morning with fruits, coconuts and dry sweets like ladoos), Sankhudi Bhoga (in the midday with freshly cooked food which includes rice, dal with many types of curries, including fish and meat and other local delicacies), Sandhya Dhupa/Raja Bhoga (in the evening with pithas—a wide variety of rice, coconut and jaggery-based dumplings, pancakes, fritters like Kakara, Arisha, Monda, Chhena Podo, Birikanti, Chnadrakanti). In many places, the Goddess is bid farewell with Lakhe Balita Deepa (a lamp with 100,000 wicks).

Saja Puja or Astra-Shastra Puja

Although similar to the Ayudha Puja, there are two important aspects to it in Odisha—the worship of vehicles and occupational tools. Worshipping one's occupational tools is an extension of a spiritual custom that dates back to when there were Chhattis Pataka

(36 different occupations) in Odisha. On the day of Dussehra, vehicles are washed and decorated with red cloth and bangles; workers clean the tools of their trade and worship them along with household deities in a ritual called Saja Basiba. The Saja is usually placed near the household deities. This ritual symbolizes reverence for the tools or instruments that represent each Jati's source of power. While the brahmana Jati worship pothi (scriptural books) and lekhani (pen or stencil), kshatriya Jati worship weapons, vaishya Jati worship pen and notebooks, farmers worship ploughs and artisans worship musical instruments and tools, etc.

A less strict version of the home Puja starts on Dvitiya (the day after Mahalaya) with Ankura Arpana to receive the Goddess. Ankura means fresh grass that sprouts during Navaratri, symbolizing fertility, regeneration and prosperity. It involves the ritual consecration of the vessel and infusing life into the symbolic image of the Goddess called Ghata Sthapana. The ghata (a pot) is filled with Ganga Jala and other auspicious items, dressed up like a Devi with saree, sindura, bangles, jewellery, etc. and placed on a terracotta bowl filled with sand and Panchashasya (five grains) and anchored by four banana plants. On Maha Panchami, a photo of Lalita Devi (embodiment of Kali, Lakshmi and Sarasvati) is worshipped with Pancha Upachara (five offerings) and chanting of the 'Lalita Sahasranama'.

On Shashti Puja, the favorite food of all the children is offered to the Goddess. The priest ties a red thread on the hands of family members as a measure of protection and blessings. Saptami, Ashtami, Navami involve the actual Puja, where the Goddess is worshipped with a new saree and all the shringara (symbols of beauty) of a married lady. Ladies have purificatory baths with haldi (turmeric), wear alta (red dye on the feet) and new clothes on Maha Ashtami. On all three days, Puja and Bhoga is offered three times a day. Until Navami, only vegetarian Bhoga is offered. Although non-vegetarian food is cooked on Navami, it is not offered as Bhoga to the Goddess (unless doing Bali with proper rituals).

On Dashami, the Goddess is bid farewell with gifts—saree,

jhuntia (toe rings), paunjhi (anklets), sindura, haldi and a basket with little packets of grains, lentils and whole masalas wrapped in sala leaves. The final ritual is Shanti Puja, where the priest adds a little Ganga Jala and haldi into the kalasha/ghata, which has received the shakti of the Goddess and sprinkles this Shanti Jala on all the family members and all over the house. Then the priest ties pieces of the sprouted ankura on everybody's hands. Although gift exchange is not common, Dasahara Bheti or Dasahara Baksisha is a common tradition, where money is gifted to all the people who serve you.

Some believe that any impropriety in the Puja rituals will incur the wrath of Ma Kali who can then only be appeased by blood. As a preventive measure, people wear red on their body (symbolizing spilled blood) or paint red dots in their homes as a wounded person is unworthy of a sacrificial offering to the Devi.

Royal Family Rituals

Shakti is the presiding deity of the Khandayats (kshatriyas) and the royalty in Odisha. Even today, all the family members of the royal families gather at their ancestral palace to worship at their Kuladevi temple as per centuries old traditions. All the archaic rituals such as Khanda Puja (sword worship), Bali (animal sacrifice), Aparajita Puja (prayer for invincibility) and Kanaka Anjali (rich gifts to the Goddess) are followed in great detail.

A typical royal family festival starts with the Suniya Puja 27 days prior to Dussehra, where the royal calendar is updated, depicting the reign of the present royal incumbent. Dussehra Puja holds sentimental value for the people as the king symbolically performs his duties as a father and a kshatriya. On Dussehra, the king honours Ma Durga as his own daughter and sends her back to her husband's home with Kanaka Anjali, gifts worthy of his power. Then, he raises his sword as a kshatriya's sign of power and promises to protect his people.

Odisha's Ancient Shakti Tradition

During the ascendancy of the Shakti sect, the Goddess was worshipped as per tantric rituals. During this period, Matrika Puja was highly prevalent in Odisha as is evident from two Chausathi Yogini temples at Hirapur and Ranipur-Jharial, as well as the popular worship of Grama Debi (Devi) (patron Goddess of the village) and Khetra Debi (Devi) (patron Goddess of the city). But today, barring the Shakti Peethas, the Goddess is worshipped mostly as per Vaishnava/Vedic rituals. According to various accounts of the 51 Shakti Peethas across the Indian subcontinent, as many as three are in Odisha, including two (Tara Tarini Peetha, Brahmapur and Bimala Peetha, Puri) of the four (Bimala, Tara Tarini, Kamakhya and Dakhina Kali) most important peethas. In fact, the first documented reference to Shakti worship can be found in some versions of the Mahabharata, which points to Biraja Peetha, also in Odisha.

In addition to the Bimala, Tara Tarini and Biraja Peethas, there are 11 other Shakti Peethas revered in Odia culture. These are: Ma Kakatapur Mangala (Kakatapur), Ma Samaleswari (Sambalpur), Ma Hingula (Talcher), Ma Charchika (Banki), Ma Sarala (Jhankada-Jagatsinghpur), Ma Cuttack Chandi (Cuttack), Ma Bhattarika (Badamba), Ma Sureswari (Sonepur), Ma Ramachandi (Konark), Ma Gauri (Bhubaneswar) and Ma Bhagabati (Banapur).

All the Shakti Peethas in Odisha strictly follow the Shodasha Dinatmaka Puja. Purity and sanctity are the prime needs and under no circumstances can the temple worship be shorter than 16 days. The celebration is in Shodasha Upachar. It is customary for the Devi to be worshipped in 16 different avataras during the 16-day festival at the temples.

Prominent Regional Celebrations

Puri—Ma Bimala Peetha, Durga Madhaba (Madhava): While Goddess Durga is worshipped as the consort of Shiva almost all over

India, it is only in Puri that she is worshipped as the tantric consort of Jagannatha (a manifestation of Vishnu). Ma Bimala, whose shrine is within the Jagannath (Jagannatha) Temple in Puri, is considered the presiding Goddess of this temple. Jagannath is considered to be Bhairava and Bimala as Bhairavi and a special 16-day Puja known as Shakta Gundicha is conducted during the Durga Puja in Jagannath temple. According to the lore, Madhaba visits the Bimala temple every night till Ashvina Amavasya.

After Amavasya, Bimala and Madhaba together visit the Narayani temple at Dolamandapa Sahi. This goes on for eight more days. However, the rituals of Shakta Gundicha are observed secretly and women are barred from visiting the Bimala shrine during these days. The Durga Madhaba Sakta Gundicha is flagged off with a Kara Baithaka (handshake) between the priests of Ma Bimala and priests of Sri Jagannath and is received by the Puri Gajapati (king of Puri) who seeks the blessings of Durga Madhaba.

While the Jagannath temple follows traditional Vaishnava rituals throughout the year, during Durga Puja, animal sacrifice is made before the Goddess Bimala—an unusual departure from the otherwise bloodless rituals performed in the temple.

Jajpur—Ma Biraja Peetha Ratha Jatra: The Biraja (Viraja) Shakti Peetha in Jajpur, on the banks of river Baitarani (Vaitarani) is considered as the Oddiyana Peetha (Oddiyana is an ornament worn by women around the navel). According to the Tantra Chudamani, Sati's navel fell in Utkala, the old name for Odisha, in the Biraja Peetha. Sri Adi Shankaracharya, in his Ashtadasha Shakti Peetha Stuti, describes the Goddess as Girija in Odisha. The only one of its kind, this dui bhuja (two-armed) Mahishasura Mardini Murti, represents the earliest form of Shakti worship in Odisha. This Peetha observes a ratha jatra (chariot festival) where the Goddess is moved around the temple complex continuously for nine days in a beautifully decorated chariot called the Simhadhvaja (lion emblem). It is believed that a darshana of the Goddess in the chariot can liberate one from a lifetime of sins. A novel tradition here is to pray to Goddess Biraja to receive oblations on behalf of one's ancestors instead of praying to Vishnu as is customary everywhere in India.

Sambalpur—Ma Samaleswari, Dhabalamukhi: Ma Samlei, a form of Durga, is the presiding deity of Sambalpur and a strong religious force in western Odisha. During Mahalaya, thousands of devotees come to the temple to have a darshana of Ma Samlei in Dhabalamukhi Besha (a white costume) which lasts for two and a half days instead of the red color costumes she wears the rest of the year. It is a popular belief that the darshana of Ma Samlei in the Dhabalamukhi Besa will absolve all sins and sufferings since it is as good as getting a darshana of Goddess Ganga. It is customary to worship Ma Samlei with a different traditional musical instrument for the 16 days of Durga Puja. Various cultural events like music and dance are organized at the temple as well as in the villages.

In western Odisha, Durga Puja is celebrated from Pua Jiuntia to Bhai Jiuntia. Pua Jiuntia is celebrated on Mulasthami, observed by mothers to please Sri Dutibahana for the long life and prosperity of their sons. On Bhai Jiuntia or Maha Ashtami, the sisters worship Durga for their brothers. Bhai Jiuntia is the tribal version of Rakshabandhan—sisters fast all day and offer prayers to the Goddess in the evening with flowers, fruits, holy grass, rice, coconuts and light lamps. The following day, they tie the Jiuntia around the brother's neck. Village girls dance to the tune of Dalkhai (another name for Durga) after breaking their fast.

Kalahandi—Ma Manikeswari, Chattar Jatra: Ma Manikeswari is the Kuladevi of the Kalahandi Royal family. Chattar Jatra is a traditional victory festival celebrated in the town of Bhawanipatna, Kalahandi during Durga Puja. A bamboo covered with black clothes and with a silver plate on top containing the Dashamahavidya Yantra (10 aspects of the Devi) represents Ma

Manikeswari in the Jatra. After performing the traditional Sandhi Puja in the Manikeswari temple on Maha Ashtami night, the ceremonial Chattar of Goddess Manikeswari is taken to Jenakhal, about 3 kilometres from the temple where secret rituals are performed in the early hours of Maha Navami. When she leaves the temple to kill the asuras, no one is allowed to see her because she is in a ferocious form. The Jatra starts on Mahanavami during the return journey.

With the reverberations of traditional drums like Jena Badya, Nisan and Ghanta, the Chattar is accompanied by dancers performing Ghumura, a tribal martial dance. Devotees follow the Chattar and make animal sacrifices as a mark of the fulfillment of their wishes. Although the government has strictly banned animal sacrifice, devotees don't follow the rule and thousands of animal sacrifices reportedly take place in this festival. At the main gate of the temple, the Maharaja of Kalahandi performs a puja to receive the Chattar from the priests and takes it inside the temple. Kalahandi's Nuakhai (celebrating new harvest) is on Dasahara, but the royal family eats Nua (new harvest) with Buddha Raja (Bhairav) on Navami after receiving the Chattar.

Cuttack—Cuttack Chandi: Ma Cuttack Chandi is worshipped as the living Goddess of the city of Cuttack. During Durga Puja, she is worshipped in Shodasha Avatara (16 forms), as is common in many temples. After Harisayana Eksdashi in the month of Ashadha, an elaborate Sayana Utsav (sleep ritual) is observed on Radhahtami. The priests worship the Goddess's benevolent Gouri form. Seven days later on Mulastami, the Devi is awakened from her sleep because of the tradition of Akala Bodhana (untimely awakening). At the Amrita Bela (auspicious moment), the Goddess is awakened by a sacred bath called Sahasra Kumbha Snana (bathing with a thousand pitchers). Thereafter, the usual rituals of Durga Puja are followed.

Over the decades, Durga Puja has gradually evolved from being a seat of ancient Shakti traditions and deeply ethnic rituals to one that is more contemporary—involving the community, invoking the arts and generating an atmosphere of celebration and commerce with enormous social and economic significance for the region.

8

Kerala Marg in Uttar Pradesh

GIRIRATNA MISHRA

It was the first day of Vasanta Navaratra and, as usual, my wife and I were busy with the preparations. My daughters, who usually wake up well after sunrise, got up early due to the hustle and bustle in the house. Eight-year-old Aparajita, the elder one, emerged rubbing her eyes, and asked her mother, 'What is happening? What are you doing?'

'I am making preparations for Vasanta Navaratra. Get ready quickly so that you are in time for the Puja.'

Aparajita giggled and wondered, 'Just last October we celebrated this festival. Now, again in April! Are the festivals not yearly? Usually, festivals are celebrations of food and toys. Why does this festival come with so many restrictions? Also, I remember both of you washed my feet, offered me my favourite dishes, gifts and money and did my Puja. Why do you do this when I am your daughter? Since all the festivals are connected to some deity, whom do we worship during Navaratra?'

My wife was amused. She replied, 'All these questions will be answered by your father...'

With the baton in my hand, I said, 'You have your bath, get ready and let us finish kalasha sthapana and Puja. Then we will sit and discuss this.'

Aparajita was ready in no time, dressed in new clothes, and sat with us for the Puja. This time, she was accompanied by her four-year-old sister, Geetika. When we concluded the morning session of Puja, I took some books out and began explaining.

The Sanskrit word 'Navaratra' stands for a specific time defined as, 'नवानां रात्रिणां समाहार:' (group of nine nights). While interpreting this word as per grammar, Navaratra stands only for the time and not any specific act.[1] Some scholars say Navaratra stands for karma done during this particular period of time. However, that is not true; Navaratra represents a specific time period.[2] That specific time is considered auspicious due to the stellar movements. It has been celebrated in Aryavarta since time immemorial. It is the source of eternal energy, which is beyond limits and never exhausting. Also, the energy, which is an attribute of Shakti, can never be destroyed. The Sadhana done for nine days (mentioned as nights) charges the seeker with an immense energy. The word 'Navaratri' is a localized form of the correct Sanskrit word, Navaratra.

The statement given above is the gross meaning of Navaratra, the para meaning is immensely deep.[3] Let us understand the meaning of number nine first.

'Nava' stands for number nine. Nine has an important role in Shakta Sadhana. Shri Yantra has nine triangles,[4] Bhagavati has a body with nine orifices,[5] she manifests herself in nine forms, and so on. To be precise, it can be said that nine is her favourite number. 'Why is it nine?' is a subject of realization and is the supreme learning of Shakti Sadhana. This cannot be explained in mere words.

The other part of the word Navaratra is ratri, that is, night. There are various reasons behind the use of the word. Grammatically,

---

[1] Ref. Panini Sutra—प्रत्यन्ववपूर्वात् समालोम्न: तत्पुरुषास्याङ्गुले सङ्ख्याऽव्ययादे: (5.4.75), (5.4.86), अह: सर्वैकदेशसङ्ख्यातपुण्याच्च रात्रे: (5.4.87).

[2] नवरात्राभिधं कर्म नक्त्रव्रतमिदं शुभम्।
धर्मार्थकाममोक्षार्थमनुष्ठेयं द्विजातिभि:॥

[3] In Shakta Mata all the aspects of the three meanings, Sthula (gross), Suksma (subtle) and Para (beyond these) have to be considered. This is because Shakta Sadhana is based on Trika Siddhanta.

[4] नवयोनीर्नव चक्राणि दीधिरे नवैव योगा नव योगिनीश्च। नवानां चक्रे अधिनाथा: स्योना नव मुद्रा नव भद्रा महीनाम्॥ (Shri Tripura Mahopanishad-2)

[5] तेन नवरन्ध्ररूपो देह: ॥12॥ (Shri Bhavanopanishad)

it stands for date (रात्रिशब्दस्य तिथिपरत्वात्[6]). This is supported by Damarakalpa too, where it is mentioned, 'If ratri is not considered as an indicator of date, we will have to give up the meaning of Navaratra, if in case the date increases or decreases.'[7] That is, depending on the tithi, sometimes, Navaratra will have eight days and sometimes, 10 days. If night is not taken as a count of date the term would become Ashtaratra (eight nights) or Dasharatra (10 nights) and the essence of Navaratra would be gone.

This is just a verbal meaning. The para meaning of this word ratri is different, Mahamaheshwar Acharya Abhinavagupta Ji explains this while saying, 'One who does not shine due to Surya, Soma and Agni. These sun, moon and fire are nothing without Para Prakash. These are made to shine by Samvid Prakash.'[8]

The Vaidika source of origin, operation and destruction of the three worlds are Soma, Surya and Agni (अग्निषोमात्मकं जगत्). These three are due to Samvida Prakash. Here Samvida is Shri Para Shakti and Prakash is Parameshvara Shiva. Hence, these three are attributes of Samvida Shakti and Parameshvara Shiva. As they are dependent on Parameshvara Shiva and Samvida Shakti, they cannot make their source shine. The word 'ratri' or night, as in Shivaratri and Navaratra, have the same meaning. These festivals are indicative of the supreme power, who is the source of all and is beyond worldly sources. As night is devoid of the light of sun, moon and fire, this is closer to the characteristic of Shri Para Shakti and Parameshvara Shiva. Hence, is considered auspicious to realize them.

All this description was something new for my elder daughter, and she looked at me with surprise. After a while, she asked: 'How long have we been celebrating this Navaratra?'

'Since the beginning of time. Or you can say that time started

---

[6]Navaratrapradipa

[7]तिथिवृद्धौ तिथिह्रासे नवरात्रमपार्थकम्।

[8]यन्न सूर्यो न वा सोमो नाग्निर्भासयतेऽपि च॥ न चार्कसोमवह्नीनां तत्प्रकाशादिना महः। किमप्यस्ति निजं किं तु संविदित्थं प्रकाशते॥

when Navaratra started. This is why the first day of year is the first day of Vasanta Navaratra.' I smiled and added, 'If you want, you may wish us an incredibly happy new year!'

History of Navaratra

As Shakti is beyond the boundary of time, so is her Sadhana. Shakti and her Sadhana have bestowed her seekers with grace since time immemorial and this is also true of Navaratra. Shruti[9] says, 'To save from death, Prajapati bestowed eternity to Devas through Navaratra.'[10] The Tandya Mahabrahaman, (an anga or limb scripture of *Samaveda*) also talks about a Shakta Satra which continued for 36 years on the banks of Yavyavati river.[11] It is said that flesh was offered in purodash[12] in this Satra. In this, Trivrtta Mantras continued for nine samvatsaras; panchadasha stotras for nine; 17 stotras[13] for nine and 21 stotras for nine samvatsaras.[14]

Here, as per Mimamsa Sutra, samvatasara stands for a day.[15] The Shrauta-yajna[16] is on the frame of Mimamsa. Hence, here, day for samvatsara is acceptable. These examples are enough to understand that Navaratra has been observed since time immemorial.

My daughter asked: 'We recently celebrated this festival in October, then again in April! Why?'

'My dear daughter! We celebrate this festival four times a year.'

---

[9]Vedas and Upanishads that have been revealed.
[10]नवरात्रेणामृतत्व प्रायच्छत—Tandya Mahabrahamana (22.12.1)
[11]एतेन वै गैरिवीति शाक्तस्तरसपुरोडाशो....(T.M. – 25.7.2). Satra is a sacrifice.
[12]Offering given during Vaidika yajna, a kind of cake.
[13]Term for year. A stotram is a hymn.
[14]नवत्रिवृत: संवत्सरा...(T.M. – 25.7.1)
[15]अहनि वाभि संरव्यवात् (M.S. – 6.7.41)
[16]A yajna based on Vedas, the shruti texts.

Navaratra through the Seasons

Shri Devi asks Bhagavan Shiva in 'Shri Tara Khanda' of *Shri Shakti Sangam Tantra*, 'When is Navaratra and what shall be done during this festival?[17]' To this, Bhagavan Shri Shiva replies 'Since nine Shaktis are united there, it is called Navaratra.[18] The one supreme Shakti Devi pervades in nine forms. This Navaratra is of two types, named Shayan and Bodhan.'

Shayan is in Chaitra month and Bodhan is in Ashvina month. If both are observed, a human being earns siddhis. It is said that these two seasons are vulnerable to diseases and hence are called Yama danshtra (bitten by Yama). Hence, seekers shall observe Navaratra Vrata during these seasons.

In *Shri Mahakaal Samhita* and 'Shri Guhyakali Khanda', it is said that there is no difference between Vasanta and Ashvin Navaratra. Earlier, only Vasanta Navaratra was celebrated in the three worlds.[19] These two Navaratras are famous. However, there is a total of four Navaratras as described in *Shri Skanda Purana*, 'Manasa Khanda' and *Shrimad Devibhagavat Mahatmya*.[20]

In *Shrimad Devibhagavata*, the names of months during which four Navaratras are observed are Chaitra, Ashvin, Ashadha and Magha.[21] Among these, Navaratra of Ashadha and Magha are Gupta Navaratra. Gupta Navaratra will be discussed some other time.

My daughter had been listening carefully. Now she had a query. 'Okay... Who is worshipped in this festival, Shri Lakshmi ji or Shri Sarasvati ji?'

To which I laughed and replied: 'I know you are very devoted to those Devis. I will explain it to you.'

---

[17]देवेश श्रोतुमिच्छामि (16.1)

[18]This is one more definition of Navaratra.

[19]यथा च शारदीयार्चा वासन्त्यर्चा तथैव च। नानयोर्विद्यते भेद: स्वल्पोऽपि निगमादिषु।। आसीत् पूर्वं महापूजा वासन्त्येव जगत्त्रये। (13.123)

[20]अथवा प्रीतये देव्या नवरात्रचतुष्टये। श्रृणुयादन्यमासेऽपि तिथिवारर्क्षशोधित।। (5.7)

[21]चौत्रे आश्विने तथाषाढे, माघे कार्यो महोत्सव:। नवरात्रे महाराज पूजा कार्य विशेषत:।।

Navaratra as per Nava Durga

In general, it is known that Shri Shailaputri, Brahmacharini, Chandraghanta, Kushmanda, Skandamata, Katyayani, Kalratri, Mahagauri and Siddhidatri, are the nine forms of Devi worshipped during Navaratra. However, there is more to it. The above nine forms are worshipped during both Navaratras. But during Ashvina Navaratra, there are three kalpas (procedures) for Shri Durga Puja:[22]

- Shri Katyayani Kalpa, Shri Dasha Bhuji Durga (Shri Durga with 10 arms) and Tritiya Kalpa (third kalpa)
- Shri Bhadrakali Kalpa, Shri Shodasha Bhuji Durga (Shri Durga with 16 arms) and Madhyama Kalpa (medium kalpa)
- Shri Ugra-Chanda Kalpa, Shri Ashtadashabhuji Durga (Shri Durga with 18 arms) and Uttama Kalpa (best kalpa)

There are detailed dhyana mantras for these forms of Devi. Without getting into details, let me highlight some aspects:

- Uttama Kalpa—The name of Shri Nava Durgas of this Kalpa are Rudra-Chanda, Prachanda, Chandogra, Chanda Nayika, Chanda, Chandavati, Chandarupa, Atichandika and Ugra-Chanda. During this kalpa, the prabodhana[23] is done on Ashvina Krishna Navami and kalasha is established on Ashvin Shukla Pratipada. Nine Durgas are worshipped.
- Madhyama Kalpa—The names of Nava Durgas are Shailaputri, Brahmacharini, Chandraghantha, Kushmanda, Skandamata, Katyayani, Kalaratri, Mahagauri and Shri Siddhidatri. During this kalpa, the prabodhana is done on

---

[22] इयं हि शारदी पूजा मूर्तिभेदात् त्रिधा मता। तत्तद्वर्ष्यमधिष्ठाय नृणां गृह्णाति सार्चनम्॥ ये ऽष्टादशभुजां देवीमुग्रचण्डाभिधां प्रिये। (13.593 – 594)
ईश्वरीं षोडशभुजां भद्रकालीति नामिकाम्॥ (13.599) दुर्गादेवीमर्चयीत सप्तम्यादिदिनत्रये। दशबाहुधरां देवीं महासौन्दर्यशालिनीम्॥ (13.602)

[23] To invoke the deity.

Krishna Chaturdashi (a day before), kalasha is established on the first day of Navaratra and usual worship on Shri Murti or Yantra is done for the period of nine days.
- Tritiya Kalpa—The names of Nava Durgas are the same as above.

Kalasha is established only on the first day. Ashtadashakshara (18 syllable) mantra japa is done till Shashthi (sixth day). On the same day, prabodhana is done. On Saptami (seventh day), nine leaves are kept on the kalasha and then onwards, Navaratra worship is done.

There is one more tradition of Nava Durgas—Hrilekha, Gagana, Rakta, Mahocchushma, Karalika, Iccha, Gyana, Kriya and Durga.

In the Vaishnava tradition, during the nine nakshatras of Sharad ritu (the autumn season), these nine forms of Devi are worshipped: Shri Devi in Hasta Nakshatra, Amrtodbhava in Chitra, Kamala in Svati, Chandrashobhini in Vishakha, Vishnupatni in Anuradha, Vaishnavi in Jyeshtha, Vararoha in Mula, Harivallabha in Purvashadha and Sarngini in Uttarashadha Nakshatra.

Shri Sarangini is considered as inherent Shakti of Bhagavan Vishnu, by whose grace Shri Ramachandra slayed Ravana.

As per *Shri Mahakaal Samhita*, 'Guhyakali Khanda', the Ashvin Navaratra may be observed with any of two worship procedures, to earn the love of Kali, Purana based or Tantra based.[24]

Navaratra According to Region

According to *Shri Shakti Sangama Tantra*, 'Shri Tara Khand', there are three different ways of Navaratra celebrations based on region, Gauda, Kashmir and Dravid.[25] Their detailed rituals, as per region, are as follows:

The one who celebrates the Navaratra as per the said procedure

---
[24]पूजाया: कथितं चात्र द्वैविद्ध्यं मुनिपुङ्गवै:।। पौराणिकं तान्त्रिकं च कालिकाप्रीतिसिद्धये। (13.610)
[25]नवरात्रव्रासक्तो नवनाथो भवेद्ध्रुवम्। गौडकाश्मीरद्रविडमार्गेण त्रिविधं भवेत्।। (16.6)

undoubtedly becomes Navanath. In 'Shri Sodashi Khanda Gauda', Kashmir and Dravid Krama are defined:

- Gauda Marg: From Nepal up to Kalinga, 18 regions follow Gauda Marg.
- Kerala Marg: Entire Aryavarta up to Samudra (Indian ocean), follows Kerala Marg.
- Kashmir Marg: Rest of the 19 regions fall under Kashmir Marg.

Dravid Krama is more famously known as Kerala Krama.

So, the Marg of Navaratra Sadhana in Uttar Pradesh is the Kerala Marg. In case of Bihar Mithila and regions adjacent to Bengal, they follow Gauda Marg, whereas some districts follow Kerala Marg due to their cultural association with Uttar Pradesh.

There is yet another classification found in the same scripture, which is based on sunlight. These are named as Ashvakranta, Rathakranta and Vishnukranta. We shall discuss them some other time. Apart from this, there is one more division in Shri Durga Sadhana, which is of North and South India. I will not emphasize this. Some difference in procedures of worship are obvious due to differences in region.

My daughter asked me, 'Is there anything special in our state? Who do we celebrate this here in Uttar Pradesh?'

I explained to her.

Navaratra in Uttar Pradesh

Uttar Pradesh has a great history of Shakti Upasana. Shri Vindhyavasini, who slayed Shumbha and Nishumbha, and Shri Raktadantika, who slayed Raktabija, reside here with full grace. Shri Rama, whose Navaratra Sadhana is famous in the world, was the king of Ayodhya. These facts also establish that Navaratra has been celebrated in Uttar Pradesh since ages.

Uttar Pradesh has famous Shakti Peethas like Shri Vindhyachal, Shri Kashi Vishalakshi, Shri Alopa Shankari, Shri Kalyani Devi, Shri Shitala Devi, Shri Lalita Devi, Shri Pateshvari, Shri Shakambhari Devi and many other great mandirs, which charge the region and people with divine bliss.

There is a famous anecdote about Adi Sankara, where his pupils asked him: 'When Sanatana Dharma is eternal, why does it exist in Bharata only?' Adi Shankara replied, 'There is a mystic triangle whose three points are Shri Sarada Peetha, Shri Kanyakumari and Shri Kamrup Kamakhya. The centre of this mystic triangle is Kashi. This makes the region so sacred that Sanatana Dharma exists here. Hence, the root cause behind the flourishing Sanatana Dharma is a constant energy recharge by Shakti. This energy is experienced and the seeker gets charged when he celebrates Navaratra.

In Uttar Pradesh, the festival is observed in two ways. The first is based on the Shastras, which is limited to a few people who are typically Shakta, are initiated in Shakta Mata and are well-versed with the Shastras. They follow the procedures mentioned in scriptures. However, most people celebrate this festival as per family and social traditions.

Navaratra According to the Shastras

The practices followed during this includes: Prabodhana, Kalasha Sthapana, daily worship, special Puja, Havana, Kumari Puja and Vrata.

Puja Vidhana

There are various rituals, just as there are many kalpas and Puja Paddhatis. However, there are some rituals which are generic.

The seeker shall establish ghata (kalasha) on the first day. He shall install a flag 16 hands high on a mast on a square and flat ground and make a mandapa. A Murti of Shri Durga with four arms or eight arms shall be established (these days, pictures are also used). If the sadhaka does Chakra Puja, he may place that Yantra also. If in case these are not available, he may place *Navakshara Mantra*. The ghata shall be behind the throne of Ma Bhagavati.

The seeker shall engage five, three or one brahmins, as the order of preference goes, and ensure that either *Shrimad Devibhagavata* or *Shri Durga Saptashati* is recited daily in front of Devi.[26] The seeker shall recite the mantra given by Shri Gurudeva and worship Bhagavati thrice in a day, i.e., morning, evening and midnight. This shall be done with Panchopachara, Shodasopachara or Rajopachara.[27]

Special Puja

There are various streams in which Mahanisha Puja is celebrated. Specifically, in the Avadhuta cult of Aghoracharya Baba Kinaram Ji, the bali is given. This is also true of various other mandiras. Some seekers initiated in Dasha Mahavidya karma practise mantras of Bhagavati during this period, with specific rituals prescribed.

There are two famous Vishesha Puja (special worships) called 'Nava Patriki Pujana' and 'Kadahi Puja'.

Nava Patrika Pujana is done on Ashvina Shukla Saptami, in which, leaves of banana, kacci (yam), turmeric, jayanti[28] Bael (bilva), pomegranate, ashok, giant taro and rice are tied with fruitful branch of bael. This is again tied in a banana leaf and is then bathed in Gangajal at the Puja Mandap, decorated as Devi, and placed on the right of Shri Ganesha. The ritual prescribed for this worship is not mentioned here.

In Kadahi Puja, a kadahi (wok) full of prepared halva is offered to Bhagavati on the eighth or ninth day at the time of parana (before kalasha visarjana). After performing this Puja according to the prescribed rituals, a seeker shall do visarjana with full devotion

---

[26]नव पञ्च त्रयश्चौको देव्या: पाठे द्विजा स्मृता:।
[27]Respectively, five, 16 or royal offerings
[28]Sesbania sesban Merrill

and request Bhagavati to arrive again. The Puja is performed by the common folk and is quite popular in the rural areas of eastern Uttar Pradesh.

The Havana shall be done daily with recitation of the 'Navarna Mantra'. This may be done with other Shakti Mantras that the diksha seeker is initiated in. At the time of visarjana, the Havana based on *Shrimad Devi Bhagavat* or *Shri Durga Saptashati* shall be done. If the *Shrimad Devi Bhagavat* is recited, Havana shall be done as per this scripture, or else if Shri Durga Saptashati is recited, Havana based on this scripture would done.

Aparajita said, 'Now that so many things have been explained, I still don't understand why you worship me.' I explained that it was called Kumari Puja.

Kumari Puja

As per Shiva Sutra, 'Iccha Shakti herself is Uma Kumari.' So, the Kumari is manifestation of Iccha Shakti only. In Yamala, there are three types of Kumaris—Para, Apara and Parapara. Hence, she is Adya Shakti who deliberates herself in three forms and then nine as Nava Durga and so on. This has many more secrets which you will learn as you do Sadhana. There are various rituals of Kumari Puja. Let me tell you the one mentioned in *Shri Mahakaal Samhita*.[29] The little girls are a direct manifestation of such Devi Kumari, as their hearts are free from any kind of worldly deceit.

Girls aged between one and 16 years are considered as Kumari. They have certain names: One year—Sandhya; two years—Sarasvati; three years—Tridha-Murti; four years—Kalika; five years—Subhaga; six years—Uma; seven years—Malini; eight years—Kubjika; nine years—Kalasangharsha; 10 years—Aparajita; 11 years—Rudrani; 12 years—Bhairavi; 13 years—Mahalakshmi; 14 years—Kulanayika; 15 years—Kshetrama and 16 years—Chandika.

A Kumari in the age group of seven to nine is considered the

---

[29] 13.1183–1407

best. It is prescribed that she shall be of bright complexion, must be from a good family, her parents shall be alive, all her limbs shall be intact, her hair shall be long, teeth shall not be jutting out and she must not be engaged to someone. The number of Kumaris shall be odd, as in three, five, seven and nine. If multiple Kumaris are not found, even one can be worshipped. Most beautiful amongst them shall be placed as Mukhya Kumari.

As per *Shri Shrividyaranava Tantra*, the girls of all castes are eligible for Kumari Puja. Hence, there is no such restriction.[30] This shows that Shakti Sadhana does not have any kind of social restriction.

The Kumaris shall be brought to the place of Puja to the accompaniment of music. They shall be made to stand in line, with eyes directed at the ground. The seeker shall do pranayama, apasarana and digbandhana. He shall wash the feet of Kumaris and sprinkle that water on his head. He shall spread rice grains in all directions so that troubles may be removed. This is done to avoid the hinderances of various secondary Devatas that entered with Kumaris. The seeker shall hold the right hand of Kumari with the left hand and then while placing right foot first, he shall take her to throne. Others shall recite hymns as given in the scripture.

First of all, the Puja of Mukhya Kumari is done. In this sequence—first nyasa of 18 Kumaris is done on her body. Then, nine Devis are worshipped, who are Shuddha, Kalika, Lalita, Malini, Vasundhara, Sarasvati, Rama, Gauri and Durga. Two Devas shall be worshipped. A five-year-old boy shall be worshipped as Batuka and a nine-year-old boy shall be worshipped as Ganesha. Then worship of eight Bhairavas and then again eight Devis—Mahamaya, Kalaratri, Sarvamangala, Damaruka, Rajarajeshvari, Sampadprada, Bhagavati and Kumari. Followed by the worship of six attendants—Anangakusuma, Manmatha, Madana, Kusumatura, Madanatura and Shishira.

---

[30]ब्राह्मणी सर्वकार्येषु जयार्थं नृपवंशजाम्। लाभार्थे वैश्यसंभूतां सूतार्थं शूद्रवंशजाम्॥ दारुणे चान्त्यजातीनां पूजयेद्विधिना नर:। (1.18)

After worship of Mukhya Kumari, other Kumaris shall be worshipped with the same rituals. After that, the food shall be offered. It is important that when they eat, there shall be utter silence and no music shall be played. All seekers shall stand with hands joined. They shall recite the Stotra as mentioned in *Shri Mahakaal Samhita*. After food, they shall be offered readied betel leaves and the leftover food shall either be given to jackals or buried in ground.

The conduct of the Kumaris and the way they eat indicate the future of the seeker, his family and his country.

This worship, which has prevailed for long in Uttar Pradesh, is now celebrated only in a few peethas and in the homes of a few seekers who are well-versed with the Shastras.

Vrata

As per *Shri Mahakaal Samhita*, the Navaratra Vrata has some strict rules, as the seeker shall fast, observe mauna,[31] do japa, perform Kumari Puja and organize a feast for seekers.[32]

As per Navaratra Pradeepa, the Navaratra Vrata can be done by anyone in this world. There is no restriction of caste and religion.[33] There is a complete chapter dedicated to the description of the dos and don'ts for the seeker performing Navaratra. It is said that seeker shall bathe in a river or waterfall. He shall wear only two pieces of cloth. Apart from this, Brahmacharaya shall be followed, where the seeker shall sleep on floor and shall not keep any thought in mind. Above all, devotion is a must, without which there is no use of these efforts.

Nishabhedana[34] is good during Navaratra.

There are a few seekers who celebrate Navaratra as per these

---

[31] Silence of mind and tongue.
[32] होमो जप: कुमार्याचा साधकानां च भोजनम्। उपोषणमथो मौनं प्रभूतफलहेतवे।। (13.604)
[33] स्नाते प्रमुदितैहृष्टैर्ब्राह्मणै: क्षत्रियैर्विशै:। शूद्रैर्भक्तियुतैम्लेंच्छैरन्यैश्च भुवि मानवै।। स्त्रीभिश्च कुरुशार्दूल तद्विधानमिदं श्रृणु।।
[34] Post night Puja, mantra japa till morning

rituals. These rules are followed by learned scholars. A large section of people follows simple practices, which are mostly based on devotion.

The general celebrations are primarily based on Bhakti. A long period of slavery has led people of Bharata to be devoid of the Shastras. They are left with only the names of celebrations and gross rituals, followed in the name of tradition. The activities of general seekers are the same as that of those who follow Shastras. However, Mantras and rituals are not in practice to that extent. For example, kalasha sthapana is done. But the seeker will place them while reciting name of the mother only and not the Mantras prescribed. Prescribed Mantras and rituals lead the seeker to the feet of Bhagavati though it is greatness of the caring mother that seeker who does these rituals without Shastra rituals also gain the merits.

General seekers certainly are unaware of Kerala Marg and Kalpa. However, their devotion fills all these gaps. This Navaratra celebration involves *kalasha sthapana*, daily Puja, sangeet, Durga Puja, Jagarata (Jagarana), Havana, Kumari Puja, Vrata and pilgrimage.

Kalasha Sthapana: As mentioned above, people will do kalasha sthapana at the time of the muhurta. This is a gross practice, which may or may not be supported by prescribed mantras. If a brahmin is invited, he may do the same. However, if not, this is done with devotion only. There is no separate prabodhana done in case this is performed by one's own self.

Daily Puja: The general seeker offers sandalwood paste, sindura, garlands, flowers, dhupa, deepa and the prasada[35]. This would be followed by some paatha, whatever is possible. The rituals here are followed by devotion towards mother with mantras if the brahmin is engaged and with name of the mother, when done by one's own self.

---

[35]Prasada means bliss; this is bliss of Bhagavati

Sangeet: Ladies of the house sit together in the evening at the house and sing the 'Devi Geet'. In eastern Uttar Pradesh, Avadhi songs prevail and in the region of adjoining Bihar, Bhojpuri, Magadhi and Maithili songs are sung. Whereas in western Uttar Pradesh, local variants of Hindi are used for songs. This singing is supported by dholak and manjeera.

In almost the entire region, ladies' groups also perform the song in local Mandirs when they are free from daily household works.

Durga Puja: Durga Puja came to Uttar Pradesh from Bengal. This is celebrated during Ashvina Navaratra by town-based organizing committees. In this, a stage is set up, in which, Shri Mahishasurmardini Vigraha, along with Shri Mahalakshmi, Shri Mahasarasvati, Shri Ganesha and Shri Kartikeya, is installed with full fanfare. Nowadays, this is quite famous and youngsters actively participate. The morning and evening Puja is organized in celebration pandals and people from across the city come to witness the great celebrations. Some committees also organize Jagarana and public Havana. Kumari Puja is organized on the last day of event.

In some areas of Kashi and Prayagraj, Bengalis have been celebrating this festival since centuries.

Jagarata (Jagarana): Devotee groups organize an overnight devotional song event, in which Devi geetas are sung with full fanfare. In this, some singing artist is invited to sing the Mata ki bhente.

Havana: General seekers perform Havana on the day of visarjana. This Havana is based on *Shri Durga Saptashati* and Navarna. The entire family of the seeker participates in this Havana, inviting the brahmin who is offered food and dakshina and then the entire family takes prasada.

Kumari Puja: This is done on the ninth day by people. The girls are invited to house, first they are worshipped, they are offered the feast and then some gifts are given to them, then seekers request them to bless the family. It is seen that groups of girls go from one house to another during this event. This ritual generally does not involve any prescribed ritual and is Bhakti based.

Vrata: The pivot of Navaratra for the common man is his vrata. This is done with utmost devotion and care. A few days before, the markets are full of important items required for Navaratra Puja and vrata. People following this are visibly caring about what should be done and what not. The seeker tries to follow as much as he can. Although sleeping on the floor, bathing in the river and following mauna may or may not be followed, then also the devotion pervades.

Eating habits are changed during this period because the seeker is seen to be dissolved in thoughts of Devi.

Pilgrimage: Seekers pay visit to some Shakti Peetha during Navaratra. They perform Puja and bring prasada and good fortune to their homes. In Uttar Pradesh, people usually visit Shri Vindhyachal, Shri Kashi Vishalakshi, Shri Alopa Sankari, Shri Kalyani Devi, Shri Sitala Devi, Shri Lalita Devi, Shri Pateshvari, Shri Shakambhari Devi and various other mandirs. Those who have some commitments visit distant mandirs like Shri Mata Vaishno Devi and others. Shri Vindhyavasini is the deity of Bihar also. So, many people from Bihar and other parts of the country visit here during Navaratra celebrations.

After listening to all this, Aparajita asked, 'Ultimately, what do we get from this celebration?'

I said, 'With all these celebrations, the seeker feels like a new-born. All their malign influences are destroyed during these nine days. The ninth day is the new birth for the seeker. The seeker who celebrates this festival with full devotion is released from bonds, earns Brahma jnana and unites with the charana kamala of Ma. This is represented by the kalasha with ripened barely.'

After listening to all this, I saw that she calmed a little, I could see a different shine in her eye. She told me, 'Please narrate this to me every Navaratra so that I may thoroughly understand the essence of Navaratra.'

I smiled and replied to her while touching her lovely cheeks, 'I will write this for you my dear, the rest is your devotion and practice. May Bhagavati Shri Nava Durga bless you with her Divya Anugraha.'

9

Temples and Tribes in Andhra

RAMACHANDRA MURTHY KONDUBHATLA

*N*avaratri is celebrated in the Telugu states of Andhra Pradesh and Telangana with a great amount of enthusiasm and ceremonies. This is true of both Vasanta Navaratri and Sharada Navaratri.

'Nava' is nine and 'ratri' is night. So, Navaratri means nine nights. 'Nava' also means new. People who live in fear of the asuras look forward to a new beginning. There are nine ways of worshipping God—Shravanam (hearing), Keertanam (singing of paeans), Smaranam (chanting god's name), Paadasevanam (worshipping of feet), Archanam (performing Puja), Vandanam (genuflecting), Daasyam (dedicating oneself to God), Sakhyam (be a friend of God) and Atma Nivedanam (submitting one's self).

Vasanta (spring) and Sharada (winter) bring along with them many seasonal diseases. People pray to Parameshvari to come to their rescue. Sage Vyasa tells King Janamejaya that people get rid of the fear of death by worshipping Devi. In Chaitra (March–April), the first nine days, from Paadyami to Navami, the first lunar day to the ninth are considered Vasanta Navaratri. After about six months, at the beginning of winter (Sharada) season in Ashvayuja (Ashvina), the first nine days, from Paadyami to Navami, are called Sharannavaratri or Sharada Navaratri. In Andhra, Vasanta Navaratri culminates in Sri Rama Kalyanam (wedding) followed by Sri Rama Pattabhishekam (coronation). Sharada Navaratri ends with Dussehra on the tenth day. During the 10 days of Sharada Navaratri, the Devi is worshipped and a number of cultural programmes are held.

Panchanga Shravanam

Ugadi, the Telugu New Year Day, is on Chaitra Shuddha Padyami, the first day of Vasanta Navaratri. It marks the advent of spring. New leaves begin to sprout and flowers blossom. Panchanga Shravanam, or formal listening of the annual calendar reading, is organized. Panchanga Pathanam (reading) or Keertanam (rendering) and Panchanga Shravanam (hearing) have been in vogue since time immemorial. Madugula Nagaphanini Sarma, a sahasravadhani,[1] says all of it is nothing but the worship of Kaala-Purusha—a personification of time. 'Panchangam' means five limbs of time—tithi, vaara, nakshatra, yoga and karanam. There is a reference to the measurement of time in the Vedas, from 'Nimesha' to 'Kalpa'. 'Ugadi' stands for Yuga+Aadi, meaning the beginning of the year. The Panchangam forecasts the rainfall, crops, wars, diseases and other things of human interest.

In the earlier times, kings used to have Panchangam read by scholars in their courts on Ugadi. Over the years, Panchangam readers such as Pitaparti Subrahmanya Sastry, Madhura Krishna Murthy Siddhaanti, Malladi Chandrasekhara Sastry and Sankaramanchi Ramakrishna Sastry, left their imprint. Nowadays, it is customary for Chief Ministers, ministers and other dignitaries to be among the audience when Panchangam is read and interpreted by the pundits on the Ugadi morning.

Chaitra Navaratri

It is during this season that Maha Vishnu, in his seventh incarnation, descended on earth in a human form as Sri Rama. The first festival

---

[1] A person who can debate with 1,000 persons at the same time.

of the year, Ugadi, is celebrated for nine days till Sri Rama Navami. Bhadradri, the Sri Rama temple at Bhadrachalam, on the banks of the Godavari river in Telangana, is an important place of worship for Vaishnavites. According to Ramanjaneya Acharya, the chief priest of the temple, the 5,000-year-old Murtis of Sri Rama and Sita Devi are Svayambhuva or self-manifested. Kancharla Gopanna (1620–1680), popularly known as Bhakta Ramadasu, made this temple famous by involving himself its renovation and reconstruction—at the cost of his job and freedom. He was a great devotee of Sri Rama and also a composer of Carnatic music. His devotional lyrics in praise of Sri Rama are an important part of south Indian classical music.

At the Bhadrachalam temple, kalyanam (wedding) of Sri Rama and Sita Devi is celebrated on Navami, and also Sri Rama's coronation on the tenth day. For Sri Rama Kalyanam, the chief minister or the endowment minister carries holy turmeric rice and jewellery on their heads.

Vasanta Navaratri is celebrated in the villages as Sri Rama Navami. On all the days the devotees worship Sri Rama and read the Ramayana. Pandals are erected, the Murtis of Sri Rama and Devi Sita are set up on platforms. The Puja goes on for nine days. People participate in the Puja every day and take prasadam, consisting of water mixed with jaggery and soaked black gram. The practice of mass feeding too is observed.

Sharada Navaratri

Sharada Navaratri is celebrated by the Telugu people with gaiety and enthusiasm, as Devi Navaratri. Nine goddesses representing Devi are worshipped on nine days: Shailaputri or daughter of the mountain, Brahmacharini, Chandraghanta, Kushmanda, Skandamata, Katyayani, Kalaratri, Mahagauri and Siddhidatri. The tenth day is Vijaya Dashami, when Ravana's effigies are burnt. Even at Bhadrachalam, the Devi is primarily worshipped during Sharada Navaratri. This continues for eight days in the name of Ashta Lakshmi vratam.

Stage plays are organized in a big way at Devi Chowk, a popular centre in Rajamahendravaram city. Loudspeakers blare songs from films on Ramayana and poems from stage plays such as *Sri Ramanjaneya Yuddham* (battle between Rama and Anjaneya or Hanuman). *Sri Ramanjaneya Yuddham* is one of the five immortal plays in Telugu, the other four being Satya Harishchandra, Chintaamani, Gayoopaakhyaanam and Krishna Raayabaaram.

In the play, Yayati, the king of Kashi, is responsible for the clash between Sri Rama and his ardent devotee Anjaneya. They come face to face, indulging in rhetoric, listing what one did for the other. It turns out to be a battle between Rama-vanam (Rama's arrow) and Rama-japam (chanting of name of Rama). When Rama uses his arrow, Anjaneya goes on chanting Rama-namam (Rama's name). Ultimately, Anjaneya falls. Believing that his devotee is dead, Rama becomes emotional. He is about to end his life when Anjaneya gets up, reminding Rama that he is a chiranjeevi, one who cannot die.

Tandra Venkata Subrahmanyam wrote *Sri Ramanjaneya Yuddham* in 1944–5. Earlier, there was another play on the same theme, named *Hanumadrama Samaram*, written by Baddireddi Koteswara Rao. However, *Sri Ramanjaneya Yuddham* caught the imagination of the public, sending the earlier version into oblivion. Betha Venkata Rao, a great actor and a singer, was well known for his portrayal of Anjaneya in this play. He died when he was in the process of getting his make-up done, and his body in Anjaneya's attire was taken round the town in a big procession before cremation.

Sri Ramanjaneya Yuddham also got popularized with the 1958 and 1975 films by the same name; N.T. Rama Rao played Sri Rama in the later version.

Sharada Navaratri is celebrated in all the villages of Telugu states. The Vaishya (business) community actively participates by sponsoring the events. They also perform Pujas in the pandals with family as it is an auspicious time to launch new business ventures. It is also the time they worship their account books.

The main Navaratri celebrations are held at Kanaka Durga Temple in Vijayawada, Bhramaramba-Mallikarjuna Swamy Temple at Srisailam, Bhadrakali temple in Warangal and the Shakti Peethas at Pithapuram, Draksharamam, in Andhra Pradesh and Alampur in Telangana.

Vijayawada Kanakadurga

Durga is considered the Universal Mother, including as the mother of three mothers—Parvati, Sarasvati and Lakshmi. Goddess Kanakadurga, presiding over Indra Keelandri in Vijayawada, is considered as 'Durga in gold'. Sri Durga Malleswara Swamy Temple, built in the Dravidian style, is the only shrine where the Devi sits on the right side of her consort. Traditionally, the female deity is seated on the left of the male deity. The fact that Durga sits on the right indicates that Shakti is predominant here. The invocation to the Divine Mother by the fifteenth-century Telugu poet Bammera Pothana, greets the devotees as they enter the sanctum sanctorum. It hails the Divine Mother as Mugurammala moolaputamma (mother of all the three mothers) and Universal Mother. Circumabulating the main mandapam and viewing the glittering golden gopuram (tower) is done first, before one enters the temple. Kanakadurga is seen amidst the glow of oil lamps with benign smile.

For abhishekam (holy bath) and other purposes, water is fetched from the Krishna river in a brass vessel at 3 a.m. every day. Six couples are given the privilege of the first darshana in antralaya.[2] They offer silk clothes to the deities in a ritual called Sri Ammavaari Vastraalankarana Arjita Seva. Khadgamala is another important ritual where devotees worship the deity's sword for success in business, studies or any other pursuit. Kings used to perform this Puja before embarking on wars.

The most important annual festival here is Dussehra, which is

---

[2]The inner sanctum.

celebrated for nine days (Navaratri) culminating on the tenth day as Vijayadashami. Kanakadurga is given different svarupas on different days:

Ashvayuja Paadyami—Swarna Kavachaalankruta Durga Devi or golden armoured form. The story goes that King Madhava Varma of Vijayavatikapuri announced death sentence to his son since he was found responsible for the death of a boy. Pleased with the king's selfless commitment to dharma, Durga revives the child and rains gold on Vijayavatikapuri.

Dvitiya—Sri Balatripura Sundari Devi, Bala mantra is believed to be very powerful. Children are taught Bala Mantra, most important of all Devi mantras, so that they do well in their studies.

Tritiya—Sri Gayatri Devi as Veda Mata. The Goddess appears with panchamukha (five faces) and blessing hands. The triumvirate of Brahma, Vishnu and Maheshvara are believed to dwell in her.

Chaturthi—Sri Annapurna Devi. She feeds all living beings, holding a golden vessel in one hand and a diamond-studded ladle in the other.

Panchami, also known as Lalita Panchami—Sri Lalita Tripura Sundari Devi. She is believed to have existed even before the Trimurti of Brahma, Vishnu and Mahesha as the principal source of power.

Shashthi—Mahalakshmi Devi. She is the symbol of everything auspicious, an embodiment of eight forms of Lakshmi. The Shakti triumvirate Mahakali, Mahalakshmi and Mahasarasvati ended the tyranny of asuras. Mahalakshmi displayed tremendous valour to annihilate Asura Hala.

Saptami, also known as Maha Saptami—Mahasarasvati Devi. The goddess of learning, clad in white and seated on a lotus is playing the veena with hamsa vahana (swan boat) at her feet.

Ashtami, known as Durgashtami—Durga Devi is worshipped. Durga Devi killed an asura by name Durugudu. Hence the name Durga. She wears a gold crown and sits on a lion.

***Navami*, also known as *Maha Navami*—**Mahishasuramardini or slayer of Mahishasura. The Divine Mother, eight-armed, sitting on a lion is seen piercing Mahishasura and his men with her trident. She is said to have self-manifested in this form on Indrakiladri.

***Vijaya Dasami*—**Raja Rajeshvari. Serene and benign-looking, she is seen sitting on a lion with a sugarcane in one hand. She is also called Aparajita (invincible).

During the nine days of Navaratri, the city of Vijayawada reverberates with the chanting of her name, 'Jai Kanaka Durga', 'Jai Bhavani', 'Jai Shambhavi' and 'Jai Kali'. On the concluding day, the Murtis of Ganga, Durga and Malleswara Swamy are taken on a highly illuminated hamsa vahana for a ride on the Krishna river. It is called Teppotsavam. 'Teppa' in Telugu means boat and 'Utsav' is celebration. Thousands of people gather to watch the spectacle. In the evening, on all the nine days, Pancha Haratulu or five aratis, are offered to the Goddess on the banks of the Krishna.

Food plays important role in the festivities, and each day has its own menu. On the first day for Shailaputri, Katta Pongali (a sweet preparation with rice) is offered. According to the custom followed at Srisailam, Kadambam (sambar rice), blackgram vadas, Ravva Kesari (sweet with ravva-semolina) and Panakam (jaggery water) are also offered to Shailaputri. Pulihora (yellow tamarind rice) is offered to Bala Tripura Sundari. Gayatri is given coconut rice and payasam (sweet dish). Annapurna Devi is offered vadas made of black gram and sorghum. Lalita Devi is offered curd rice. Mahalakshmi's favourite dish is Kesari, a sweet made of rava. Sarasvati, Jaganmata, is offered sweet rice and ginger vadas. Durga Devi is given vegetable curry and pulusu (tamarind preparation). The same food menu is followed at home as well during Navaratri.

Durga is considered as the Goddess of Harvest. In *Devi Navaratrulu*, Sri Vasavi Kanyaka Parameswari Devi, Vanabala Vasavi, Lalita Tripura Sundari, Chandi, Gajalakshmi, Dhana Lakshmi, Panchamruta Gayatri, Kalika Devi, Sarasvati and Mahishasuramardini are some of the forms in which the Goddess is worshipped.

In Srisailam, Navaratri is celebrated the same way as is done at Vijayawada's Kanakadurga temple except on the last two days. On the ninth day, it is Siddhidayini on a horse and on the tenth, it is Bhramaramba Devi, the presiding goddess of Srisailam. Navagraha Mandapaaraadhana, Chandi havan, Panchakshari, Bala Anushthanam and Chandi Parayanam are performed during the nine days. On Vijaya Dashami, Chandi Yagam, Rudra Yagam, Vahanaseva and Alaya Utsavam are conducted.

Navaratri at Home

In middle-class Telugu households, Sharada Navaratri or Devi Navaratri involves all members of the family in the celebrations. Those who live away from home in different parts of the country, make it a point to reach their parents' place to be together during the festival. The sons-in-law are especially invited for the occasion. The elders observe a fast, living on fruits and milk for nine days. Others, whose health does not permit rigid fasting, skip one of the two meals in a day. Those who cannot do even that observe a half-day fasting on the last three days, from Saptami to Navami.

Flowers, fruits, coconuts, kumkuma, camphor and aromatic materials are kept ready. The floor is cleaned. Cow dung mixed in red soil is applied in the place of worship, creating a platform. The place is decorated with flowers, mango leaves arches, turmeric powder and kumkuma. Rangavali or rangoli is drawn. Pancha Pallava, five tender branches of five trees, are placed on the dais. The lady of the houses observes fast the previous night. The next morning, she places the pratima (Murti) of the Devi with 18 arms—

holding different weapons including a disc, a sword and a trident. An image of the goddess mounted on a lion, piercing the asura with her trident, is also placed. In case such a Murti is not available, a copper plate inscribed with the words, 'Aim, Hreem, Kleem' is used. Members of the family take a head bath early in the morning, wear silk sari, dhoti or pyjama and kurta, and sit on a lion skin or a wooden plank facing east or north for the Puja. They sip water thrice for achamanam, chant the 'Gayatri Mantra' and sit in dhyana for ten minutes before taking the sankalpa. Thereafter, Ganapati Puja is done followed by swasti punyahavachanam. The jyoti (light) that is lit in the morning must be kept burning, by putting oil regularly, for all the ten days. The Murtis of Sun, Ganapati, Shiva and Vishnu are kept on four sides on the platform. 'Gauri Panchakshari,' 'Bala Sharadakshari,' 'Panchadashi' and 'Shodashi' are mantras recited in praise of the Devi. 'Sahashra Namaavali' and 'Ashtothara Shata Naamaavali' are also rendered. *Devi Puranam, Saundarya Lahari, Durga Saptashati* and other stories about Devi are read as part of Puja on all the nine days.

Guru Puja, Gau (cow) Puja, Kumari Puja and Suvasini (married women) Puja are also performed every day. On Padyami, the first day, a two-year-old girl called 'Kaumarika' is worshipped. On the second is it three-year-old Trimurti; on the third day, a four-year-old Kalyani; on the fourth day, Rohini, a five-year-old girl, is worshipped. On the fifth day, it is Kalika, a six-year-old girl; on day six, it is Chandika, a seven-year-old; on seventh day, eight-year-old Shambhavi is prayed to. On eighth day, a nine-year-old girl is worshipped as Durga and on Navami, it is Subhadra, a 10-year-old girl. The belief is that by worshipping little girls who are treated as goddesses, people would ward off poverty, enemies, disease and grief.

On the evening of Dussehra, people go to Shami (Jammi or *Prosopis cineraria*) tree and pluck some leaves to be exchanged between friends, youngsters and elders as an expression of goodwill. Students go to their teachers with small gifts, and touch their feet to obtain their blessings. In Telugu, they have songs like 'Ayya vaariki chaalu pappu bellalu' to be sung on this occasion while meeting the teachers. The legend goes back to Dvapara Yuga, when Pandavas were employed in the court of Virata during their exile and their weapons were hidden on a Shami tree.

Bommala Koluvu—Golu

Bommala Koluvu, a display or exhibition of dolls and toys, is an integral part of the Navaratri festival in the Telugu region. Clay, sandalwood, teakwood or dried coconut shells are used to make dolls to depict the village life, culture and tradition of Telugus. The koluvu, which means court or durbar, shows a figurine of a boy and a girl together looking at elephants, horses, camels and other animals on display. They exhibit court life, royal procession, rath yatra, scenes depicting harvesting, and everyday activities. There would be kings riding elephants and a series of dolls and toys narrating puranic stories.

These displays are typically thematic, narrating legends from the Ramayana, the Mahabharata and the Puranas. The toys and dolls are arranged on three steps or tiers covered with bright cloth.

Nowadays, clubs and associations organize the displays. The underlying purpose of the show is to encourage agriculture and make children familiar with farm tools and rural life. The clay is obtained from dredging and desilting of irrigation canals. It has significant connection with the agricultural economy. The practice of koluvu is prevalent in all the southern states.

Display of dolls and toys is called Golu and in some places as Kolu, Bomma Habba, Bommai Kolu, depending on the local language. Organizing Bommala Koluvu in a way integrates the modern and uprooted people and helps them reconnect with the rich culture and traditions.

Friends and relatives visit each other to see Bommala Koluvu. The hosts and the guests together participate in the worship by singing

A Photograph of Sharada Peetha in Kashmir in 1893 by the British Scholar Aurel Stein

Durga Patachitra from Bengal (Vakyavagisha)

Kolu in Tamil Nadu (Sriram Sivasankaran)

Bhoga in Odisha (Tapasi Mohapatra)

Paalkis of Devi Sharvari and Devi Gayatri at Jagatsukh's Chachauhali Mela in Himachal Pradesh (Divya Prasad)

Ghatasthapana and Jzaunra from Himachal (Divya Prasad)

Bathukamma in Secunderabad, Telangana (Prakash Reddy Family)

Bathukamma—Good Old Days (Prakash Reddy Family)

Bathukamma in Telangana (Anuradha Goyal)

Centenerian Grandmother Applying Tika on Her Great-Great-Granddaughter on Dashami in Nepal (Kripa Joshi)

Garba in Gujarat (Anuradha Goyal)

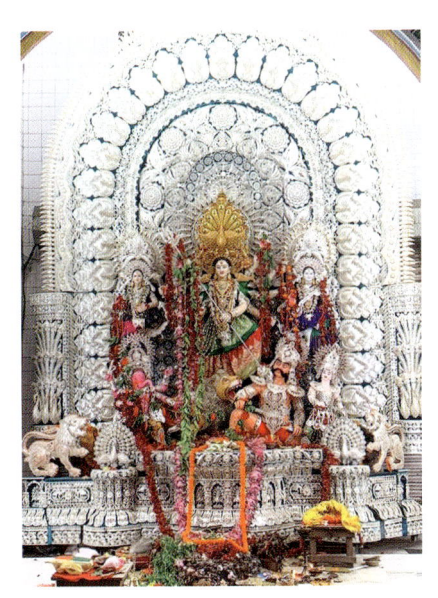

Medha at Bhubaneshwar, Odisha (Gayatri Tripathy)

Mrinmayee Devi Puja by the royal Family of Aul in Odisha (Avantika Devi)

Raja of Kalahandi, Odisha Receiving the Chattar of Maa Manikeswari (Rituja Devi)

Teppotsavam in Andhra Pradesh (P. Vijayakrishna)

Sharada Devi Sond Phool Alankaar in Mangaluru, Karnataka (G. Aditya Bhat)

Karni Mata near Bikaner in Rajasthan (Anuradha Goyal)

Sanjhi at Uruswati Museum near Gurugram, Haryana (Anuradha Goyal)

Vidyarambham in Kerala (Rajesh B.R. Bhagavath)

Durga Puja (Arya Swami)

hymns. Sometimes even the neighbours join in the singing. Food consisting of sweet items is offered to the goddess and distributed among the guests. There is chit-chat regarding the display. Some music programmes are also organized. The guests are given small gift bags. Married women are given kumkuma, fruits and new clothes.

Banni Festival

Banni festival is observed only in Devaragattu village in Holagunda mandal of Kurnool district in Andhra Pradesh. Banni in Kannada means 'Please come'. On Dussehra night, two rival groups indulge in mock stick-fight merrily injuring one another. The Karrala Samaram (stick-fight) is celebrated by hundreds of people and watched by thousands who descend on the village from Karnataka, Tamil Nadu, Andhra Pradesh, Telangana, Maharashtra and other states.

Legend has it that two asuras, Mani and Mallasura, were bothering and torturing saints and noblemen in the Devaragattu area. People prayed to Lord Shiva and he appeared in Kumaravataram on a hillock, assuring protection from the asuras; he vanquishes them. He came to be known as Sri Mala Malleswara Swamy. However, just before dying, the asuras prayed to Sri Malleswara Swamy to let them have human sacrifice annually. The Swamy promised the asuras a fistful of blood from Kambarabhira family once a year.

Persons who are ardent and dedicated devotees of Mala Mallikarjuna Swamy are known as Goruvaiahs. Dressed in black, they consider themselves as the adopted children of Malleswara Swamy. They are present in every village around Devaragattu and belong to the Kanche Beera dynasty. One of them would pierce a thick needle into the muscle at the back of the knee, from one end to another, causing blood to flow. He then throws the blood on two stones that represent the asuras Mani and Mallasura.

On Vijaya Dashami, the priest performs Ganapati Puja, Kanaka dharana and nischitardham (engagement) of Malleswara Swamy with Parvati. The deities are carried in a palanquin by a group of people followed by thousands of people wielding flaming torches and long sticks with metal ring tips. They dance to the drumbeat.

The stick-wielders from Nerani, Neranithanda and Kothapeta villages together take on the rival group comprising people from Aluru, Sulluvai, Yellarthi, Arikera and Netravatti villages. They start from their villages in processions at about 10 p.m. All processions merge on reaching Devaragattu. At 12:10 a.m., people from Nerani, Neeranithanda and Kothapeta villages gather at dollina banda (a huge stone) and take a pledge to protect the Murtis and then take milk pots into their hands. At 12:40 a.m., the villagers go to the top of the hill. At 1:10 a.m., the priests celebrate the kalyanam (wedding) of Mala Mallikarjuna Swamy and Parvati.

People perform ksheeraabhishekam (milk bath) of the deities. At 1:20 a.m., they put the Murtis in the palanquin and start to climb down the hill. The palanquin is carried by persons from Sigaluru family of Holikote village in Karnataka. The members of this family come to Devaragattu for the festival every year without fail. They are emotionally attached to the people from Nareni, Narenithanda and Kothpeta villages. Then they are stopped by the rival villagers. At 1:45 a.m., the procession reaches Aswatha Narayana Katta. Then the sticks rise into the air and the fight starts. One group tries to force the other group to take the procession to their villages which is an act they consider auspicious.

After the stick fight, the Goruvaiahs and Devadasis dance. During this time, the palanquin carrying Murtis of Swamy and Devi are kept on Simhasana Katta (a bund on which there is a flat platform). Some people play flute, others dance to a tune swinging tridents and sounding damarukams (dholaks) with their hands. Then they go into a trance beating themselves with bamboo plates uttering something incoherent as though they are possessed.

A Goruvaiah from Balluru village of Halahari Mandal breaks an iron chain, 23 times at every knot, weighing 20 kilograms. After performing the feat, he is lifted into the air by admiring crowd of devotees amidst slogans and whistles. Basivinis (Devadasis) who come from Adoni, Aluru, Guntakallu towns and some other parts of Rayalaseema are tossed into air by people from a particular community from Nerani village. Then coloured water is sprinkled just like vasantotsavam. The Murtis of Mallamma and Malleswara Swamy are carried to a Shami tree where all the sticks are placed. People of both the groups worship the god and goddess. Then the palanquin is taken towards Basavanna Gudi (Temple of Basava) where the chief priest talks about the future that is in store for the people. Then the Murtis are taken back to their abode on the hill.

Shakti Peethas

Andhra Pradesh has three Shakti Peethas—Bhramaramba Devi at Srisailam in Kurnool district, Puruhutika Devi Pithapuram and Manikyamba Devi at Draksharaamam in East Godavari district. Jogulamba Devi is in Telangana at Alampur of Gadwal district.

Bhramaramba Devi: Srishailam is the abode of Srishaila Mallikarjuna Swamy located on an 800-foot hillock on the right bank of the Krishna river also called Pataala Ganga. It is one of the 12 Jyotirlingas across the country and Goddess Bhramaramba Devi is one of the Mahashakti Peethas. The mountain on which the shrine is situated is called Srigiri, Siridham, Sriparvatha and Srinagam.

The temple is believed to have been there since Satavahanas' time in the third century. Subsequent dynasties like Ikshvakus also known as Parvatiyas (devotees of Parvati), Vijayanagara kings, Kakatiyas, Prolaya Vemareddy and Maratha king Chhatrapati Shivaji added to the temple. Like the entry arch was added by Vithalamba, wife of the second Harihara Raya of the Vijayanagar dynasty.

Puruhutika Devi: It is a part of Kukkuteswara Swamy's temple, on the outskirts of Pithapuram town near Kakinada. Pilgrims take a dip in the Pada Gaya Sarovaram (lake) here. Puruhuthika temple has on its walls Ashtaadasa or 18 Puranas painted. Puruhutika Devi Murti has four hands holding a bag of seeds (beeja), an axe (parasu), a lotus (kamala) and a dish (madhu patra).

Manikyamba Devi: Draksharamam, near Amalapuram is where Daksha Yajnyam is believed to have taken place where he came from all the way across the Vindhyas. Inscriptions on the temple reveal that it was built between the ninth and tenth centuries CE by the Eastern Chalukyas. Manikyamba Devi is the consort of Sri Bheemeswara. The temple of Bheemeswara is considered to be one of the Trilinga Kshetras. Famous Telugu poet Srinatha wrote *Bheemeswara Purana* narrating the story of the Shiva and Sati.

Jogulamba: The Jogulamba temple near Kurnool was built by the Chalukyas of Badami, at the initiative of Pulakesin-II in the seventh century. At Alampur, they built a complex of nine temples for Brahma called Nava Brahma temples. Jogulamba temple and Nava Brahma temples were also damaged during the Islamic invasions. A new temple was built again, after centuries.

10

Satvika in Punjab and Haryana

ANURADHA GOYAL

Come Navaratri and all us young girls would dress up in our best attires to be the Kanjaks. Everyone we knew in the neighbourhood invited us home to wash our feet, worship us, pamper us and shower us with gifts. We hardly understood the Devi, whose swaroop or forms we were worshipped as, we just knew it was our day and we were important. In hindsight, it is my earliest memory of connecting with my inner shakti that has the power to give and to bless.

I remember my Dadi creating Sanjhi[1] on our walls during Sharada Navaratri. It is not an inherent tradition in my community, but it was her Manauti or a vow and she practiced it till she could. That tradition in my family died with her but not without introducing me to the Devi who comes and lives with us for nine days.

Jagrata or the night-long celebration of the Devi, singing her glory and dancing along, is another memory that reminds me of how the devotion for the mother brought everyone together across all kinds of divides on a single platform.

As a young professional, living in Delhi in the late 1990s, I observed that the newly launched international fast-food joints went vegetarian for the nine days of Navaratri. I am a born vegetarian, but in north India, many hardcore non-vegetarians turn strictly vegetarian during Navaratri. However, for multinational food joints,

---

[1] A manifestation of Mother Goddess.

better known for their non-vegetarian menu, to go vegetarian told me of the extent to which the festival is followed by people.

Naraate is how Navaratri is known in Punjab, just a little localization of the word that is universal within the Indic calendar. In Haryana, it becomes Naurate, to flow with the sound of the language.

Sharada Navaratri that is from Shukla Pratipada to Navami of Ashvina month, or the first nine days of the bright half of Ashvina month, remains the most popular Navaratri. It roughly falls in October. Chaitra Navaratri that culminates in Rama Navami is also celebrated with great fervor around April. Magha and Ashadha Navaratri are rarely known in this region. Any practitioners of Shakta tradition do so in absolute privacy.

Both Chaitra and Sharada Navaratri come at the time of seasonal transits. Chaitra brings in the summers and Sharada is the harbinger of winters. It is considered the time to purify the body, mind and spirit to prepare for the upcoming season. These nine days and nine nights are devoted to cleansing the body by fasting, and the mind and soul by soaking oneself in the devotion of Jagatjanani—the mother of this universe who is also the Prakriti or Nature. *Devi Bhagavata Purana* calls these times as 'Yamadamshtra', likening them to the teeth of Yama (the god of death) for living beings, as they bring along all kinds of diseases.

Fasting

It is no wonder then that fasting is the most common way of observing Navaratri in Punjab and Haryana. It is a tradition that is not followed as much ritualistically as it is by the free will of the observer. Each person, depending on their bodily capacity, circumstances, devotion and inclination to keep the fast choose their own regime for the fast. How much and for how long you fast are totally individual choices. People fast anywhere from one to nine days. On one end of the spectrum are people who undertake *Nirjal*

Nirahar Vrat, meaning they take no water or no food for nine days. This is very rare. Many people do only nirahar, which means they do consume water or sometimes milk but no solid food. Then there are those who consume milk and fruits once a day. The most common mode of fast though is one meal a day prepared using the alternate food grains.

Traditionally, during fasting, you give up anna or grains of all kinds. Phalahaar or a fruit-based diet, that typically includes milk and fruits, is recommended. Some alternates to everyday grains like kuttu or buckwheat, sabudana or sago and *saunkhiya chawal* which is a variety of small round rice not considered grain in typical sense can be consumed. Sendha namak or a type of rock salt is used instead of common sea salt.

At my home, when we used to fast for nine days, we ate a meal around afternoon—usually made of kuttu ka atta. It could be parantha, puri or pakode made of purple hued kuttu flour. Sanghade ka atta or flour made of water chestnut is another flour that can be consumed but one needs to be an expert cook to handle this flour. sabudana khichadi, kheer made of saukhiyan rice and aalu or potato chat are other options. People usually plan a menu for the nine days of Navaratri. These days most restaurants and even some airlines offer the food for those fasting with these options.

In most families, the fast is done for seven or eight days, culminating on the Ashtami or Navami in Kanya Puja, after which the regular food is resumed. Some people fast only on Saptami or Ashtami, a day before the Kanya Puja. Some fast on the first day of Navaratri and then on the seventh or eighth. Within a family, too, different people will often follow their own choice of fasting every Navaratri, mostly driven by the inner voice and willpower.

Those who do not fast for any reason would abstain from having any tamasik food like non-vegetarian food, eggs, onion and garlic. Is this a way of cleaning our bodies as we transit through the major change in season? Probably. It ensures that we go on a simple yet vitalizing satvik diet on a regular basis. When everyone around you follows this routine, it becomes a part of Ritucharya,[2] making it easy and festive.

Going vegetarian and sticking to satvik food that is nourishing and vitalizing, for nine days is one of the most followed rituals in Punjab and Haryana during Navaratri. Well, there was a reward at the end of the fasting season as we shall soon see.

Kanjak Pujana

Kanjak is how Kanya or Kumari Puja is known in Punjab and Haryana.

Devi Bhagavata Purana, in its description of Kanya Puja Vidhi, says that girls between the ages of two and 10 should be invited home as Devi Swaroops and worshipped. Girls below the age of two have not yet developed their senses so they are not eligible. It is assumed that after the age of 10, girls will start menstruating, hence, they are no longer Kanyas. If a girl starts menstruating before 10, she should also not be invited. Thus, the girls who can be treated as different Swaroops of Devi are those who whose senses have developed and have not yet started menstruating or stepped into womanhood.

It goes on to describe the Swaroop of Devi that girls represent at every age, each of which bestow certain kinds of blessings or protects you from different kinds of negative forces in life. The names of these Swaroops are as follows:

2-Year-Old—Kumarika
3-Year-Old—Trimurti
4-Year-Old—Kalyani
5-Year-Old—Rohini
6-Year-Old—Kalika
7-Year-Old—Chandika

---

[2]'Ritu' meaning season and 'charya' meaning regimen or discipline, indicating a seasonal cycle.

8-Year-Old—Shambhavi
9-Year-Old—Durga
10-Year-Old—Subhadra

It prescribes inviting a Kanya home every day for worship. One can also increase the number of Kanyas by one everyday so that on the ninth day, you worship nine Kanyas. You can also multiply the numbers while maintaining the ratio.

In practice though, Kanya Puja is performed either on Ashtami or Navami depending on the family tradition, by inviting nine or more girls. One or two boys of same age, called Launkra, are also invited along and worshipped the same way. All the kids invariably come from the neighbourhood. Besides age and availability, there is no other criteria for who can be invited.

They are seated respectfully on an Asana. The head of the family washes and cleans their feet. Tilak is applied on their foreheads. A Kalava or Mauli a sacred red and yellow thread, is tied on their wrists. A red Chunri decorated with sequins is offered to them. Gifts given to them include items of Shringara or ornamentation like bindis, bangles, jewellery, etc. along with a little cash. These are the minimal things beyond which one is free to gift anything they wish. A formal Puja is done for the Kanyas and members of the host family touch their feet and seek their blessings. Then, it's time to offer food to the visiting Devis. All that one offers as Puja to a deity in a temple is offered to the Kanjaks.

The most common food made for Kanya Puja includes halwa, puri and black chana. Kanyas, who are considered the Devis visiting your home, are fed with love and devotion. Practically, the girls get so much food from all the homes they visit that they can eat it all for a few days! The food and gifts received by the girls belong to them and no one in their families will even touch them. My own memories of being a Kanya are formed around all the small gifts my sister and I used to get and the piles of halwa puri that would collect on the dining table for us to eat.

Kanya Puja is also performed in the temples. Prominent Devi temples see groups of girls who can be invited by anyone for Kanya Puja. It is a convenient way to find Kanyas, if there are not many in your surroundings. It is also performed by the people who undertake pilgrimage to their Kul Devi or Isht Devi temples during Navaratri and hence are not at home to perform this Puja.

Sanjhi Devi

Popular media has acquainted us with the Durga Puja of Bengal where the Goddess is created, worshipped and then merged back in the elements. Punjab and Haryana have their own version of creating the Devi image before Navaratri, worshipping her for nine days on a wall at home and then bidding her farewell by leaving her in the waters till she is created again next year using the mud from the same place. Here she is called Sanjhi Mata. 'Sanjhi' has two literal meanings, the first being 'evening' from 'Sanjh' or 'Sandhya' and the second from Punjabi where it also means 'shared' or 'common'. Both the meanings reflect in the way she is always worshipped every evening for nine days along with people in the neighbourhood.

In my childhood, I used to make stars, sun, moon, birds, plants and many other decorative elements using clay brought from a pond. These decorations later form the Sanjhi. Small sticks are used to create rays and other designs. The clay pieces are dipped in white paint and left to dry in sun. Once dry, they became a canvas to be painted with rust colored Geru and decorate using whatever is available. All this is done by Amavasya, a day before the Navaratri begins.

Come the first day of Navaratri, the chosen wall of the house is given a coat of fresh cow dung, making it shuddh or purified. It is ready to be the sacred space to host Sanjhi Mata. Absolute cleanliness is maintained around this area, for it is the abode of Devi.

All the stars kept ready are arranged and pasted on the wall to create the image of Devi, almost like a collage or a jigsaw puzzle. Her face may be created using these stars or a pre-made colorful face bought from a potter can be used. Hands and feet are sometimes created using stars and can also be realistic imitations of the limbs. Any material can be used to decorate the Devi, be it cotton, sequins, lace or anything that will beautify her. One of the Devi's hands is depicted raised with the palm facing outwards, which can be interpreted as Abhaya Mudra symbolizing the divine protection and fearlessness. Ample jewellery like bangles, earrings and necklaces adorn the Devi. Some families also choose to drape her in full clothes like ghagra and choli. A red Chunri is finally put on the Devi to complete the Swaroop that is ready to be worshipped. How you create your Sanjhi is really a matter of how creative you feel.

These days, prefabricated Sanjhi figures are available in the market that you can simply hang on your wall and worship. What a lost opportunity for our annual creativity sojourn, especially for kids who would remember creating the Devi for the rest of their lives like I do, apart from the first-hand experience of srishti (Creation), sthiti (Sustenance) and laya (Dissolution) that represents the universal cycle of life.

Elaborate Sanjhi creations sometimes have multiple figures surrounding the main figure of Sanjhi Mata. At times, children or brothers are shown accompanying the figure of the Mother. In some villages they make Ulta Chor, a reversed figure of a thief, who it is believed is someone who tried to run away with the jewellery of the Sanjhi Mata but could not. A sun and moon are seen in almost all Sanjhi decorations. Birds and animal figurines create the environment surrounding the Sanjhi Devi.

Every evening after sunset for nine days, an Arati is performed. All the children, especially girls from the neighbourhood get together with a thali holding a deep (lamp) and prasada. Together they sing Arati for Sanjhi Mata. Most of these songs welcome Sanjhi and ask her to bless everyone in the family specially the brothers. Prasada is offered to the Devi and then distributed among all those present. The neighbourhood community comes together to worship Devi. People visit all the homes that have put up Sanjhi. Some elders impromptu reward the young girls singing Sanjhi Arati. In small villages, collective Sanjhi is made by the women of the village where everyone comes together to celebrate as one big family. This may have roots in the fact that villages used to comprise of one big extended family.

At places, grandmothers make all the girls sit around Sanjhi and tell them the story of Sanjhi that goes like this: Once upon a time, there was a pious and wealthy couple who followed their dharma. They had everything but no children. One day, the lady of the house was busy with her Puja in the courtyard when a sadhu visited her. He sensed that she was not happy and asked her the reason of her unhappiness. She explained that they had everything in life but it all felt worthless without children. The sadhu told her to make a Swaroop of Sanjhi Mata in Ashvina Navaratri and worship her for nine days. She followed the advice and was blessed with children. Just as her wish was fulfilled, Sanjhi Mata fulfills everyone's wish. As they say in every Phalashruti,[3] anyone who tells or listens to this story also gets his or her wishes fulfilled. Young girls typically wish for a good husband and the well-being of their brothers and families. However, when one prays to Sanjhi Mata, what you wish for is strictly between the devotee and her.

Sanjhi is put up only during the Sharada Navaratri that culminates in Dussehra. On the morning of tenth day, all the clay parts are removed from the wall, collected in an earthen pot and taken to a waterbody. Ideally, it has to be Pravahit or immersed in the flowing water. In case there is no river or canal close by, people also leave it in a pond or tank. Visarjan or sendoff of Sanjhi in water is again done collectively. Some villages have a tradition of boys breaking the Sanjhi pots when girls leave them in the pond. They stop it from reaching the other end of the pond which is considered

---

[3] The rewards of listening to a story or an episode from the scriptures.

inauspicious but it is all done in jest. It is a kind of farewell that the village gives to the Devi till she is invited again next Navaratri.

Sanjhi is a tradition that is followed every year in some families, while in others it is a kind of thanksgiving when a wish is fulfilled like when you have a new born in the family, and that may also include the new born of your cattle. So, if your family has been blessed with milk or sons, you invite Sanjhi during Navaratri and worship her. Barota or the image of a young one is depicted along with Sanjhi, when a newborn comes in the family.

Punjab has three main regions—Majha, Doaba and Malwa. Sanjhi is more prevalent in Malwa, the southern part of Punjab. It is also prevalent in some parts of Haryana.

Songs of Sanjhi

> Jaag Sanjhi Jaag,
> Tere mathe laggan bhaag
> Tenu kudiyan pujan aaiyaan
> Teri pattiyan suhaag
> Pehli Arati karan tayaar
> Jeeve Sanjhi mera veer pyar
> Veer pyar diyan do jodiyan
> Do Shiva/Krishna duale khadiyan
> Tu khol mata hattadi
> Mein pujan teri pattadi
> Mein pujan tere pair
> Niranjan saade aaya / teri kaaya
> Mein har ka darshan paya
> Govind saade aaya
> Main har ka darshan paya

(This is repeated seven times so that the same Arati is offered seven times. The only word that changes is the number of Arati being performed.)

Sanjhi ta mangdi hara hara gobar
Main kithon liaavan Sanjhi hara hara gobar
Veera ta mera gauaan da paali
Mein uthon liaavan Sanjhi hara hara gobar
Tu le meri Sanjhi hara hara gobar

Sanjhi ta mangdi peeli peeli mitti
Main kithon liaavan Sanjhi peeli peeli mitti
Veera ta mera zameenan da malik
Mein uthon liaavan Sanjhi peeli peeli mitti
Tu le meri Sanjhi peeli peeli mitti

Meri Sanjhi taan mangdi laal laal chudiyan
Mein kithon liavaan laal laal chudian
Veera ta mera banjara da saathi
Mein uston liavaan laal laal chudian
Tu pa meri Sanjhi ni laal laal chudian

Sanjhi ta mangdi chitte chitte chawal
Main kithon liaavan Sanjhi chitte chitte chawal
Veera ta mera kariyane di hatti
Mein uthon liaavan Sanjhi chitte chitte chawal
Tu kha meri Sanjhi chitte chitte chawal

Sanjhi ta mangdi peele peele laddu
Main kithon liaavan Sanjhi peele peele laddu
Veera ta mera halwai da sathi
Mein uthon liaavan Sanjhi peele peele laddu
Tu kha meri Sanjhi peele peele laddu

Sanjhi ta mangdi chhaj bhare gehne
Main kithon liaavan Sanjhi chhaj bhare gehne
Veera ta mera suniare da sathi
Mein uthon liaavan Sanjhi chhaj bhare gehne
Tu pa meri Sanjhi chhaj bhare gehne

Meri Sanjhi taan mangdi laal laal chunniyan
Mein kithon liavaan laal laal chunniyan
Veera ta mera bajaji da saathi
Mein uston liavaan laal laal chunnian
Tu pa meri Sanjhi ni laal laal chunnian

Meri Sanjhi taan mangdi girian chhuvaare
Mein kithon liavaan laal girian chhuvaare
Veera ta mera kariane da saathi
Mein uston liavaan girian chhuvaare
Tu kha meri Sanjhi ni girian chhuvaare

This song is in Punjabi, but it exists in Haryanvi as well, with the same lyrics and verses, talking about all that the girls need to create and worship Sanjhi. It talks about the clay they need from the ponds, the cow dung from cows, clothes from a cloth merchant, jewellery from a jeweler, sweets from a Halwai, bangles from a bangle maker and dry fruits that come from far off. Lyrics are modified as the life around changes. In a modern version I once heard, black high heel sandals were also mentioned. In a way, the songs touch every fabric of society and their presence becomes a part of Sanjhi through their works. Is this not an oral documentation of the society as the girls saw around? To me, this is also an indication of how different people who constitute the society came together in our festive celebrations, directly or indirectly.

Mein tenu puchhan Sanjhi
Ke tere bhai

(Sanjhi Replies)

Satt bhateeje mere nau, das bhai
Sattan da mein byah rachaya
solan di badhai

Or

Bhaian di mein liti sagai
Bhateejeyan di badhai

This repeats as each person worships Sanjhi with Thali in hand. Brothers feature prominently in the songs of Sanjhi. My interpretation is that in a woman's life, her link to her native family and land is through her brother. He is the pivotal support system in her life, whose presence is required at all major life events even in her marital family. His well-being and prosperity are wished time and again.

Sowing the Seeds

On the first day of Sharada Navaratri, barley seeds or Jaun are sown in small clay pots called Khetri. In two to three days, the seeds germinate and green shoots start sprouting. By the tenth day, grass-like blades of barley stand tall in the earthen pot. The Khetri is kept close to the Sanjhi, if Sanjhi is observed, otherwise it is kept near the temple of the house.

The belief is that the growth of Jaun is indicative of the coming year. If the growth is delayed or stunted, a difficult year is expected, a lot of hard work may be required. If the leaves are partially yellow and green, then it predicts a mixed year ahead. If the growth is good, it indicates a happy and prosperous year ahead.

On the tenth day of Sharada Navaratri is the festival of Dussehra, the day Sri Rama killed Ravana in Lanka. In my Agarwal community, a figure of Ravana is drawn on the floor on this day with cow dung, and nowadays with dough, depicting his 10 heads. It is worshipped with many things along with the Jaun that have grown during Navaratri. After Ravana Puja, sisters worship their brothers, put Tilak on their foreheads and hang the Jaun on their ears, in a Rakhi-like ritual, wishing well for the brothers. Brothers in turn give gifts to the sisters.

Ram Lila

Sharada Navaratri is also the time for performance of Ram Lila. During my childhood, every village, town, different parts of big cities held an annual performance of the Ramayana called Ram Lila. Every evening, people would gather at a common place, where mostly children would perform the Ram Lila. During the day, the same children would collect money to build the effigies of Ravana, Kumbhakarana and Meghnada that would be burnt on Dussehra. People would happily contribute money and materials for the effigies.

Ram Lila in big cities was enacted by actors but in most neighbourhoods, it was done by locals. Everything was planned within the neighbourhood. Ram Lila was performed and watched by the people we knew. There were enough impromptu improvisations to include current affairs in the dialogues. This was another opportunity to nurture creativity and artistic instincts.

Ram Lila, though not really connected to the Devi Puja, does coincide with the celebration of Navaratri in Punjab and Haryana.

Jagrata

Jagrata or Jagran—the night-long celebration of Devi—is very common in North India. It is not really tied to Navaratri dates; it can be organized on any convenient date throughout the year. Still, people choose to organize them a lot more during Navaratri, as these are the days of the Devi. Just like Ganga Snan is beneficial anytime but it is especially beneficial during the month of Kartik, Jagran is also considered more beneficial during Navaratri. In fact, Jagran of one night is recommended during the nine nights of Navaratri in our scriptures.

Jagrans are organized by families, communities or by neighbourhoods bringing together the devotees of Devi to collectively celebrate the mother. When families organize Jagrata to thank the Devi for fulfilment of a wish, they personally invite everyone around for the Jagran. Invitation cards used to be sent but these days of course WhatsApp messages also work. You are in a way inviting everyone in your circle to be a part of your celebration.

Jagrans are open to anyone who wants to join. *Devi Bhagavata Purana* recommends the worship of a Murti of the 18-armed Durga riding the lion and that is what we see being practiced Jagratas to date. *Mata ki chowki* or darbar is set up, with a big Murti of Durga riding her vahana—Simha or the lion. In absence of Murti, a painting or photograph may be used. A kalasha sthapana is done. At the beginning of Jagrata, usually late in the evening, an Akhand Jyoti is lit up in front of the Murti. Professional singers are invited to sing bhents. Bhent literally means a gift, it is a stuti—a song telling the glory and brave deeds of the Devi, as she annihilated different asuras. The story of two sisters Rukman and Tara is narrated in between. This goes on till early morning and ends with the sunrise when Bhog Arati is performed and prasada is distributed. Jagrans are also followed by Kanya Pujan, just the way Kanya Pujan is done on Ashtami or Navami.

Prasada typically is made of halwa, puri and black chana. Distributing mithai or sweets is also common. Additionally, different types of fruits and dry fruits are also kept. Bhandara is the name given to the meal hosted by the organizers for everyone present at the Jagran.

People wear *Mata ki Chunri* or red scarfs that says 'Jai Mata Di' on their heads. Most women choose to wear auspicious colors like red and yellow. As the singing picks up momentum, people inadvertently break into dance. It is not unusual to see some people get possessed and the common phrase for it is *'Mata Aa Gai'*. I would say that it is a higher energy realm that one goes to.

Popular literature and stereotype always left me with an impression that it is a folk way of celebrating the Goddess. I would much later read in scriptures like the *Skanda Purana* that Jagran is a prescribed way of celebration for Devi. She is pleased when her devotees stay awake the whole night singing songs for her, along with music and dance. I now understand it as a long-standing tradition being followed by the devotees of the Devi.

What remains with you from *Mata ka Jagran* is the high energy created with enthusiastic singing and collective participation of everyone who is present there. It is not a passive event where only the professional singers sing; they do lead the singing though. It is an active night where everyone participates and expresses their devotion for the Jagat Janani—the mother of the world.

Devi Temples in Punjab and Haryana

Devi temples can be found in every village, town, neighbourhoods in the cities in Punjab and Haryana. In fact, the area I was born in is called Mata Rani Mohalla. However, the region also has its share of Shakti Peethas and Shakti Sthalas.

Jalandhar is known for Devi Talao Mandir that forms an important Devi Kshetra. Amritsar has ancient Durgiana mandir. Patiala is known for its Kali temple. Chandigarh, the city named after ancient Chandi Devi temple is surrounded by many important Devi temples like the immensely popular Manasa Devi and Kalka Devi. Jayanti Devi's abode is not too far. Kurukshetra is home to the Bhadrakali Devikoop temple that finds a mention in the Mahabharata. Jind, the erstwhile state that is now split between Punjab and Haryana, was named after Jayanti Devi, the presiding Devi of the region. Agroha Dham near Hissar has a temple dedicated to Mahalakshmi, the Kuladevi[4] of Agarwal community.

The days and nights of the Devi during Chaitra and Ashvina Navaratri are thus spent being Satvik, focusing on the divine mother and celebrating her presence as Kanyas, as Sanjhi and as Durga riding her lion, remembering every form in which she manifests to guide us.

---

[4]The form of the Goddess worshipped by a specific kula, meaning community.

Note

I would like to thank Smt. Usha Gupta of Panchkula for the conversations we had about Sanjhi celebrations, along with all those who uploaded Sanjhi songs on the internet creating a link for all of us who live away from Punjab.

11

Vidya Dayini in Kerala

SAJEESH KUMAR N.

The origins of present-day Kerala are shrouded in the clouds of stories and legends. According to the most popular, the land that forms Kerala has been raised from the depths of the ocean by Parashurama, an avatar of Vishnu. Parashurama waged a series of epic wars against the Kshatriyas to seek revenge for the death of his father. At last came a moment, when Parashurama was moved by remorse and offered severe penance atop a mountain. On his way to profound atonement, he threw his mighty axe that had annihilated the Kshatriyas into the distant ocean. The mighty axe guided the waves to part ways and form a linear stretch of land extending from Gokarna to Kanyakumari. Thus, emerged from the ocean the 'divine' land and with this legend, Kerala has also earned the sobriquet, 'God's Own Country'.

Befitting the name, this progressive southernmost state of India has consistently achieved one of the highest human development indices, presenting to the world a 'Kerala Model of Development'. A model that could achieve a very high level of human development without attaining a corresponding level of economic growth. The 'proud' Malayalis have always attributed this unique development model to communism and the influence of foreign traders who came to Kerala to propagate faith and barter spices. Contrary to popular perception, one can argue that it is the legends and traditions, which had their roots in local culture and religion, that have played as big a role as any foreign influence in shaping the social and cultural fabric of Kerala. It is the smart interweaving of certain socially relevant messages with the religious, social and cultural symbolisms and practices through underlying stories and legends that transformed Kerala into a modern society. These socially-driven transformational messages are part of many of the popular festivals in Kerala, including state festivals like Onam and religious festivals like 'Navaratri'.

Before understanding the Navaratri traditions and practices, it is important to understand how many of the popular festivals in Kerala acquired a distinct local flavour entrenched in local customs, practices and ethos. Keralites have adapted many of the Hindu festivals to suit their cultural fabric. Reformist leaders extensively used the stories and legends concerning these festivals as transformational tools to drive socially-driven overarching messages. That's how Maveli and Onam became such an inseparable part of Kerala's cultural moorings—the same way as Vidyarambham, a part of Navaratri celebrations, has been embedded in the cultural consciousness of Malayalis.

The Onam story relates to an asura king called Mahabali who ruled Kerala. His subjects started worshipping him because of his greatness. That was enough for Indra to get jealous. Indra went to Vishnu, seeking a solution to curtail the ever-growing glory of Bali. Vishnu acquired the form of Vamana and Bali was pushed to the land of asuras—Patala: Vamana granted a wish to Bali before the latter went to Patala; an opportunity to come and see his subjects on earth on the day of Onam. The benevolent king wanted all his subjects to remain prosperous and live in peace when he visited them on Onam day every year. This *Bhagavata* story was adapted to the local context by connecting it to one of the rulers of Kerala to drive the message of egalitarianism.

The spirit of reformist ethos that is captured in the story behind Onam can be traced to many festivals of Kerala. Even the Navaratri celebrations, which transcend different regions of the state, predominantly focus on worshipping Devi Sarasvati, the goddess of learning, thereby exhorting people the importance of learning and according it a credible religious sanction. In popular Kerala culture, Vidyarambham ceremony, the ceremony of initiating children to formal learning conducted on the Vijaya Dashami day after the end of Navaratri has the greatest significance. It is followed even today and is one of the most popular traditions. One cannot undermine the significance of this festival in transforming Kerala as one of the most literate states in the country.

Stories and Legends

Navaratri or Nine Nights is a composite festival celebrated across the state of Kerala every year. The festival falls in either September or October. However, the festival dates are decided in consonance with the Malayalam calendar and based on the local tradition and customs. Nine days of Navaratri are reserved for the special worship of the nine forms of Goddess Shakti/Devi. The final three days of Navaratri—Durga Ashtami, Maha Navami and Vijaya Dashami—are earmarked for the worship of Goddess Sarasvati, the goddess of wisdom and learning. As per Malayalam tradition, the Puranic origin of Navaratri is linked to 'Devi Mahatmyam' in the *Markandeya Purana* with Kali, Lakshmi and Sarasvati representing strength, wealth and wisdom, respectively.

There are large numbers of Durga or Bhagavati temples in Kerala that celebrate Navaratri festival in elaborate ways. Every district of Kerala has one or more famous Bhagavati temples. Two of the most famous temples that people gather in large numbers during Navaratri are the Chottanikkara Bhagavati Temple in Ernakulam and the Mookambika Temple in Kollur, near Mangalore in Karnataka. They are also connected by a common legend. These two temples date back to Adi Shankaracharya's era. In Chottanikkara, Bhagavati is believed to represent the forms of all three Devis. Hence, the idol is draped and worshipped in white as Sarasvati in the morning, in red as Lakshmi in the afternoon and in blue as Durga in the evening.

As per legend, Adi Shankaracharya was saddened by the fact that there was no Sarasvati temple in his native Kerala. So, he did penance at Chamundi hills to please the Devi. She appeared before him and granted a boon. Shankara requested Devi to accompany him and stay at his homeland. To this, the Devi replied that she was common to all people and could not stay at one place. However, at Shankara's insistence, she agreed to follow him on one condition: that she would stay at the place from where he turned back. She also assured him that he would hear the sound of her anklets as a sign that she was following him. Shankara started the walk towards his homeland followed by Devi. Shankara could hear the sound of her anklets. While they were crossing the hills of Kodachadri, Shankara turned back to check Devi, as he could not hear the sound of her anklets. In compliance with the condition, Devi Sarasvati stopped there. The spot where she stopped is believed to be the site of the Kollur Mookambika temple. Shankara realized his mistake and tendered an apology. He pleaded with her to go with him to his homeland.

But the Devi did not relent. However, after repeated insistence, she agreed to a compromise. She relented to go to Chottanikkara in his homeland and to appear before devotees in the morning. But she made it clear that she would return to the spot where she stopped at Kollur Mookambika in the afternoon and reside there for the rest of the day. As a result, the door of the main sanctum of the Chottanikkara Temple is opened early in the morning and the door of the sanctum at the Mookambika Temple is opened in the afternoon after the doors are closed at Chottanikkara. It is believed that Sarasvati leaves Chottanikkara temple once the doors are closed and reaches Mookambika before the doors are opened there. Thousands of people throng these temples during Navaratri and on Vijaya Dashami to pay obeisance to Devi Sarasvati.

In the city of Thiruvananthapuram, the state capital, festivities of Navaratri start with a traditional procession of Murtis coming from Nanchinadu in Tamil Nadu to the Padmanabhaswami Temple in the city. As a custom, the Murti of Goddess Sarasvati from Padmanabhapuram Palace in Kanyakumari district, the Murti of Kumaraswami from Kumanarakovil in Velimala and the Murti of Goddess Munnootty Nanga from Suchindram Temple are brought to the city, accompanied by a ritualistic procession that reminds one of the cultural and historical connection the royal families of Travancore had with a part of Tamil Nadu. While Goddess Sarasvati is carried on an elephant, Kumaraswami rides on a silver horse and Munnootty Nanga proceeds on a palanquin. At the end of the procession, the members of the royal family of Travancore accord them a grand welcome and receive the Murtis at the eastern gate of the Padmanabhaswami temple.

The Murti of Goddess Sarasvati is placed in a Mandapa near the temple. The members of the royal family of Travancore keep their books and weapons in the Mandapa before the Murti for the Navaratri Puja. The Murti of Kumaraswami and Munnootty Nanga are taken to the Aryasala temple and the Chenthitta temple respectively and placed there for the rest of the Navaratri period. A Navaratri Mandapa with stone pillars and women holding deepa in their hands, can still be seen at the Padmanabhapuram palace, which is otherwise a huge, wooden structure.

According to legend, the Murti of Sarasvati worshipped in the Mandapa is the same that used to be worshipped by the great Tamil poet Kambar (or Kavichakravarthy Kamban). Realizing that he was getting old, Kambar offered the Murti to Kulasekhara Perumal, the king of Venad, on a condition that the rituals performed by him should be preserved and continued. Kings who succeeded Kulasekhara Perumal, including the Maharajas of Travancore, continued the tradition of paying obeisance to the Murti since then.

The practice of bringing the Sarasvati Murti to Thiruvananthapuram was initiated in 1839 by Maharaja Swathi Thirunal, the music-loving king, who was well-versed with ragas and compositions. The aesthetics and detailing of the procession represent the meticulous and systematic way it was designed by the king years back. Maharaja Swathi Thirunal believed that the Murti of Goddess Sarasvati represented knowledge, Kumaraswami, a symbol of military might and Munnootty Nanga, a symbol of power.

A music festival is organized at the Navaratri Mandapa near Sri Padmanabhaswami Temple during the festival in Thiruvananthapuram. The Mandapa opens only for the nine days during Navaratri. During the musical festival, only oil lamps and no artificial lights are used to lit up the Mandapa. No arrangements of chairs are normally made for the audience and they listen to the performances seated on the floor, especially on the steps at the eastern gate. The Mandapa is decorated with jasmine and the heavenly aroma of sandalwood and camphor elevates the environment to a different level. Musical offerings are made from 6–8 p.m. every day during Navaratri. In the old days, specially-made earthen pots were hung using coir ropes at different places in the Mandapa to amplify the sound.

The music for the Navaratri concerts was originally composed and codified by Maharaja Swati Thirunal himself. He composed songs in nine ragas—Shankarabharanam, Kalyani, Saveri, Todi, Bhairavi, Panthuvarali, Shuddha Saveri, Nattakurinji and Arabhi, which are performed as main pieces on each day of Navaratri. Even today, those ragas composed by Swathi Thirunal are sung during the festival. Nearly every noted musician has performed at the festival. Traditionally, only male singers performed during the festival. However, in 2006, female singer Parassala Ponnammal performed in the Mandapa for the first time, thus initiating a new tradition for women singers to take the Mandapa after a good 300 years.

On Vijaya Dashami, after the rituals, the Kumaraswami Murti is carried on a silver horse in a procession from Aryasala temple to a Mandapa about four kilometres away. In the times of the monarchy, members of Travancore's royal family used to exhibit their valour by performing martial arts before the Murti, in front of the Mandapa. This was discontinued later.

Navaratri epitomizes the triumph of good over evil. Navaratri takes place at around harvest time. During Navaratri, Durga, Lakshmi and Sarasvati are worshipped as three different manifestations of Shakti or cosmic energy. To treasure different manifestations of the mighty goddess, Navaratri is divided into sets of three days. On the first three days, the Goddess is invoked as powerful force called Durga who manifests to destroy all our impurities, vices and defects. In the second set of three days, the mother goddess is adored as a giver of spiritual wealth Lakshmi, who is revered and blesses her devotees with endless wealth. The final set of days is spent in worshipping the mother as the goddess of wisdom and knowledge Sarasvati.

People need the blessings of all three divine manifestations of Goddess to have complete success and attainment in life. Hence, she is worshipped for all nine days. Though traditional families in Kerala worship her different manifestations on all nine days, people at large celebrate the last three days of Navaratri festival. Durga Ashtami, Maha Navami and Vijaya Dashami are considered more important than other days in worshipping Devi.

People of Kerala celebrate Navaratri in a befitting manner. Sarasvati Puja is performed during the last three days of Navaratri. This is similar to the Ayudha Puja celebrated in other parts of India. On Durga Ashtami day, a ceremony called Puja Veppu is performed in the evening. Just before Puja Veppu, all studies and work that require any kind of skill, are halted till it is resumed on Vijaya Dashami. After that, a Puja is performed for Goddess Sarasvati, during which beaten rice, roasted paddy and jaggery are offered to the Devi. The following day is known as Maha Navami and it is devoted to the worship of Sarasvati. Students abstain from reading any books or using any study materials on Maha Navami day. Puja is performed both in the morning and in the evening. On Vijaya Dashami, which follows Maha Navami, after a Puja in the morning, the books and implements are removed from the Puja room—the ceremony is called Puja Eduppu.

There are certain communities that celebrate the festival on all days of Navaratri, exhibiting the images of gods, animals and toys of different variety. This exhibition of images of Gods on Navaratri is called 'Koluvaipu'. Koluvaipu or Bommai Kolu is popular in southern part of Kerala, especially in places like Thiruvananthapuram. Different toys mainly representing different forms of Vishnu and Durga are decorated on pedestals having three, five, seven, nine or 11 steps. Kolu refers to showcasing and displaying miniature forms of gods, goddesses, animals, birds, spiritual personalities and art work to name a few.

Every morning, noon and evening, special Naivedya are prepared and offered to these Bommais. On the day of Vijaya Dashami, these Bommais are taken out and put to sleep again to be used next year. Traditionally, Bommai Kolu is celebrated by the Tamil brahmin families who are settled in Kerala. Similar traditions are also followed in parts of Karnataka and Tamil Nadu.

Vidyarambham Tradition of Navaratri

Though the traditional Navaratri celebrations are important for Hindus in Kerala, the ritual or practice that captured the imagination of popular culture of the state is Puja Veppu and the Vidyarambham. The Vidyarambham or Ezhuthiniruthu celebration especially has been so popular that it has transcended religious boundaries. Many Muslim and Christian families also follow this tradition nowadays. If there is one religious practice that has helped Kerala in its tryst to be an educated and progressive society, then it must be Vidyarambham.

Very few families observe the nine-day worship during Navaratri. Instead, nearly all Hindu families celebrate the last three days of the Navaratri: Durga Ashtami, Maha Navami and the tenth day culminating into celebration of the victory of good over evil on Vijaya Dashami.

On the eighth day of Navaratri, i.e., Durga Ashtami, followers keep their tools for Puja at temples. More importantly, students keep their books and study materials for Puja in the Puja room or temples for worship. This unique practice in Kerala during Navaratri is called Puja Veppu. Lot of people perform Pujavepppu at their homes also. If it is done at home, a Murti of Sarasvati is placed on a wooden stage. Then a garland of jasmine and a lotus flower is placed on the Murti. The stage is then decorated by placing different types of fruits and harvest such as sugar cane, apple, banana, oranges, etc.

The traditional Kerala oil lamp called Nilavilakku is also placed in front of the Murti and lit. In the evening, oil lamps are lit all around the podium on which the Murti is placed and Puja is performed. Beaten rice, jaggery and roasted paddy are given to the Devi as Naivedyam. Special Kerala payasam (rice pudding) and unniyappam are also prepared and offered to Sarasvati during the Puja. Unniyappam is a small snack round in shape made from rice, jiggery, banana, coconut and ghee.

The Puja Veppu day is special for children, as they are not allowed to read, write or use any study materials, that too with the consent of their parents and elders. Quite unlike other days, efforts of elders in the family are directed towards stopping any kid unknowingly or mischievously opening the book and reading! It is believed that there are two types of knowledge, Vijnanam or scientific knowledge and Jnanam, the spiritual knowledge. The essence of observing Puja Veppu is to turn to Jnanam and not Vijnanam. The spiritual knowledge or Jnana helps to develop inner strength, which is the real purpose of worshipping Sarasvati during the last three days of Navaratri.

Puja Veppu ends on Vijaya Dashami. It is the tenth day after Navaratri and commemorates the day Durga emerged from the collective energies of all gods, riding on a lion to slay the demon Mahishasura. This Durga form also symbolizes the dispelling of ignorance and conceit from people and enriching them with the seeds of knowledge and wisdom. The ceremony that concludes Puja

Veppu is called Pujaeduppu. The time for the break-up of the Puja marks the beginning of learning and work. In conformity with the message of Navaratri, the tools and books that are kept in temples or Puja rooms are taken out and children resume reading from them, leading to a path of new awareness.

On Vijaya Dashami, another very special event is held in most of the temple premises and places of cultural importance in Kerala. It is Vidyarambham—the beginning of formal learning. Vidya means 'knowledge' and Arambham is 'beginning', hence Vidyarambham. Vijaya Dashami is considered auspicious for the beginning of learning in any field. On this day, thousands of people throng temples and places of cultural importance to initiate their children into the process of learning. On this occasion, children between the ages of three and five years are given instructions and guided to write alphabets in Malayalam for the first time, on a tray of sand or rice grains. According to the customs followed in Kerala, children are initiated into formal learning i.e., reading and writing, only after the completion of this ceremony. Like during other festivities, children are made to bathe and dress in new, traditional attire before the ceremony. Normally, children are made to sit on the lap of a teacher, priest or the eldest member of the family. Initiation into the universe of syllabary usually commences with the writing of the following mantra:

ॐ हरि: श्री गणपतये नम: अविघ्नमस्तु श्री गुरुवे नम: श्री सरस्वती सहायम्

> Salutations to Hari (Vishnu), Shri Ganapati who shall remove all obstacles and salutation to Guru with the help of goddess Shri Sarasvati.

After the teacher or an elder member of the family helps the child write letters on the rice or sand spread on a tray by holding the index finger of the child, the words *'Om Hari Sri Ganapathaye Namah'* are written on the tongue of the child with a piece of gold dipped in honey. *'Om Hari Sri Ganapataye Namah'* signifies all 51 letters of Devanagari script that form the embodiment of the Naadarupini Devi—the goddess of sound. The practice is meant to introduce the children to the world of language, letters, music and arts. Writing of letters on sand with the guidance of a master denotes practice. Similarly, writing on a tray of grains represents the beginning of the acquisition of knowledge that can lead to prosperity. The practice of writing on the tongue of the child invokes the blessings of the Goddess of Learning to shower her grace in the attainment of the wealth of true knowledge and wisdom. Like on any other auspicious occasion for the Hindus, the ritual also involves an invocation to Lord Ganesha for removing any obstructions during the process of learning. It is believed that the index finger represents our ego and by holding the index finger, the Guru guides the child to give up the burden of ego to attain true knowledge and wisdom.

As per the beliefs, on the day of Vidyarambham, Sarasvati and teachers or gurus should be presented with Gurudakshina as a mark of respect and thanksgiving. After the ceremony, for many days, the elders in the family hold the index finger of the children and make them practice alphabets on a tray of sand or rice so that the child becomes familiar with those letters and how to write them. People belonging to different religions nowadays celebrate Vidyarambham with equal enthusiasm, owing to the concept of initiation to learning this ceremony represents.

Vidyarambham ceremonies are organized in many places across Kerala during Navaratri. Some of the important temples where Vidyarambham is celebrated with much of enthusiasm include Guruvayur Sri Krishna Temple in Trissur, Bhagvati Temple in Attukal, Thiruvananathapuram, Chottanikkara Devi Temple in Ernakulam and Panachikkadu Sarasvati Temple in Kottayam. Another place where Vidyarambham is performed with grandeur is Kollur Mookambika Temple near Mangalore. Kollur is believed to be the abode of Goddess Sarasvati, hence it is considered really fortunate if children could perform Vidyarambham through pandits at Mookambika Temple. Though Vidyarambham is performed at the temple every day, the ceremonies on Navaratri are special and attract larger crowds.

Thousands of people also throng at Thunchan Parambil in Malappuram, the birthplace of Thunchath Ezhuthachan, the father of the Malayalam language, to conduct Vidyarambham for their children. Ezhuthachan refined the Malayalam language and made it popular with the common people and incorporated in his writings whatever is good with a strong sense of worship and righteousness. The sand collected from his erstwhile home is used by many people in Northern Kerala to start the Vidyarambham process. Even budding writers and poets come to Thunchan Parambil to offer their first work on this day.

Vidyarambham or Ezhuthiniruthu, is one of the major festivals of Thrikkavu Sri Durga Bhagavaty Temple at Ponnani in Malappuram district also. This ancient temple is revered as one of the 108 Durga temples that were consecrated by Sri Parasurama and the ritual of Vidyarambham is quite elaborate at this temple. Thousands throng the Sarasvati temple at Panachikkadu in Kottayam during Navaratri to take a dip in the mysterious holy pond whose source is unknown yet.

This temple is also known as Dakshina Mookambika (Mookambika of south). Though, the main deity of this temple is Lord Vishnu, the temple is known as Sarasvati temple. Massive gatherings are also witnessed at the famous temples at Thekkegram (Palghat), where there are no Murtis, only huge mirrors. Devotees bow before their own reflection, to indicate that God is within them.

Vidyarambham and Tryst with Literacy

Kerala has been known for its high rate of literacy for years now. Even at the time of independence, the rate of literacy in Kerala was double the national average. Often, this success is attributed to foreign influence and social reforms brought by rulers and governments pre and post-Independence. However, one of the aspects which is seldom highlighted is the power of certain stories, traditions and festivals, and their role in shaping Kerala society.

Vidyarambham has played a significant role in Kerala's tryst with total literacy. In Kerala, learning was not considered as a tool for material advancement alone. It was considered a way of paying reverence to Goddess Sarasvati. As a result, every member of a Hindu family who was between the ages of three and five invariably went through the Vidyarambham ceremony. Since the vow was taken before the Goddess, everybody wanted to fulfil that commitment and believed that not taking it seriously would attract the wrath of the all-powerful Goddess.

It is the religious sanction and the legend behind it that drove people to continue with the learning that was initiated during Vidyarambham. Today, this practice transcends even religious boundaries in Kerala. It is not difficult to assume a link between the spirit of social transformations in Kerala and the underlying messages behind those rituals and legends some of the festivals intended to drive. The religious sanction ordained to the Vidyarambham festival created the spirit of social transformation by inculcating the value of the learning within Kerala society. This single ceremony as part of Navaratri would have contributed as much as the combined effort of all social reformers or educators to guide Kerala towards the attainment of total literacy. In myriads of festivals celebrated by Malayalis, the Navaratri festival and Vidyarambham ceremony therefore holds a special place owing to the message it carried and propagated through generations.

12

Dandiya and Garba in Gujarat

PULAK TRIVEDI

In India, we worship and celebrate Motherhood as the divine feminine. This instantly reminds everyone of Navaratri, the World's longest dance festival. The name is self-explanatory, Navaratri meaning celebration for nine (nava) nights (ratri). It is often referred as the celebration of Bhakti and Shakti, two of the most powerful forms of Goddess Durga.

The aspect of Bhakti refers to devotion. The idea of Bhakti has been talked about in our scriptures for centuries. The concept of Bhakti and Shakti in Navaratri originates from a rather simple philosophy. It is used to explain the simple fundamental that pure devotion to people/tasks gives us shakti (energy) to rise above all obstacles and achieve our aim.

Tradition has it that the demon king Mahishasura was an ardent devotee of Brahma. He worshipped so sincerely that one fine day, Brahma appeared before him and granted him a boon: That no man, God, animal, Yaksha,[1] Gandharva[2] or any other species would be able to kill him. However, Brahma said that he could grant total immortality and asked Mahishasura to choose how he would like to die. So, the asura chose death by an unborn woman.

Over the years, the king grew in strength and power, and along with that came arrogance. He defeated every king on earth, but this

---

[1] Semi-divine deities.
[2] Divine musicians and singers.

did not satisfy him. He decided to wage a war against Indra, the *king of heavens*. Indra was so worried that he went to the Trinity—Brahma, Vishnu and Shiva—to seek their help. As the Trinity was constrained by the boon Brahma had bestowed, its constituents decided to invoke Goddess Durga by combining their energies. Goddess Durga fought Mahishasura for nine days and eventually killed him. And hence, the Goddess is also known as Mahishasura Mardini.

This is one of the prime reasons why the festival is related to worshipping the feminine, Shakti or Goddess Durga. People worship the nine forms of Goddess Durga/Shakti on this day.

These nine forms are:

1. On the first day, she is worshipped as Shailaputri, an incarnation of Goddess Parvati. Dressed in red outfit, she is portrayed as the direct incarnation of Mahakali. The Goddess drives the bull Nandi with a Trishual and lotus.
2. She is worshipped as Brahmacharini on the second day. This form is the Sati avatara of the Goddess. She holds a rudraksha mala and a kamandalu. Everything about the Goddess symbolizes peace and tranquility.
3. On the third day, the Goddess is worshipped as Chandraghanta with a half-crescent moon on her forehead. She is a fierce 10-armed goddess riding a tiger to destroy every evil on her way.
4. She is worshipped as Kushmanda on the fourth day. The word Kushmanda is a combination of three words: 'ku' meaning little, 'ushma' meaning energy and 'anda' meaning egg. This avatara signifies her as the creator of the universe.
5. People worship Goddess Durga as Skandmata on the fifth day, i.e., Panchami. She is a four-armed deity with lotus in two of her hands, a kamandalu and a bell in the other two. Lord Kartikeya is seated on her lap. It is for this reason that Lord Kartikeya is also known as Lord Skanda.

6. Goddess Durga is worshipped as Katyayani on the sixth day. She rides a lion and symbolizes valour.
7. It is believed that the Goddess is in her most fierce form on the seventh day. Worshipped as Mahakali, tradition has it that the Goddess appeared in a white attire but her skin turned black in rage during a battle with the demons Nishumbha and Shumbha.
8. On the eighth day, also known as Ashtami, Goddess Durga is worshipped as Mahagauri. The day symbolizes perseverance.
9. The goddess is worshipped as Siddhidatri on the ninth day, i.e., Navami. This day stands for knowledge and perfection.

The tenth day is celebrated as Vijaya Dashami or Dussehra to market the victory of good over evil. In its true sense, this festival symbolizes the victory of good over the evil qualities that reside in a person. The idea is to overpower the evil with the pure and vibrant energy which we receive upon worshipping the Goddess.

Shakti Peethas in Gujarat

The Ambaji temple located in Banaskantha district of Gujarat is a prominent Shakti Peetha of India and a very popular destination for devotees from all over India. Also knows as the Arasuri Amba Temple, it is located on the Arasur hills, near Sarasvati River. The most interesting part about the temple is the fact that there is no Murti of the Goddess. There is a yantra which is the centre of worship for devotees. There is an akhand jyot (eternal flame) at the temple which is believed to have existed for centuries. Lakhs of devotees from various parts of the State visit the temple on foot, to pay their respect to the Goddess. People come to Ambaji to pray to Goddess Amba. This temple is believed to exist since the Pre-Vedic period and it occupies a central place in the religious identity of the state.

The Pavagadh Temple is yet another place which attracts devotees from various parts of Gujarat and India. Kalika Devi is worshipped in the temple here on the hill top. The temple is situated 762 meters above the sea level and is located in the Panchmahal district in Gujarat. The temple dates back to tenth or eleventh century. It is believed that the temple was established by the great Sage Vishwamitra after a long tapasya. Another tale has it that Luv-Kush, sons of Lord Rama, attained moksha at this place. Devotees trek up the hill from the based at Champaner to the hill top during Navaratri, even though there is easy ropeway available to reach close to the top of the hill.

Both the places are thronged by pilgrims during Navaratri.

The Grand Festivities

In Gujarat, the festival is accompanied by nine days of traditional dance called Garba. The nine days see the state turn into its most vibrant form. The word 'Garba' evolved from the Sanskrit word 'garbha' meaning the womb. Tradition has it that people perform the Garba around a lit earthen pot, which symbolizes life or Shakti, the Goddess.

Navaratri here is not just a festival but a way of life. People wait for its arrival and dress up in traditional attires. The women wear a chaniya choli and the men adorn the kediyu to perform the garba. People also perform the 'Dandiya Ras' which is accompanied by the use of 'Dandiyas' (wooden sticks). The Dandiya Ras is related to Sri Krishna's worship and traces its origin to the Gop culture of Saurashtra and Kutch. The traditional songs often recount the tales of valour of Goddess Amba and are a form of evocation. There are also songs from the episodes of Sri Krishna and the gopis, and they too form an integral part of the culture of Navaratri in Gujarat.

Children across the state build a small hill or mound, also known as the gabbar. They often start the preparations a couple of weeks in advance and visit each and every house in their respective localities to collect donations. No house ever lets these children leave empty handed. It is believed that the Goddess rests in the gabbar and during Navaratri, people perform the Arati and then do the

Garba around the gabbar.

There are a number of styles in which the Garba is performed. Some of the most common and popular styles are Ek Taali (single clap), Bey Taali (two claps) and Tran Taali (three claps). Other styles include the Dodhiyu, Hinch, Raas, etc. The Dodhiyu style consists of six steps in total. One of the most important aspects about this style is the coordination between the performers. It is for this reason that is generally performed in small groups.

Gauf is a combination of Dandiya and Raas. The performers generally begin with the Dandiya and then use the dupattas hanging in the middle from above to perform the remaining dance.

The Ek Taali, Bey Taali and Tran Talli are simple in terms of the steps. The performers clap once in a complete step in Ek Taali. Similarly, they clap twice and thrice in a complete set of Bey Taali and Tran Taali respectively.

Different Types of Garba

Tippani: This type of Garba is native to Saurashtra. It is also known as 'malt dance' or 'tippani nritya'. It is believed that this form originated amongst the labour community to break free from their mundane lives. It is generally performed by the Koli community. The sticks used by the women in the dance as known as 'tippani'. They have an iron or a wooden block attached to them, called Garbo.

Hudo: This is native to the Bharwad community (shepherd community). It is widely believed that the concept of this dance originates from the sheep fights as the performers copy the sheep ramming their heads into each other. It is performed by men and women. Apart from Navaratri, this dance is also performed at the popular Tarnetar festival which is held in Surendranagar district.

Raas-Garba: This is a curious combination of Dandiya and Garba. It is generally done in pairs where the performers coordinate with the tunes of music and bump their respective dandiyas with each other. The simplest version has five steps in it. A large number of people dance to the tunes of songs dedicated to the life of Lord Krishna for this style.

Padhar: This form of dance is generally performed by the fishermen community in Gujarat, especially in Nal Sarovar region. The performers have small sticks in their hands and their dance steps are similar to rowing a boat.

Considering the fact that the festival is an occasion to revere and worship the feminine, it holds a special significance in each and every household of Gujarat. A large number of families request the Goddess to visit their homes and bless them. Women, in particular, hold deep regard for the Goddess.

People sow wheatgrass in a small pot, do the anushthana for nine days and appeal the Goddess to visit their homes for nine days. Families pray and do the Arati twice a day and even fast for nine days. The families also establish an akhand jyot in their house for those nine days and then immerse all the holy materials in water body. There are a few people who fast for nine days straight without food. They only take water or lemon juice during the nine days.

On the ninth day, the family organize a small feast which they offer to the Goddess and do the Garba to appease Shakti.

The Arati sung by people during Navaratri is a form of invocation to the Goddess. The hymn recalls the tales of valour in honour of the Goddess and the devotees request Shakti to bless them with her divine energy and spirit to achieve success and salvation.

One of the most popular Arati is 'Jay Aadhya Shakti'. The word 'Aadhya' means 'excellent' or 'opulent'. Therefore, the Arati signifies the power of Goddess in the universe.

Here are a few stanzas of the Arati:

Jaya Aadya Shakti
Maa Jaya Aadya Shakti
Akhand Brahmaand Neepavya

Akhand Brahmaand Neepavya
Padave Pandit Ma
Om Jayo Jayo Ma Jagadambe

Dwitiya Bay Swarup
Shivashakti Janu
Maa Shivashakti Janu
Brahma Ganapti Gaye
Brahma Ganapti Gaye
Har Gaaye Har Ma
Om Jayo Jayo Ma Jagadambe

The Arati begins by proclaiming victory to the Adi Shakti who bears the whole universe. It goes on to describe the various Swarups of Devi on all tithis till the Purnima on the fifteenth day.

Local Traditions and Beliefs

Apart from these popular styles, there are various local traditions and folklore spread across each and every region in Gujarat. These are based on local culture, stories of ancestors, rulers and local deities.

Sadu Mata Ni Pol in the World Heritage City Ahmedabad has a special tradition which is followed by the men of Barot community every Navaratri since the last 200 years. The local legend and stories have it that the men here perform Garba due to curse given by a woman named Sadu, who is now worshipped as a goddess. The Sadu Mata Ni Pol in Ahmedabad is thronged by lakhs of tourists who wait to watch the men perform the Garba. And it is no ordinary Garba! The men wear sarees and perform the Garba.

Legend has it that Sadu was a beautiful woman who lived in present-day Patan. She was married to Harisingh Barot who lived in Ahmedabad. The then Gaekwad king learned about Sadu's beauty and sent a proposal for marriage. As her husband was not home, Sadu asked the messengers of king to return once he was back. The word spread like a forest fire by evening and turned into a deadly battle between the Barots and Gaekwads. However, there were a few Barot families who hid themselves and did not participate in the battle. The enraged and hurt Sadu cursed the community that they will not be able to bear sons. This curse is still relevant today. A large number of Barot families in the pol still adopt sons.

The men perform Garba in saris to atone for the curse.

Apart from that, the temple of Goddess Sadu Mata is thronged by people from various parts of the state to thank the goddess for fulfilling their wishes. The men wear a saree to thank the Goddess if their wishes are fulfilled.

Similarly, Garbi—an offshoot of Garba—is performed by young girls every year in various parts of Saurashtra, especially Rajkot. Community leaders, social organizations and people at large organize the festivities for nine days to watch the young girls perform Garbi. It is believed that the Goddess resides in those girls for the nine days and people present them with gifts, cash, sweets etc each day.

The Dandiya Makers

One of the most interesting aspects of the festival is the fact that while it is a prominent Hindu festival, it holds an important place in the lives of the Muslim community of the state. A large number of Dandiya makers in Gujarat are Muslims and, hence, they wait eagerly for Navaratri like they wait for the moon during Eid.

The firms that make Dandiyas are spread across Godhra. Each maker produces an average of 50,000 dandiyas per season, and the prices range from ₹10–30 per piece, depending on demand and sales. The profits earned during each season help them survive throughout the year.

Such is the vibrance, diversity and fiesta of Gujarat's Navaratri. A festival which is a form of joy for some, for others it is a period of faith, worship and reverence and for others, a means of livelihood.

13

Shakti in the Shivaliks of Jammu

MANU KHAJURIA

Worship of the female Shakti in the hills is as old as our Sanatana civilization. The Adi Shakti is worshipped in her different manifestations in the Jammu region. Hundreds of Shakti shrines, many of which are cave shrines, are to be found in Jammu, a province with 10 districts. Historical and literary sources establish that Devi Pujan or Shakti worship is an age-old practice in this northern Himalayan region. Adi Shakti or the supreme feminine divine is attributed with the powers of creation, nurturing and dissolution. The worship of Shakti is considered essential for peace and prosperity. For the Dogras of Jammu, a martial race, Shakti must be invoked for victory in the battlefield.

A large part of the Jammu region is located under the shadow of the Trikuta mountains, the abode of Mata Vaishno Devi, a form of Durga. In fact, if there is anything that has been universally identified with this region, it is the Vaishno Devi Cave Shrine, with its holiest of holy Pindis[1] of Maha Lakshmi, Maha Kali and Maha Sarasvati. Vaishno Devi attracts a large number of religious tourists, even more than the better promoted and picturesque Kashmir Valley. From Sukrala Mata in Kathua district bordering Punjab to the Bhadrakali in Bhaderwah in Doda district and Machhail Mata in Kishtwar, which is a district closer to the Kashmir Valley, the region is steeped in Shakti worship.

---

[1] Arrangement of three stones that are worshipped as the three forms of Devi.

Sheetla, Cheechi, Bhoomeshwari, Kalka, Sarthal, Pingla, Chountra, Mangala and many more are worshipped as divine mothers. The Bawe Wali Mata Temple, dedicated to Goddess Maha Kali, is the presiding guardian deity of the city of Jammu. The same role of a protector is also attributed to the Shakti Svarupa in the Mahamaya Temple located on a hilltop in a forested area, bordering Jammu city. Many sub-regions have their own presiding deities and devotees believe that the Supreme Mother watches over and protects them.

The feminine divine has also been acknowledged as a fierce warrior and her blessings are sought after, during battles. The war cry of Jammu Kashmir Rifles, which earlier was the State Force of the Dogra kingdom of Jammu Kashmir, is *'Durge Mata ki Jai'*. One of the greatest warriors of India, the master of white-out operations and mountain blitzkriegs was Dogra General Zorawar Singh, whose janmabhoomi was Himachal and karmabhumi Jammu, was also a Shakti worshipper.

Details of Shakti Puja are also found in the folk songs and ballads sung in the local Dogri language. One of the ballads describes how even Shri Rama worships the Devi:

Kshatri Brahman Simarde, Puja Paath karai;
Ramchandra Mata ji Simarde Lachhman da bhai[2]

Kshatriyas and brahmins remember the Goddess by praying and performing the religious rituals;
Ramchandra, the brother of Lakshmana, also meditates upon the Mother Goddess.

Navaratri in Jammu

Navaratri, the Hindu festival where Adi Shakti is celebrated and worshipped, comes four times a year, according to the lunar calendar. Vasanta Navaratri or Chaitra Navaratri comes during the

---

[2]Devotional song from Padmashri Shiv Nirmohi's book *Duggar ki Lokgathayen*.

spring season in Chaitra (March–April); Ashadha Navaratri, also called Gayatri or Shakambhari Navaratri, is celebrated in Ashadha (June–July); the Sharada Navaratri is celebrated during Sharada (beginning of winter, September–October) and the Poushya/Magha Navaratri in the month of Pousha (December–January). Of these, the Sharada Navaratri and the Chaitra Navaratri are most important and celebrated with great fervour in the Jammu region.

Navaratri, or the nine nights of celebrating the feminine divine, is called 'Naraate' in Dogri. In Jammu, people sow barley grains in an earthen pot on the first day of Navaratri. This ritual is called 'Khetri' and the barley that is grown is 'Saankh'. This is symbolic of the feminine powers of creation and fertility. Traditionally, Dogras fast for eight days. Only certain foods are allowed during these eight days of fasting. On the ninth day, devotees break their fast. Kanya Pujan is done on this day and in many homes, havan is also performed. The Saankh is then taken to the nearest water body and immersed there.

In Jammu, Kanjak or Kanya Pujan is done in most homes on the ninth day. Kanjak in Dogri refers to pre-pubescent girls. They are considered to be the purest embodiment of Ma Durga, the divine feminine herself. People invite at least nine Kanjaks as a representation of the nine forms of Devi Durga to their homes or in temple premises on the last day of Navaratri. These little Durgas and the feminine divinity they represent, are revered. The Kanjak Pujan ritual involves a ceremonial washing of the feet. A bhog or prasada of puri, chana and halwa is offered to the Kanjak or Kanya. People also gift bangles, red dupattas and a token amount of money as shaguna[3] along with this bhog.

People of Jammu visit different temples on those nine days, especially Bawe Wali Mata, Vaishno Devi and other Shakti shrines across Jammu. Mata Vaishno Devi Shrine in Katra sees a heavy rush of pilgrims who come to pay their obeisance during the auspicious

---

[3]Token money given as blessing.

days of Navaratri from all across the region and the country as well. Fairs and colourful cultural activities are organized during Navaratri. Markets bear a festive look and are abuzz with shoppers.

Annual Navaratri Festival in Katra

In order to showcase and highlight the regional culture, heritage and traditions of the area, the Jammu and Kashmir State Tourism Department has instituted the Navaratri Festival as an annual event to be held in Katra, the base camp for visiting Shri Mata Vaishno Devi, for all the nine auspicious days of Navaratri. This has become the main highlight of Navaratri in Jammu and Kashmir, and attracts devotees from far and wide. The festival showcases the religious traditions as well as the popular culture of the region.

A 'Shobha Yatra' is taken out in Katra town to mark the first day of Navaratri. The nine swarups of Goddess Durga are a part of the Shobha Yatra tableau. Stunning flower decorations and rich displays showcasing Hindu culture and traditions mark the way from the grand entrance gate at the base of the mountain all along the 13-kilometre route to the main Bhavan, where the cave shrine is. Every year, the theme for the decorations is different. For example, the highlight of 2019 was a golden gate at the Cave Shrine's entrance that featured nine forms of Goddess Durga. The work on the gate began more than two months before Navaratri and was built using about 12 kilograms gold, 1,200 kilograms copper and 1,100 kilograms silver. A group of devotees donated money for this grand gate.

Various activities are planned as part of the festivities, including presentation of 'Mata Rani ki Kahani'[4] and 'Rama Leela', 'Prabhat Pheris',[5] devotional song competition, cultural programmes and even wrestling competition. An international wrestling competition is organized every year in the town by the Jammu and Kashmir Indian

---
[4]Story of the Mother Goddess.
[5]The ceremonial procession in the morning.

Style Wrestling Association. One of the most popular events during the Katra Navaratri Festival is the All-India National Devotional Song Competition. This competition attracts a lot of singers from across faiths and is televised widely. Interestingly, the competition has been won by Muslim singers too.

Shat Chandi Mahayajna is also organized by the Shri Mata Vaishno Devi Shrine Board during Navaratri at the Holy Cave Shrine of Shri Mata Vaishno Devi Ji. It commences on the auspicious occasion of beginning of the Navaratri amidst chanting of Vedic Mantras and performance of other religious ceremonies for peace and prosperity, and concludes with Purna Ahuti[6] on Maha Navami.

During Navaratri, the Bhawan and the area surrounding it are elegantly decorated with flowers brought from various parts of the country and even abroad. The board also makes elaborate arrangements for the sanitation, security, drinking water, special foods permitted during the fast and uninterrupted power supply all along the track and in the Bhawan area.

Kaan Sakhiyan

Just as there are Bomai Kolu in South India, Durga pandals in the east and Dandiya/Garba in western India, there is Kaan Sakhiyan in the Jammu region. It is a unique regional celebration during Navaratri, now mostly restricted to villages and small towns.

Kaan Sakhiyan predominantly involves young girls organizing Puja rituals and feasts for Goddess Durga. There is excitement amongst children of the neighbourhood, when Navaratri is approaching. Girls form groups and there is a healthy competition amongst the different groups to organize a better and bigger celebration. A consensus is reached amongst the girls regarding the house that will host the Goddess. This process is called '*Mata Rakhni Hain*', which translates to hosting the Goddess. Once the house that will host

---

[6]Final offerings to the fire during a Yagna

the Goddess is decided, girls get busy with the rituals involved. A clay Murti of Durga Mata, is made and decorated. Earlier, 'dabbad' or coins with holes and 'kaudi' or shells were used for decoration. Amongst the girls, one becomes Pachailan or Priestess in charge of the worship of Mata. This Pachailan is responsible for leading the other girls in her group for all the rituals for eight days of Navaratri.

In villages, Pachailan would knock at the doors of her group's homes in the morning. After a bath on the riverside, these girls carry water from the river in a lota (vessel) and perform the ritual of worship and adornment of the Durga Murti they had made. They use the same water for Saankh (barley) grown during these days. The lighting of diya (lamp) and dhupa (incense) accompanies the singing of devotional songs called Bhente that is followed by Arati.

An evening Arati is conducted by the girls on all nine days. They sing to put Goddess Durga to sleep. Usually in the evenings as was practised earlier, girls would carry their plates of food and eat it together after the evening Puja rituals and prayers. In colloquial language the girls would inform their families that they were going to have their meals together by saying '*chuti karne jade*' that literally means washing of the mouth after a meal. On the first eight days of Navaratri, the girls get food from their homes and eat together every evening.

On Navami, Kanjak Pujan is performed and on the same day the girls would play Kaan Sakhiyan. One amongst the girls takes on the role of Kaan or Kanha (Krishna) and others those of the sakhiyan or friends of Kanha. A day before, the girls would prepare for this enactment, making paper crowns and collecting appropriate items for dressing up. The parents of the girls and all the villagers or the neighbourhood in case of a town would come to see the Kaan Sakhiyan tableau. The Pachailan distributes naivedya/prasada to all those who come to pay obeisance to Durga Ma and the offerings of petty cash made by them would be later equally distributed amongst the girls. On the last day, the girls bring flour and sugar from their homes and Babru (puris made with fermented dough) are made.

The celebrations come to an end with the immersion of the *Mata ki Murti* and the Saankh in the river.

This unique celebration strengthens the community cohesion, spreads divine thoughts collectively and also becomes a good way to pass on traditions to the next generation. Though this Duggar tradition, the perfect way to foster community spirit, is fast disappearing from cities.

Navaratri Fasting

It is a common practice for the Hindus of the Jammu region to fast all seven or eight days. Those fasting have a list of strictly vegetarian foods they can and cannot consume. Even those not fasting, avoid meat, alcoholic drinks, onion and garlic. During the fasting period, many people eat only one meal a day, at sunset. Flours like kuttu ka atta (buckwheat flour), singhade ka atta (water chestnut flour) and sabudana (sago) are allowed. Dreu or buckwheat is used to make rotis, puri, chila and even as a batter for paneer or alu pakoda (fritters). Instead of regular salt, rock salt or sendha namak is used. Dairy, fruits and potatoes are allowed. People make a variety of potato dishes like zeera alu (boiled potatoes tempered with cumin seeds), dahi wale alu (boiled potatoes cooked in curd). Sabudana kheer is also a popular sweet dish made during the Navaratri. Many food joints in Jammu city add Vrata special thali in their menus during Navaratri.

With Jammu becoming more cosmopolitan and in a modern digital age where it is easy to access and even travel to different regions, the adoption of other regional cultural practices is bound to happen. Dandiya, a famous Gujarati dance performed during Navaratri, has enamoured Jammu too and has started making inroads in the city of temples lately. The Bengali community in Jammu has, for instance, formed the Jammu Durga Puja Committee and celebrates Durga Puja with enthusiasm and gaiety.

Nava Devi Darshan Yatra

Nava Devi Darshan Yatra is undertaken by many devotees in northern India on the auspicious occasion of Navaratri, covering nine prominent Devi temples that now fall in different States.

The Yatra starts from the Chandi Devi Temple in Chandigarh. This temple is dedicated to Mahakali and is nestled in the Shivalik hills, The temple draws a large number of devotees, especially during Navaratri when special prayers are offered and the temples bear a festive look, with elaborate flower decorations.

The Manasa Devi Temple in Panchkula is the second temple devotees throng after Chandi Devi Mandir. Manasa Devi is a Shakti Peetha. It is believed that Sati's head fell at this spot. The Mata Manasa Devi temple was built on this site by Raja Gopal Singh of Manimajra in 1815.

The third temple in this Nava Darshan Yatra is Mata Naina Devi Mandir, which is approximately 115 kilometres from Mata Mansa Devi Mandir, situated in Bilaspur district of Himachal Pradesh. Naina Devi Temple is the place where Sati's eyes had fallen and the Temple was constructed by Raja Bir Chand. The temple is located at considerable height and it is a 1.5 hour-trek from the road. Stunning views of Govind Sagar Lake are visible from the temple premises.

Mata Chintpurni Mandir in Una district of Himachal Pradesh is the fourth Shakti Peetha on this nine Devi Darshan Yatra. This is approximately 112 kilometres from Mata Naina Devi Mandir. This is where Ma Sati's feet fell.

Bagalamukhi Mata Mandir located around 34 kilometres away from Chintpurni Mata Mandir, is the fifth mandir darshana in this Yatra. The temple is located in Kangra district. It is believed that the temple was built in one night by the Pandavas during their ajnaata vaasa in the Dvapara Yuga.

The sixth Shakti Peetha, Jwala Devi Mandir, is 26 kilometres from Baglamukhi Mandir is and situated in Jwalamukhi village in Himachal's Kangra district. It is believed that Sati's tongue fell on this spot and it is worshipped in the form of an eternal fire or jyoti. It is believed that Jwala Devi fulfils all wishes and especially the devotees who offer special prayers to her during Navaratri always remain carefree.

Brijeshwari temple in Nagarkot, Kangra is the seventh Shakti Peetha in the Nava Devi Yatra and where Sati's left breast fell.

Twenty-four kilometres away from the Brijeshwari temple is the Chamunda Mata Temple dedicated to Mahakali, and both Shiv and Shakti reside here.

From here, devotees travel into the Jammu region to offer their obeisance to Vaishno Mata in Katra. Vaishno Devi is the last of the Nava Devi Darshana Yatra that devotees set out for, during Navaratri, to seek blessings from the Mother Goddess.

14

Kamakhya of Kamarupa in Assam

PARTHASARTHI MOHANTA

Navaratri and its observance is not as widespread in Assam as it is in many other parts of India. The celebration of Navaratri is limited mostly to Kamakhya Devi Dham, one of the foremost Shakti Peethas of the Indian subcontinent.

In fact, all the four Navaratris at four different times of the year are observed at Kamakhya Dham. The primary among them is the Navaratri during the Hindu calendar month of Ashvina, which coincides with the advent of autumn. The second Navaratri is observed at Kamakhya in the month of Chaitra, coinciding with the end of the spring season and onset of summer. The third is in the month of Ashadha, which coincides with the monsoon season. And the fourth Navaratri is celebrated during the month of Magha, which is in the winter season. Of these four Navaratris, the most widely observed ones are during the months of Ashvina and Chaitra, while the other two Navaratris are known as Gupta (or secret) Navaratris.

The Navaratri during the month of Ashvina is the most popular at Kamakhya Dham. What sets the observance of this Navaratri at Kamakhya apart from those in the rest of the country is that it is observed over a span of 15 days that are marked by many unique rituals. This Navaratri stretches from the Navami (the ninth day) of krishna paksha (the dark half of a month) in the month of Ashvina to the Navami of shukla paksha (the new moon period).

The *Kalika Purana* has extensive sections on the Devi, as she is worshipped in Kamarupa, Kamagiri or Kamakhya. Some of these accounts involve Naraka as the king of Kamarupa. In many parts of *Kalika Purana*, it is stated that Devi, as Kamakhya, has companion goddesses—Yoginis and Nayikas. We are told that Yoginis number eight in some places, 64 in others and in yet other places, the number runs into crores. We are also told that Goddess Durga has eight associates as Shaktis—Ugrachanda, Prachanda, Chanogra, Chandanavika, Chanda, Chandavati, Chamunda and Chandika.

The Navaratri during the month of Ashvina has some special rituals. Five bratis who lead their lives strictly according to Vedic rules and regulations and carry out all the tasks at the Kamakhya Dham, are assigned the task to perform all the rituals associated with the observance of this Navaratri.

The first brati is called the Pujari, who's only assigned task is to carry out the Puja. The second brati is the Bidhipathak, who is well-versed in the observance of all *bidhis* (rituals). The third brati is known as Hota, whose role is to light the fire of the yagna as per laid down procedures. The fourth brati is Brahma, whose role is to conduct the daily Pujas and japa (daily chanting of mantras). The fifth brati is called Chandipathak, who has a vital task: that of reciting the Chandi during the 15 days of Navaratri.

The five bratis conduct Pujas and all other rituals as per the scriptures, every morning, mid-day and evening during the fortnight-long observance of Navaratri. The five bratis partake habishyanna (boiled food and fruits), which is cooked inside the temple premises.

An essential part of this Navaratri is Kumari Puja—the worship of young maidens who are considered to be forms of the Devi. On Pratipada (the first day), one Kumari (maiden) is worshipped, while on Dvitiya (the second day), two are worshipped. The number of Kumaris worshipped on Tritiya (the third day) is three, four on Chaturthi (the fourth day), five on Panchami (the fifth day), and so on Shahsti (the sixth day), Saptami (the seventh day), Ashtami (the eighth day) and Navami (the ninth day) as well.

Kumari Puja is, in fact, one of the most important Pujas associated with Kamakhya Dham. According to the Shastras, a powerful asura named Kola forcibly occupied Svargarajya (the celestial abode) and started torturing the Devatas. The Devatas beseeched Mahakali to save them, and she assumed the form of a young maiden (Kumari), and went to Kola to beg for alms.

Charmed by the sight of the Kumari, Kola took her to his palace, seated her on a bejewelled throne and asked his servants to serve her food. She finished whatever was served to her and asked for more. Kola, who had come under her spell, offered her anything she wanted. Mahakali, in the form of the Kumari, thereafter devoured Kola's entire kingdom and then Kola himself. The Devatas were overjoyed, and started celebrating and worshipping the Kumari who had vanquished Kola. That is how the practice of Kumari Puja began. Any pre-pubescent girl is considered a Kumari. Generally, girls between six and 10 years of age, irrespective of their caste, are chosen as Kumaris for Kumari Puja.

Another important and integral ritual during this Navaratri is the Mahasnana of the Devi. The Mahasnana is a highly elaborate ritual where the Devi is bathed with 31 substances.

The Navami Puja is followed by sacrifices of buffaloes, goats, pigeons and water gourd. Devotees offer mostly buffaloes and goats for the sacrifices. The sacrifices are followed by another important ritual—the homa or the havan, a Vedic fire ritual.

Apart from the Kamakhya Dham, the autumnal Navaratri is also observed by all families who reside in Nilachal Parvata, where the temple is situated. All these families of priests are connected to the Kamakhya Mandir, being those of purohitas, pandas and others. All the households observe the Navaratri by setting up a ghot, a metal vessel containing water. The households at Nilachat Parvata worship Devi on Saptami, Ashtami, Navami and Dashami of the fortnight-long Navaratri.

Yet another unique aspect of the observance of Navaratri in Assam is that, unlike other parts of India where people fast, devotees who celebrate Navaratri (including the ones at Nilachal Parvata) consume normal food—vegetarian and non-vegetarian—on all the days. Animal sacrifice is part of the daily Puja (Nitya Puja) at Kamakhya Dham and it continues during the Navaratri period also. It is only the bratis who observe strict food restrictions.

In Kamakhya Dham, Devi Parvati is not worshipped in the form of any Murti or Vigraha. And during Navaratri, too, the worship of Devi does not involve any Murti. That's because the Devi is believed to be present in her innate form at Kamakhya. An interesting part of the Navaratri celebrations at Kamakhya Dham is that, while the Devi is not cast in the form of any Murti, a mystic representation is drawn on a parchment, and this parchment is worshipped in accordance with all Vedic rituals.

Yet another unique aspect of the celebration of the autumnal Navaratri at Kamakhya Dham is the ardharatri (midnight) Pujas on the intervening nights of Saptami–Ashtami and Ashtami–Navami. Three more Pujas which form an integral part of the autumnal Navaratri at Kamakhya Dham are the Trishulani Puja, the Matri Chakra Puja and Rahashya Puja.

The nine forms of the Devi—Shailaputri, Brahmacharini, Chandraghanta, Kushmanda, Skandamata, Katyayani, Kalaratri, Mahagauri and Siddhidatri—are also worshipped during this autumnal Navaratri.

After the last Puja on Dashami, the parchment on which a representation of the Devi is made and worshipped is immersed in the Brahmaputra which flows majestically beside the Nilachala Parvata.

Importance of Devi and Navaratri

Devi Durga is the Param Satta (paramount power) in this universe. It is the Devi who is the supreme power behind the creation, preservation and dissolution of the universe. The Trinity (Brahma, Vishnu and Maheshvara) who are responsible for their three respective roles of creator, preserver and destroyer derive their powers from Devi Durga, who is also the supreme Devi Shakti. No celestial God is complete without the power of Shakti or Devi Durga. Devi, looked up to as 'Mata' (the divine Mother) has many names, but only nine forms. And it is these nine forms of 'Mata' or Devi Shakti that are worshipped during Navaratri.

Devi Durga is eternal, indivisible and incorporeal. According to the Rig Veda, Adi Shakti Jagdamba is the supreme Goddess of the universe. It is only due to Ma Durga's wishes that humans bear the fruits of their karma (deeds).

Ma Durga is the fountainhead of consciousness and eternal knowledge.

त्वं परा प्रकृति: साक्षाद् ब्रह्मण: परमात्मन: ।
त्वत्तो जातं जगत् सर्वं त्वं जगज्जननी शिवे।।[1]

O Shiva, you are the Para Prakriti (basic, infinite and inner cosmic energy, the root cause of this creation). You are the Brahmananda Parmatman (supreme self), you are the Jagatjanani (mother of the universe).

The recitation of 'Durga Saptashati' from *Markandeya Purana* holds special significance in Kaliyuga. The 'Durga Saptashati' contains odes to all nine forms of the Devi and its recitations helps one achieve punya (saintliness). The recitation of 'Durga Saptashati' helps one break away from the illusion of worldly love and attachment and ascend Devi's Parama Dham[2] or achieve moksha or salvation.

Nava Durga: The Nine Forms of the Devi

As per *Shree Chandi Kavacha*, Brahma told Rishi Markandeo that Devi has the following nine forms who are collectively known as Nava

---
[1] From Chapter 4 of *Mahanirvanta Tantra*, Shloka 10.
[2] Ultimate and final abode.

Durga: Shailaputri, Brahmacharini, Chandraghanta, Kushmanda, Skandamata, Katyayani, Kalaratri, Mahagauri and Siddhidatri.

Shailaputri is the daughter of Giriraj, the king of mountains.

In the Brahmacharini form, the Devi represents existence, consciousness and bliss.

Chandraghanta represents vigil, with her third eye always open in readiness for battle against rakshasas.

Kushmanda, also known as Astabhuja Devi because of her eight hands, created the cosmic egg and is Surya Deva's source of power.

Devi came to be known as Skandamata after She became the mother of Skanda, also known as Kartikeya.

Katyayani is a fierce form of Devi and the slayer of Mahishasura. Her triumph over this demon is celebrated as Durga Puja.

The seventh form of the Devi, called Kalaratri is her most ferocious form. She is also known as Bhadrakali, Rudrani and Chamunda.

Mahagauri represents beauty and is fair complexioned and clad in white.

The ninth form of the Devi, Siddhidatri, is Her primary form. It is said that one half of Bhagavan Shiva's body is that of Devi Siddhidatri, which is why he is known as Ardhanarishvara.[3]

It is the worship of these nine forms of Devi that marks the observance of Navaratri.

---

[3] The composite male—female form where the right side is male representing Shiva and left, female representing Shakti.

15

Mannami and Nave Jevan in Konkan

RADHIKA PRABHU

Sharada Navaratri, or Mannami, as the festival is referred to colloquially, is celebrated with devotion and gratitude by the Konkani-speaking Gaud Saraswat community. Traditions and festivities include the Makhar Utsav at temples in Goa, the worship of Sharada Devi as the Goddess of Knowledge and the celebration of 'Nave Jevan' or new food. It is a time of revering and giving thanks to Devi, the divine feminine.

The Saraswat brahmins who settled on the Konkan Coast in present-day Goa are a part of the larger Saraswat community that trace their roots to the banks of the Sarasvati river. Tectonic changes caused the river to dry up, which led to the exodus of Saraswats to different regions of India. Today, communities that identify themselves as Saraswats can be found across the country, with different customs and languages based on their geography.

The Navaratri traditions described here are those practised by the Gaud Saraswat brahmins (GSBs), a branch of the Saraswat community that settled on the Konkan coast in present-day Goa. There is a large overlap between the practices of the different branches of the Konkani Saraswats, but for the purposes of this discussion, the discussion is limited to GSBs. Over the last millennium, due to various exigencies, members of the community spread out to present-day Karnataka, Kerala and Maharashtra. Goa remains the ancestral heartland, but the geographical spread has added regional and local flavours to all festive celebrations, including Navaratri.

The community brought their Kuladevatas, or family deities, with them as they migrated. The Kuladevatas were mostly in the form of Mahadeva and Shakti, which were initially worshipped at homes, and later at temples. This aspect of worshipping together as a family and as a community remains an integral part of the festivities. Amongst the GSBs, there are followers of both Smarta and Vaishnava sampradayas, which reflect in their multi-layered religious and social identity.

The Season of Celebration

The celebration of Navaratri can be viewed across several dimensions. It is the triumph of good over evil, as the Devi in her many forms vanquishes various asuras. The asuras are characterized by attributes such as greed, arrogance, pride, power, lust and ego, which are all well-recognized human frailties. The ability to control our senses and choose right conduct is an important and deeper objective of the festivities.

Another dimension is that of the season of celebration. The Hindu calendar contains six Ritus, or seasons, of two months each, namely, Vasanta, Grishma, Varsha, Sharada, Hemanta and Shishira. Sharada Ritu, or autumn, is characterized by clear skies after the monsoons during Varsha Ritu. The beauty of Sharada Ritu is described in Canto 10 of the *Srimad Bhagavatam*.[1] The description begins with '*ittham sharat-svaccha-jalam padmakara-sugandhina*,' which means 'the water of Sharada is clear, with fragrant blossoming lotuses'.

There is a marked change in nature at the advent of Sharada Ritu, with the muddied waters giving way to a clearer flow. The muddied waters of Varsha are interpreted as a metaphor for our

---

[1] 10.21.1, with Shukadeva describing it to Parikshit.

muddied intellect. During Sharada Navaratri, we aim to cleanse the intellect and ready ourselves to receive higher knowledge, necessary for fuller realization of the self.

Aradhana (devotion) and tyaga (sacrifice) are considered vital elements of the Navaratri celebrations. Many in the community observe vratas, the adhering to rules and regulations meant to strengthen good thought and practice. Hence, it is customary to give up onion, garlic and other tamasic food during this festival. It is also customary to give up kharkattha, a Konkani term which means anything cooked with rice before performing Pujas.

Revitalizing the mind through Devi aradhana, and the reading of sacred texts is emphasized during Navaratri. The recitation of the 'Devi Mahatmya', 'Lakshmi Asthottara', 'Lalita Sahasranama', 'Sri Suktam', singing bhajans, performing Pujas are all meant to help concentrate on the power within, remove the asuras of the mind and channel one's energies to a higher level of existence.

Navaratri preparations start out by thoroughly cleaning the home and taking care of any repairs and maintenance. The Puja room is cleaned and rangolis are drawn outside the home and near the Tulasi plant. Some of the salient traditions and practices of the community are presented next.

Devi Mahatmya Parayana

Traditionally, the 'Devi Mahatmya' is read daily in the evenings, either by a member of the family or by an officiating priest. It is read as a devotional text with a view to understanding the higher meaning it imparts. The parayana or reading begins on Pratipada, the first day of Navaratri. Some read all 13 chapters daily, while others divide the chapters across the nine days. After each reading, a wheat-based sweet naivedyam is offered to the Devi and eaten as prasada. At the conclusion of this reading on Navami, the ninth day of Navaratri, many perform a Mangal Arati and some perform the more elaborate Chandika Homam.

The recitation of 'Devi Mahatmya', not just in this community but in homes across India, is testament to a living tradition nurtured through its recital over the years. The 700 verses of the 'Mahatmya' describing the powers and virtues of the Devi is contained in the *Markendaya Purana*, which is estimated to be from fifth or sixth century CE. The Devi is worshipped as trigunatmika:[2] as Mahakali she protects against all evil, as Mahalakshmi she bestows blessings not just of material wealth but health and prosperity and as Mahasarasvati, she is revered as the giver of knowledge and inspiration. As Durga, she kills the evil asura Mahishasura, and in her many forms, she vanquishes Chanda, Munda, Madhu–Kaitabh, Shumbha, Nishumbha and Raktabija, thus restoring the forces of good.

The 'Mahatmya' is also understood to be an allegory of our binding with Prakruti, Nature. The 'Ekadasha Adhyaya', its eleventh chapter, contains the 'Narayani Stuti' which describes the Devi as follows:

आधारभूता जगतस्त्वमेका
महीस्वरूपेण यतः स्थितासि ।
अपां स्वरूपस्थितया त्वयैतदाप्यायते
कृत्स्नमलङ्घ्यवीर्ये ।।

You alone are the support of the world, by standing firm as in the form of earth; in the form of water, you overflow the entire world with your inviolable power.

Thereby, the Devi is linked to nature and through the tradition of Navaratri, we respect the earth, nature, our environment and therein the forces of the universe.

Nave Jevan

In Konkani, 'nave' means new and 'jevan' means eating of a meal.

---

[2] The three gunas of sattva (purity), rajas (passion) and tamas (darkness).

Nave Jevan is a tradition of thanksgiving during Sharada Navaratri for the community. The newly harvested rice is first offered to the divine and accepted as blessings. It is in essence the day of thanking the divine for providing the family with nourishment and plentitude. In most households, Nave Jevan is held either on Pratipada or on Navami. But family tradition and geographical location holds sway and any day of Navaratri is considered auspicious for this celebration.

The home is readied to accept the newly harvested kanasa, paddy sheaves with rice still in the husk. The lady of the house prepares for the Puja by emptying out the tandla madki, a copper vessel used traditionally for storing rice, cleaning it thoroughly and decorating it with rangoli, kumkum and marigold flowers.

The yajamana, the head of the household, sets out for the temple with offerings of coconut and bananas. Meanwhile, the newly harvested kanasa sourced from the farms is carried to the temple on a palanquin to the accompaniment of music. At the temple, the kanasa is blessed with Arati and awaits distribution to the devotees. The yajamana brings the kanasa home, places it near the Tulasi and seeks blessings. He then proceeds to the front door with the vessel containing the kanasa on his head. The lady of the house welcomes the arrival of the kanasa with Arati. Then the kanasa is brought into the Puja room and placed in front of the deity. The kuladevata is thanked and the family offers prayers together.

The kanasa is then tied into odd-numbered bunches. Each bunch includes a sheaf of paddy, a mango leaf and in some homes a jackfruit leaf is also added. To keep these bunches strong throughout the year, the twine binding it together is made from the fibers of coconut branches. These bunches are then placed ceremoniously in places of importance around the home including the Puja room, the tandla madki, the cashbox, Tulasi, baby cradle, the water source worshipped as Ganga, and at places of business, if the family owns any. The tandla madki is filled with rice and some grains of the kanasa are de-husked and added to the pot. The new rice is cooked that day to symbolize the Nave Jevan.

This is also a time when generations of the family gather at the hod, the ancestral home of the elders to celebrate the feast together. Younger generations carry the sanctified kanasa to their own homes after the celebrations.

A variety of dishes, including sweets, are cooked for the Nave Jevan feast. They differ based on family traditions and geographical location. The dishes that are most common are Gajbaje Ambat, a harvest medley of vegetables in coconut gravy, Chane Dalli Madgane, which is a chana dal, jaggery and coconut-milk based sweet dish, and Cheppi Kheer, which contains rice and coconut milk with the addition of haldi leaves. It is into this kheer that some of the kanasa is de-husked and added. Additionally, Taushe Ullel, a type of cucumber salad, is either made with coconut gravy or served plain with a seasoning. This coastal cuisine uses coconut extensively taking advantage of the local produce that is available in plenty.

It is interesting to note that the food eaten during Navaratri by the community also aligns with the principles of Ayurveda. As is common across India, communities have kept the wisdom of the ancients alive by eating seasonal and local foods based on region and climate as part of festive celebrations. By adopting these as the traditional festive foods, it has encouraged the eating of the food during a particular season.

According to Ayurvedic principles, seasonal changes affect the balance of the doshas, which can be understood as 'impurities'. Foods prescribed are based on balancing doshas, as per an individual's constitution. The principles suggest that the Pitta dosha is in prakopa, in aggravated form, during Sharada Ritu. Pitta in balance indicates good digestion and the ability to understand. Rice, chickpeas, coconut, cucumber, squash, ghee and lentils are all good for balancing Pitta dosha and they form part of the Nave Jevan festivities.

Pujas

On Mula Nakshatra, which is on Shashti or Saptami, the sixth or seventh day, many households place all the sacred manuscripts passed through the family across generations—a copy of the Ramayana, *Srimad Bhagavatam* and other religious texts considered sacred to the family—in the Puja room and pray to Sharada Devi. Arati is done daily and the books are removed only after Dashami, the tenth day.

Based on their traditions, in only a few families, Sharada Puja is performed for three days by consecrating a clay Murti according to strict protocols, rituals and vratas at home. This pratishtha is done on Mula Nakshatra day. After the Puja, a symbolic immersion is conducted and the Murti of the goddess is again placed in the family Puja room. The community conducts festive and grand celebrations of Sharada Puja by consecrating large clay Murtis of the Devi at pandals across Karanataka and increasingly in other cities such as Mumbai.

The ceremony of formally initiating young children into their first learning can be held any day after Sharada Pratishtha on Mula Nakshatra day. The belief is that knowledge gained will be internalized and will adhere when blessed by Ganapati, the remover of all obstacles and Sarasvati, the goddess of knowledge. This practice, which used to be held at homes with an officiating priest, has now moved mostly to community gatherings at temples. In temples, it is usually held on Dashami. Vijaya Dashami is one of the three days of the year where no muhurtams (auspicious times) are required to conduct any important activities as the day itself is considered wholly auspicious. Community Vidyarambha ceremonies are held in front of the consecrated Sharada Murti at the pandals.

Some families conduct the Durga Namaskara Puja at home. This is usually done on Ashtami, but is also conducted on Panchami day. The Puja is conducted by a priest and part of the ritual involves doing a circumambulation and bowing down 108 times as each mantra is chanted. The philosophy is to bow before the Devi in reverence and get rid of our ahankara, ego. This Puja is also held at temples and pandals and devotees observe a fast until the Puja is concluded.

The married women of the community celebrate Savasini[3] Pujas. The women being honoured are treated as the form of the Devi and their feet are washed by the lady doing the Puja. They are offered haldi-kumkuma, betel nut and betel leaf, flowers, bangles, a blouse-piece and dakhsina. An odd number of women are invited to grace the occasion. All the attendees follow certain observances, like a ritual head bath and fast before the Puja. After the Puja, all the Savasinis eat a meal together. This Puja is done at home and at temples, especially Devi temples during all days of Navaratri. The haldi-kumkuma ceremony held at home mostly on Lalitha Panchami does not include restrictions on numbers and invitees include girls and women from the extended family and neighbourhood who do Devi Aradhana by singing bhajans and reciting shlokas together.

Ayudha Puja, which is the worship of all implements related to one's livelihood, is celebrated on Vijaya Dashami. Pens, pencils and books are placed in the Puja room and vehicles, computers, machines of the household and those at the place of business, if any, are decorated with kumkuma, mango leaf and marigold garlands. Arati is conducted and prayers are offered for success in one's avocation.

In some GSB families, there is a custom of going to the kuladevata temples in Goa during Navaratri to offer special Pujas.

Community Celebrations—Makhar Utsava

Goa's ancient temples are living places of worship and many of them have been in their present form and location since the last 500 years. Worship of the deities has continued unabated for much longer than

---

[3] Savasinis are those who reside together.

that time frame. The temples are an integral part of life for those residing in the environs and for the diaspora whose kuladevatas are worshipped here.

A unique celebration at the temples in Goa during Navaratri is the Makhar Utsava where the Utsava Murti, the representation of the deity worshipped in the main sanctum of the temple is placed in a Makhar, a ceremonial seat where the deity is placed, adorned and worshipped. In the Goan Makhar Utsav, the Makhar is a swing of elaborate woodwork or silver which is decorated with colored paper, mirrors, intricate beadwork, embroidery and colorful flowers. The objective is to create a prafulla or joyous environment for the deities. Much as a child finds joy in the swinging of the swing, the belief is that creating such a joyous environment for the deity reflects on the devotees.

The festival is celebrated with much splendour, lights and alankara or decorations at the Goan temples such as the Sri Devaki Krishna Ravalnath at Marcel, Sri Mahalasa Narayani at Mardol, Sri Shanta Durga at Kavale, Sri Mahalaxmi at Bandora, Sri Mangueshi at Priol village and many other revered temples. The deepa stambhas or light pillars that are situated at the entrance of the temples are lit during this time and make for a serene environment.

At the Mahalasa Narayani temple, the ghata staphana is done on the first day of Navaratri. The ghata is a kalasha or copper pot used for ceremonial purposes. The Utsava Murti of the Devi is placed ceremoniously in the Makhar. Seven different varieties of dhanya or grains and pulses are put into a pot to sprout and are watered daily for the nine days. This ankurarupan or sprouting of seeds indicates prosperity and bringing to a fruition of good deeds, karma. On Dashami, the sprouted dhanya is distributed to devotees.

Worshipping the Devi during Navaratri involves a strict adherence to an elaborate set of protocols and rituals that have their origins in Vedic scriptures. Many Pujas and homams are conducted daily including the Saptashati parayana, which is concluded after nine days by the Chandika Homam. In the evenings, the Makhar is swung for about an hour to the tune of beautiful rhythmic music set to drums called tasha and shehnai as the Arati is waved continuously. Haridasas conduct kirtanas or discourses, which are centered on the virtues and powers of the Devi and related to everyday life and conduct in easy to understand narration.

The alankara differs daily as do the vahanas or vehicles of the Devi, which include Garuda, peacock, swan, lion, while the elephants are symbolic of her form as Gaja Lakshmi. On Mula Nakshatra day, three Murtis and on Navami five Murtis are placed in the Makhar. Many devotees visit the temple to worship the Devi on these days. On Dashami, the goddess is seated on a palanquin and a procession takes place within and outside the temple precincts.

At the Mahalaxmi Temple in Bandora, there is a gandha or sandalwood worship and a palanquin procession on Ashtami, which is considered the deity's favourite day. At the Shanta Durga Temple in Kavale, the procession heads to the village on Dashami and devotees await eagerly for this occasion. At all temples, the different forms of the Devi as Sarasvati, Mahishasura Mardini, Gaja Lakshmi are all celebrated and depicted through the different alankaras. Ayudha Puja is celebrated on Vijaya Dashami and is followed by the ghata visarjan, which concludes the ceremony.

In the Rig Veda, Sarasvati, the Goddess of Knowledge is praised thus:

अम्बितमे नदीतमे देवितमे सरस्वति ।
अप्रशस्ता इव स्मसि प्रशस्तिम् अम्ब नस् कृधि ॥[4]

This translates to: 'The best of mothers, the best of rivers and supreme Goddess Sarasvati, please grant us merit, O Mother, even though we are not worthy.'

Devotion to Goddess Sarasvati and the river of their origins are integral elements of the community's identity and Sharada Mahotsava is celebrated in large community-wide celebrations in

---
[4]*Rig Veda* (2nd *Mandala*, 41st *Sukta*, 16th *Rik*)

Karnataka where the community has a significant presence.

Dussehra, is the nadahabba or state festival of Karnataka. The term includes the nine days of Navaratri, and the festival is celebrated with great pomp and splendour across the state. In this region, Goddess Sarasvati is worshipped as Sharada Devi. Many devotees make the trip to Sringeri Sharada Peetham, established by Sri Adi Shankara to worship Sharadamba and ask for blessings of vidya, knowledge and buddhi, intelligence during these nine days.

The city of Mangalore is decked out in lights for the occasion. All Hindu communities celebrate the festival and the Navaratri celebrations at the Gokarnanatheshwara Temple in Kudroli, which includes worship to Sharada and Navadurga Murtis, with large tableaus depicting the many manifestations of the Goddess is ardently awaited every year.

The GSB community, which has a sizeable presence in Mangalore and in the surrounding region, celebrates Sharada Mahotsava at several pandals in the city. The Acharya Math celebrations held in the precincts of the Shri Venkataramana temple is the oldest and has been in practice for more than a century since 1923. The Sharada Murti, which is crafted from clay with much devotion by the sculptors, is ceremoniously brought into the temple precincts the night before with prayers for a successful celebration.

Sharada Pratishtha is done on Mula Nakshatra and the goddess is invoked through a variety of rituals and mantras. The Murti portrays her form as Veenadharini, the one who holds the veena, Hamsavahini, the goddess whose mount is a swan and Pustakadharini, the one who holds a book. There is a different alankara for each day and the Devi is adorned with beautiful kirita (crown), ornaments, silk sarees and flowers.

At all pandals, the decorations and themes change daily, and the Devi is portrayed in several forms including Annapurna, Devaki Krishna and Durga. At some places, hundreds of oil diyas or lamps are placed on wooden stands, which are lit by devotees. The electric lights are turned off and the Goddess is worshipped by the light of these lamps. In addition to various Pujas, there are a large variety of cultural and religious programs, including recital of kathas, singing of bhajans, children's shloka reciting competitions and donor drives that benefit educational activities. With the decline of joint family units and the inability to head to the native home, this process of celebrating Navaratri together at pandals has also taken root in places like Mumbai, where the community has a presence.

The immersion of the Murti is done on Ekadashi (eleventh day) after Vijaya Dashami. This procession called the shobhayatra makes its way through the streets of Mangalore to the accompaniment of music and the huli vesha, the famed tiger dance of Karnataka. Men and boys attired in tiger costumes and painted stripes dance energetically to the beat of the drums in honour of the Devi's favoured vahana, the tiger. The Devi's alankara on the day of the shobhayatra is ardently awaited by the community. The Devi is adorned with bugadi, the ear ornaments worn during festive occasions, the coral mangalasutra typical of the community, and her hair is adorned with sond phool, a unique arrangement of Mangalore Mallige (Mallika) or jasmine flowers which is worn by the women of the community during important events of their lives such as weddings and pregnancy.

The festivities of Navaratri conclude with a Shobha Yatra. At the place where the immersion takes place, the raft that carries the Murti circles the temple pond five times amidst the sounds of traditional music. Then the national song Vande Mataram fills the air. The tradition of singing this song was started prior to the struggle for Indian Independence and continues strong to this day. The Devi is revered as the mother of the nation, adding another meaningful layer to the celebrations. As the Murti is lowered gently into the waters, it is time to bid farewell to the physical manifestation of the Devi, with the hope that the virtues lauded and celebrated over the course of the festival stay embedded within her devotees.

Note

My sincere gratitude and thanks to my parents, Shri V.M. Pai, Purohit Shri Madan Bhat, Purohit Shri Vinayak Bhat, Shri Naresh Nayak, Smt. Srimathi Pai Kasturi and Smt. Gayathri Padiyar for sharing their knowledge on the spiritual, social and cultural aspect of Navaratri traditions in the community. Their insight underpins this essay and any mistakes in understanding are my own and are regretted.

16

Kuladevis in Rajasthan

DIWAKAR JHURANI

Rajasthan has a tradition of opening its arms to the world with the call of *'Padharo mhare des'* (Come, visit my land!). The invitation is not just to come and see the magnificent forts and enjoy desert safaris, but to experience the state's rich culture. What could be a better way to immerse into Rajasthan's culture than to experience its festivals and fairs! Navaratri is one such festival that Rajasthan has given a unique flavour too. While there are similarities with the rituals and traditions in other states, there is also ample distinction that makes Rajasthan's Navaratri a festival to experience.

Let us start with similarities. The overarching theme and story are the same, for instance, the concept of Navadurga (nine manifestations of Devi or Goddess Durga) and the underlying devotion to the Devi. The rituals of fasting and maintaining a relatively more spiritual and festive lifestyle for nine days are not too different from those practised in northern and central India. Honouring young girls (kanjaks) on the ninth day and concluding festivities with the prasada of halwa, poori and chana is also a common practice that can be observed in other Indian regions.

When one talks to locals from Rajasthan about Navaratri, one of the common features that emerges is the ritual of bali (animal sacrifice) as an offering to the Devi during the nine days. However, since the passage of Rajasthan Animals and Birds Sacrifice Act (1975) which prohibits sacrifice of animals or birds in, or within the premises of temples or places of public religious worship, the ritual is no longer observed.

There is, however, an emerging and a welcome trend during Navaratri. The festival is now being used as opportunity to inculcate a sense of respect and regard among young boys towards women, especially girls in their age group. Each Navaratri, teachers in over 2,000 government schools across 18 districts of Rajasthan, make boys perform Puja by washing the feet of female students. The rituals of applying tilak and performing Arati are also observed. The objective is clear—gender sensitization should start with boys and what better way to do it than to mix Rajasthan's culture with education.[1]

The Concept of Kuladevi

Navaratri has been a part of Rajasthan's ethos for long and its celebration has been influenced by the social structures of the state. Family clans have a huge sway on cultures and traditions in Rajasthan. The concept is not just restricted to the Rajputs, often stereotyped as the dominant group in Rajasthan. Perhaps the stereotyping is because Rajasthan is often seen as the land of forts and palaces, kings and royalty. Rajputs do have a higher influence in those areas. But other groups have influenced Rajasthan's culture and traditions as well. These include the Jats, Gujjars, Meenas and brahmins, among other. In fact, Rajputs constitute less than 10 per cent of the state population.

Navaratri is of unique importance to most social groups in Rajasthan. The Kuladevi is the guardian Devi of a clan or an extended family, called Kula. She could even be one of the ancestors seen as an incarnation of the Devi, as we shall see, in some cases.

These manifestations are celebrated in stories chronicling the

---

[1] "Teachers Use Navaratri for Gender Equality." *DNA India*, https://www.dnaindia.com/jaipur/report-rajasthan-teachers-use-navaratri-for-gender-equality-2675419. Accessed on 10 June 2021.

origins and early achievements of the Rajput groups that Kuladevis protect. The Kuladevi's power of protection is directed toward the king and his family. The goddess appears to the king (or prince) and either with him or through him protects the kula and hence the realm. Afterward, the Kuladevi's primary relationship remains with the king, who tends to her needs just as his own servants tend to his. This close mythical association between king and goddess means that the Kuladevi is identified with the royal family and conceptualized with reference to the protective functions she performs. Her temple is patronized by the royal family and is located in or near its palace.[2]

Since many of the geographical sub-groupings in Rajasthan had Rajput rulers, the concept of Kuladevi transcended just the royals and became a community phenomenon. And Navaratri becomes the most apt occasion for various communities, including Rajputs to honour their Kuladevis. Their temples, generally inside or near famous forts, host festivities. Here are some examples of Kuladevis and the Navaratri celebrations in their temples.

Karauli's Kaila Devi and Lakhi Fair

Considered the Kuladevi of Karauli's royal family, a form of Mahalakshmi (goddess of wealth) and Chamunda (goddess of death), Kaila Devi holds special significance for the Yadavs, Khinchis, and Jadaun Rajputs. Navaratri is a special occasion in the famous Kaila Devi temple (one of the Shakti Peethas) at Kaila village of Karauli. The renowned annual fair, called Lakhi Mela organized during Chaitra Navaratri, attracts visitors not just from Rajasthan but many neighbouring states. Many visitors carry with them religious flags while singing folk prayer songs, called Languriya. Interestingly, in the courtyard of the temple, there is a small temple of Bhairon and a temple facing the Kaila Devi's shrine houses

---

[2]Lindsey Harlan. *Religion and Rajput Women: The Ethic of Protection in Contemporary Narratives.* Berkeley: University of California Press, 1992.

Hanuman, also called Languriya in the local dialect. For the annual fair, many visitors choose to walk on foot. Devotees use the fair as an opportunity to seek blessings for their spouses, and to carry out mundan[3] ceremonies for their children.

The unique feature of the 17-day Lakhi Fair is the different phases that attract visitors from different geographies. The second phase, which begins with Navaratri Sthapna until the third day, attracts visitors from Delhi and Haryana. Devotees from Madhya Pradesh and Dhaulpur dominate the footfall in the third phaase (from the fourth to sixth day). The remaining days of Navaratri (seventh until the ninth day) see crowds from Gujarat, Maharashtra and southern India. An extraordinary devotee of Kaila Devi, Goli Bhagat from Agra started a unique custom, that is observed till date. This rigorous ritual called Kanak-Dandoti[4] is practised by his followers who cover 15–20 kilometres to the temple by lying prostrate, marking a line as far as their hands extend, then get up and lie down in the same position with their feet on the line they marked. They keep repeating this until they reach the temple. A few devotees choose to take rest and nourishment in between but there are ardent ones who persevere through hunger and loss of strength till they reach the temple and make the final round in front of the deity.[5]

Jaipur's Shila Mata

Shila Mata (Goddess Shila) is an incarnation of Goddess Amba and is considered the Kuladevi of Jaipur's Royal family. The name of the fort (Amber) is also derived from the name of Amba Mata. As one enters the temple, the main entrance adorns pictures of Navadurga.

---

[3]Tonsure or the act of shaving a baby's first hair
[4]From 'Dandvati'
[5]"Kaila Devi Fair." *Rajasthan Tourism*, http://www.rajasthan-tourism.org/fairs-of-rajasthan/kaila-devi-fair.html. Accessed on 10 June 2021.

What distinguishes this temple is the prasada that consists of a special milk-based delicacy called gujiyan and coconut. Another unique feature of the temple is that believers offer liquor and raw meat (generally goat or lamb) as a symbol of their devotion to the goddess.

The popular belief is that the temple was established by Sawai Man Singh of Jaipur. Mughal Emperor Akbar had appointed Man Singh as Governor of erstwhile Bengal and had tasked him to defeat the local ruler Kedar. Man Singh prayed for his victory in front of the Shila Mata Murti in Bengal. The goddess blessed him and the Murti was brought to Jaipur and installed in the Amber Fort. The Murti depicts the iconic image of Mahishasura being slayed by the Devi. During Navaratri, Maha Arati is held on each of the nine days and a special fair is organized at Amber Fort. The most important day is the sixth one, when a Chathh Fair is organized and the temple sees a particularly high footfall from locals.

Bikaner's Karni Mata

Karni Mata (considered an avatara of Goddess Durga) is the Kuladevi of the Rathore rulers of Bikaner as well as Charan community. 'Karni Mata was a Hindu warrior sage from the Charan community, who lived in the fourteenth century. Living the long life of an ascetic, Karni Mata was highly revered and continues to be revered. A museum next to her temple documents her life journey. When Rao Bika established his kingdom at Bikaner, he accepted Karni Mata as his Kuladevi.'[6] A temple dedicated to her was built by Maharaja Lunkarn Singh of Bikaner in the fifteenth century and is situated at Deshnok, around 30 kilometres from Bikaner city and is also known as the 'temple of rats', where mice are considered the descendants of Karni Mata and thus, auspicious. Chances are that a

---

[6]'Karni Mata Temple.' *Rajasthan Tourism*, http://www.tourism.rajasthan.gov.in/karni-mata-temple.html. Accessed on 10 June 2021.

few of more than 20,000 rats will harmlessly crawl over a devotee's feet and the whole act is considered a sign of good luck.
The Karni Mata Mela is hosted during Navaratri. Celebrated twice amid a 10-day period right from Chaitra Shukla Ekam to Chaitra Shukla Dashmi and once more from Ashwin Shukla Ekam to Ashwin Shukla Dashami, Karni Mata's Navaratri Mela is held in tall regard by individuals from distant places as well. Of the two fairs, the Chaitra Navaratri Mela is the bigger one in which thousands of devotees make Deshnok as their devout goal.[7]

Sikar's Jeen Mata

Jeen Mata is considered the Kuladevi of Shekhawati's Yadavs, Rajputs, Agrawals, Jangids, and Meenas. As per locals, Jeen Mata was born in Chauhan household at a village called Ghangu, of the Churu district of Rajasthan. She is considered the goddess of power (an incarnation of Durga). A popular myth that is often repeated relates to Aurangzeb. It is believed that Aurangzeb wanted to dismantle Jeen Mata's temple and the nearby Bhairon Baba temple. People prayed for the temple's safety and coincidentally (believed to have happened through Jeen Mata's blessing), Aurangzeb's army was attacked by a massive hive of bees. So fierce was the attack that Aurangzeb himself was injured. Realizing his ill-conceived act of aggression, he promised to maintain an akhand jyot (eternal flame from a lamp) at the temple.

While he kept his promise for many years and sent oil for lighting the akhand jyot from Delhi, the act was then delegated to the Maharaja of Jaipur. The practice was kept alive by Jaipur's royal family; however, the frequency was reduced and the oil for akhand jyot was supplied twice a year—during Chaitra and Sharada Navaratris. Given the relevance of Navaratri, two annual fairs during

---

[7]'Karni Mata Fair.' *Festivals of India*, https://www.festivalsofindia.in/karni_mata_fair/. Accessed on 10 June 2021.

both Navaratris are organized, when thousands of devotees visit the Jeen Mata temple.

Udaipur's Ban Mata

Ban Mata is considered the Kuladevi of the Gehlots and Sisiodiyas of Mewar region of Rajasthan. Her temple is situated in Chittorgarh and Maharana Pratap's clan also considers her as their Kuladevi. During Navaratri, Ban Mata's silver Murti is placed alongside those of Kalika, Ganesh and Bhairon. Also kept are weapons and various royal signages that are considered auspicious. An akhand jyot is lit and prayers such as 'Durga Saptashati' are recited. On the day of Ashtami (eighth day of Navaratri), Dashansh Havan[8] is conducted. Some people recall that when Udaipur's Maharana used to visit the temple on Ashtami, he would be honoured with a three-gun salute.

It is worth noting that Ban Mata wasn't born in Rajasthan, but came via Gujarat.

> The Kuladevi for the Sisodiyas used to be Amba Mata. Then, when the Sisodiyas were at Chittor, the Kuladevi became Kalika Mata. There is still a temple for her there now. Later, when the king conquered Gujarat, he asked a Gujarati princess in marriage. That princess had always wanted to marry the Sisodiya king. She had even sent him a letter telling him that. Her Kuladevi, Ban Mata, had determined to help her accomplish this aim. After the conquest, the wedding took place. When the princess left for her new home, Ban Mata came with her in the form of a pendant. That is how Ban Mata left Girnar (though there is still a temple for her there) and reached Rajasthan.[9]

---

[8] With 10 components of performing an act of homa or havan.
[9] 'Ashwa Poojan.' *Eternal Mewar*, http://www.eternalmewar.in/microwebsites/ashwa-poojan. Accessed on 10 June 2021.

Jodhpur's Aai Mata and Nagaur's Barhmani Mata

Aai Mata (an incarnation of Goddess Durga) is considered the Kuladevi of the Sirvi community of Kshatriyas. Her temple is located at Bilara, which is close to Jodhpur. The temple known as Kesar Jyoti is famous because in this temple, saffron, instead of kajal comes out of the 550-year-old akhand jyot. Devotees apply it as teeka or tilaka when they visit the temple. The temple witnesses a high influx of devotees during Navaratri, when a fair is organized.

Brahmani Mata is considered the Kuladevi of Dodiya Rajputs. Her famous temple at Merta Road, near Nagaur is the only temple in the country, where ghatasthapna takes place a day before Navaratri starts. The story goes that on one of the 'ekams' (first day of Navaratri), the area was invaded. The invasion was resisted by local priests and more than 80 people lost their lives. Since then, ghatasthapna is observed on a day before the first day, as the first day is reserved for mourning the lives lost and sacrifices made by the priests. Another story is that the priests living here, engaged in farming activities and farmers typically do not work in the field on Amavasya. In this context, the tradition of establishing ghat on Amavasya started here.

Shastra and Ashwa Poojan

The ninth day of Navaratri (Navami) is celebrated as Shakti Parva in Rajasthan. To celebrate the victory of Goddess Durga and express gratitude, many in Rajasthan worship the symbols of war. The ritual is especially common among warrior classes to worship arms, especially swords and other traditional weapons. Some people also believe that worshipping arms is in fact a way to pray for peace with a belief that they may never be used. Some families also worship Goddess Durga on Navami by performing what is called a 'talwar Arati' (a ritual to pay respects using a traditional sword dance in addition to the conventional ceremonies).

Rajasthan is also famous for its cavalry charges and Navami is marked by the worship of war animals like the elephant and the horse. This custom is particularly a trademark of the Navaratri celebration by the royal family of Udaipur. The website of the royal family of Udaipur (Eternal Mewar) gives an excellent description of the traditions around this. It reiterates that Ashwa Pujan continues to be performed and in fact, is a highlight of Navaratri celebrations. The ashwa (horses) that participate in the customs generally belong to the 'Marwari' breed, an unmistakable, universally recognized breed that is endangered. The ceremony starts with the entry of the Maharana, with a parade comprising of illustrious insignias such as two Chadiwalas carrying the long gold staff, two Gotawalas carrying the brief gold stick symbolizing the specialist of the state. Two men carrying the fly-whisk are situated at the back of the horse-drawn carriage. Ashwa Pujan, a timeless gratitude to equinity with an object of preserving artistic, religious and historic interest for cultural conservation of heritage, is conducted from a tall, raised stage from where the Maharana presides over the ceremonies.

Two men wearing Chapdas (coat of arms of the House of Mewar), two men carrying Mor Chal (peacock plumes), one carrying the Adani (velvet cloth fan) and one carrying the Meghadambar (feather fan) lend the ceremony an air of grandeur and royalty. One man carries the Karaniya, a cloth with a weaved sun symbol on one side and the moon on the other, and another carries the Chattra, an expansive umbrella, maintaining the royal glory of the yesteryears.

At the auspicious time, amidst the Vedic chanting by the Pujaris, the Maharana worships the horses. The ceremony requires an odd number of horses, from a minimum of three to a maximum of 11. The caparisoned horses are revered by putting a tilak. They are offered moong, gram, jaggery, puri and jowar, after which the Maharana performs their Arati. Before the Ashwa Pujan, the horses are taken for a bath to the lake in the morning. Over time, this has reduced to sprinkling water on the horses. Earlier in Mewar, the Maharana used to perform Gaj (elephant) Pujan as well with along with Ashwa Pujan, seated in Naginabadi darikhana. After the whole ceremony, the Maharana offers goodbye to the Sardar Umrao (nobles) by offering them a stuffed betel leaf and relieves them to carry out other devout works.[10]

Gangaur

A description of Navaratri celebrations would be incomplete without talking about Rajasthan's famous Gangaur festival. The etymology of the word comes from 'Gan' meaning Shiva and 'Gaur' from Gauri (a symbol of Shakti).

Rajasthan's women celebrate Gangaur with awesome enthusiasm and commitment, praying to Goddess Gauri or Parvati to bless them with a bountiful spring that is full of collective and conjoined conjugal concordance. They seek blessings from the goddess to bless their spouses with good health and a long life. This celebration holds uncommon centrality for married women but single young ladies too join in to pray for a great husband. Gangaur celebrates the union of Shiva and Parvati and symbolizes the matrimonial bond and saubhagya (good luck). It is believed that Parvati returns to her parental house and family to bless her companions with conjugal delight during this time. On the final day of her stay, she is given a grand farewell. Gangaur closes on a cheerful note with the entry of Shiva who comes to take his bride Gauri back home.[11]

The 18-day festival starts on the first day of Chaitra and concludes on the third day of the shukla paksha of the same month, which also happens to be the third day of Chaitra Navaratri (tritiya tithi of Chaitra, shukla paksha). The hallmark of Gangaur is women dressed in their finest attires of bandhni-ghagra-choli, paying tribute

---

[10]'Gangaur Festival.' *Rajasthan Tourism*, http://www.tourism.rajasthan.gov.in/fairs-and-festivals/gangaur-festival.html. Accessed on 10 June 2021.

[11]'Gangaur, ghoomar, ghevar...' *Deccan Herald*, https://www.deccanherald.com/archives/sunday-herald-travel/gangaur-ghoomar-ghevar-815733.html. Accessed on 10 June 2021.

to Goddess Parvati for the wellbeing of their families. Many women observe fast, restricting themselves to one meal a day and some prefer just fruits.

One primary custom of Gangaur is the collection of holy ashes from the Holika Dahan fire right after the festival of Holi. These are then used to prepare 16 balls that symbolize 16 days of fasting. On the day of Gangaur, women carry earthen pots on their heads, with a diya (earthen lamp) inside them. They go from one house to another, singing songs and collecting presents like cash, desserts, jaggery, ghee, oil and so on. This continues for the following 10 days, after which the pot is broken.

Clay Murtis of Shiva-Gauri crafted by the artisans and experts are beautified and worshipped during the Navaratri celebration. Certain Rajput families have conventional wooden dolls of the divine couple, which are repainted each year by matherans (neighbourhood painters) right around when the celebration commences. These figures are then placed inside traditional containers alongside wheat grass and flowers; wheat plays a critical part within the customs because it is a critical component of food and livelihood in India.

Individuals purchase earthen pots known locally as kunda and decorate them in a conventional Rajasthani pottery fashion called maandna. Married ladies get blessings in the form of gifts and hampers from their elders known as Sinjara, which comprises dresses, jewellery items, cosmetics and desserts. These gifts are usually sent on the final day of the celebration, which the women wear and use for the final celebration day. The decoration of hands and feet with intricate designs made out of Mehendi is another popular practice that's widespread during the Gangaur festival.

There is also a popular game that many women play during Gangaur. In a group, two young girls assume the role of groom and bride (named Ishar and Gaur, respectively). The group then assembles in a park. The two girls acting as bride and groom then take pheras (circumambulations) around a peepal tree. The pheras are followed by traditional dances and songs that the group sings together.

Different fairs with distinct practices are held across Rajasthan, the grand parades being the fundamental highlight. Customarily these parades involve a gathering of ladies, clad in wonderful attires and embellished with gems, prepared in unique Rajasthani styles, with well-decorated Murtis of Shiva and Gauri balanced on their heads. Groups of local artists too are a part of this parade as they play conventional and popular tunes. The occasion comes full circle with the inundation of the icons in bawdi or johad (wells or water stores), bidding goodbye to Goddess Gauri. Regularly, individuals from far-off corners of the town come over to witness and participate in these parades. Certain tribes in Rajasthan too celebrate Gangaur as an occasion for choosing life partners. During the celebration and fairs, many single men and women in these tribes come together to seek connections with each other. The reason behind such an assemblage is for the most part a potential marriage.

While Gangaur is celebrated across Rajasthan, the most noteworthy and outstanding celebrations happen in Udaipur, Jaisalmer, Jodhpur, Nathdwara and Bikaner. In Udaipur, a boat parade takes place on Lake Pichola in conjunction with firecrackers. Women dance to local tunes while balancing a series of brass pitchers on their heads—another unique facet of this celebration. The celebration is concluded with fireworks at the lakeside. In Jaipur, the parade moves from the Zanani-Deodhi of the City Royal residence, passes through Tripolia Bazaar, Chhoti Chaupar, Gangauri Bazaar, Chaugan stadium, and at long last concludes close Talkatora. Ancient palanquins, chariots, elephants, bullock carts and exhibitions make this parade all the grander.[12] Another unique feature of the Gangaur festival is the Rajasthani sweet called 'Ghewar'. This delicacy is often eaten by women to break their Gangaur fasts.

---

[12]'Gangaur festival and its significance.' *Times of India*, https://timesofindia.indiatimes.com/travel/things-to-do/gangaur-festival-and-its-significance/as63326660.cms. Accessed on 10 June 2021.

Adding Colour to Rajasthan's Charm

From Kuladevis to Navaratri Melas, Ashwa Pujans to Shastra Pujans, from Gangaur to Ghewar, Rajasthan adds a unique texture to India's rich tradition of celebrating the Navaratri festival. A long history of wars, migration and social exchanges with nearby regions have defined Rajasthan's way of celebrating Navaratri. The festival has not even left India's armed forces in Rajasthan untouched. Jawans (soldiers) from India's Border Security Force perform rituals during Navaratri at the Tanot Mata and Ghantiyali Mata temples, just a few kilometres from the Pakistan border. Bollywood fans will remember the 1997 war movie starring Sunny Deol—*Border*. In it, the temple which even the Pakistani tanks could not destroy is the Tanot Mata Temple near Longewala in Jaisalmer. Such is the power of aastha and bhakti towards Devi Ma—a sense of motherhood, embodied by various forms of Navadurga in the state. And Navaratri is one festival that celebrates this sacred and unbreakable bond that Rajasthan shares with the Devi Ma.

Bibliography

'Aarti Sanjhi Mata Di, by Bitta.' *YouTube*, 11 October 2018, www.youtube.com/watch?v=g6y9FsOvPu8. Accessed on 10 June 2021.

Abhisek Kumar Panda, 'The New and the Old of Durga Puja.' *The Daily Guardian*, 26 October 2020, thedailyguardian.com/the-new-and-the-old-of-durga-puja/. Accessed on 10 June 2021.

'Account of Durga Puja.' *Odisha Tourism*, odishatourism.gov.in/content/tourism/en/blog-details.html?url=an-account-of-durga-puja-in-odisha. Accessed on 10 June 2021.

Asha Prakash, 'To read or not? This is how kids today observe pooja.' *Times of India*, https://timesofindia.indiatimes.com/city/kochi/Puja-in-the-age-of-the-internet/articleshow/60871921.cms. Accessed on 10 June 2021.

Ashish Pande, 'Devaragattu Annual Banni festival celebrated with traditional stick-fight,' *India Today*, 1 October 2017.

Ashok Tharu, 'सख्या र पैयाँले गुलजार थारूको दशैं' https://www.himalkhabar.com/news/9376. Accessed on 10 June 2021.

Asmita Manandhar, 'Kathmandu's Khadga Jatras', https://royalmt.com.np/news/kathmandus-khadga-jatras/. Accessed on 10 June 2021.

Binaya Banjara, 'अक्षता: मौलिक प्रचलन' https://www.himalkhabar.com/news/9366. Accessed on 10 June 2021.

C. Keni, *The Saraswats: A compilation of facts and documents from various sources*. VM Salgaocar Foundation, Goa, 2008.

Chandra Prasad Koirala, 'Maghi Naach A Study on Performance and Tharu Culture'.

Chandrakishore, 'दशहरा: पहिले र अहिले' https://www.himalkhabar.com/news/9377. Accessed on 10 June 2021.

Devi Bhagwat Purana, Gita Press, Gorakhpur, 2016.

'Diet and Lifestyle Guidelines in Sharada Ritu.' https://www.carakasamhitaonline.com/index.php?title=Tasyashiteeya_Adhyaya#Diet_and_lifestyle_guidelines_in_sharada_ritu_.28autumn_season.29. Accessed on 10 June 2021.

'Different Kinds of Puja.' https://www.durga-puja.org/different-kinds-of-puja.html. Accessed on 10 June 2021.

Dhan Bahadur Karki, 'Why do the Dashain Tika of Mongols and Aryas differ in color?' https://english.dcnepal.com/2020/10/26/why-do-the-dashain-Tika-of-mongols-and-aryas-differ-in-color/. Accessed on 10 June 2021.

Dr Govinda Tandon, 'घर-आँगनमै दशैं-तिहार!' *Yuva Manch*, 2019.

———, 'दशैंलाई नयाँ सोच र दृष्टिकोण जरूरी छ', unpublished

———, 'विजयादशमी को महत्व र उपादेयता' *Kantipur Daily*, 5 October 2019.

———, 'सम्झना केटाकेटी बेलाको दशै-तिहारको', *Yuva Manch*, 2020.

———, *विजयादशमी सबैको लागि मङ्गलदायक बनोस्*

Dr Maheshraj Pant, 'मध्यकालमा दशैं', *Annapurna Post*, 2018.

Dr N. Mahalingam, translated by Dr B. Natarajan. *Tirumantiram: A Tamil Scriptural Classic*. Sri Ramakrishna Math. Madras, 1994.

Dr Sudhakar Malviya, *Shri Shakti Sangam Tantra Shri Sundari Khand*. Chaukhamba Sanskrit Series Office.

Dr Sudhakar Malviya, *Shri Shakti Sangam Tantra Shri Tara Khand*. Chaukhamba Sanskrit Series Office.

Dr Tirtha Bahadur Shrestha, 'दशैंका रंग बदलौं' https://www.himalkhabar.com/news/9365. Accessed on 10 June 2021.

'History of Sakti.' *History of Odisha*, https://www.historyofodisha.in/history-of-sakti-cult-in-odisha/. Accessed on 10 June 2021.

'HISTORY OF SANJHI MATA. ਸਾਂਝੀ ਭਾਊਾ ਦੀ ਪੂਜਾ। सांझी माता का इतिहास। सांझी की कहानी।' *YouTube*, 6 October 2019, www.youtube.com/watch?v=g4EXTSepilY. Accessed on 10 June 2021.

'History.' https://kerala.gov.in/history. Accessed on 10 June 2021.

J. Singh, *Siva Sutras: The Yoga of Supreme Identity*. Motilal Banarsidass, Delhi, 1979.

'Kalasha Puja—In Sanskrit with Meaning.' *GreenMesg*, greenmesg.org/stotras/puja/kalasha_puja.php. Accessed on 10 June 2021.

'Kanchi Periva Forum—Ebook # 6—Navratri Special Edition.' *SlideShare*, www.slideshare.net/kanchiperiva/kanchi-periva-forum-ebook-6-navratri-special-edition-30032334. Accessed on 10 June 2021.

Kedar Sharma, 'खुलेको फैलिएको दशैं' https://www.himalkhabar.com/news/9359. Accessed on 10 June 2021.

'Keeping Time with Tradition.' *My City Links*, https://mycitylinks.in/keeping-time-with-tradition/. Accessed on 10 June 2021.

'Legends and Rituals.' *My City Links*, www.mycitylinks.in/dussehra-in-odisha-legends-and-rituals/%3famp. Accessed on 10 June 2021.

Lal Chand Prarthi, *Kulut Desh ki Kahaani*.

M. Danino, *The Lost River: On the Trail of the Sarasvati*. Penguin Books India, 2010.

M.A. Stein, *Kalhana's Rajataraagini*. Motilal Banarsidass, 1979.

'Navaratri Festival.' *Kerala Events*, https://keralaevents.in/festivals/Navaratri-festival. Accessed on 10 June 2021.

'Navaratri Mandapam Festival.' http://ramavarma.yolasite.com/navarathri-mandapam-festival.php. Accessed on 10 June 2021.

'Navaratri.' https://www.southtourism.in/kerala/festivals/Navaratri.php. Accessed on 10 June 2021.

Nivedita, *The Master as I Saw Him*. Longmans, Green and Co. London, 1910.

'Orissa Review 2004.' http://magazines.odisha.gov.in/Orissareview/oct2004/englishPdf/shakti.pdf. Accessed on 10 June 2021.

'Orissa Review 2009.' http://magazines.odisha.gov.in/Orissareview/2009/September/engpdf/3-5.pdf. Accessed on 10 June 2021.

'Orissa Review 2012.' http://magazines.odisha.gov.in/Orissareview/2012/oct/engpdf/14-20.pdf. Accessed on 10 June 2021.

Phurpa Tamang, 'अन्यत्र बलि, रसुवामा क्षमापूजा' https://www.himalkhabar.com/news/9364. Accessed on 10 June 2021.

Prakash Pandey, 'दशैं महिमा: दशैंको टिका, जमरा, दक्षिणा र आशिर्वादको के छ महत्व?' https://www.nayacourse.com/5726/ . Accessed on 10 June 2021.

'Ready to Welcome Navarathri.' https://www.onmanorama.com/travel/kerala/2018/10/08/tvm-ready-to-welcome-navarathri-idols.html.

Accessed on 10 June 2021.

'Rig Veda' https://theveda.org.in/rigveda/02/041/16. Accessed on 10 June 2021.

R.L. Kashyap, *Rig Veda Samhita*. Sri Aurobindo Kapali Sastry Institute of Vedic Culture, Bangalore India, 2000.

Ram Mandal, 'यसरी मनाइन्छ मधेशमा दशैं' http://www.freshnewsnepal.com/news-details/4238/rashifal.php. Accessed on 10 June 2021.

Rita Dhital, Dewan Rai, 'Shades of Dashain' https://thehimalayantimes.com/entertainment/shades-of-dashain. Accessed on 10 June 2021.

Rupa Joshi, 'दशैंको सुवास' https://www.himalkhabar.com/news/9368. Accessed on 10 June 2021.

'Saanjhi: Part One.' *YouTube*, 20 August 2014, www.youtube.com/watch?v=jLruCKin5tc. Accessed on 10 June 2021.

'Saanjhi: Part Two.' *YouTube*, 20 August 2014, https://www.youtube.com/watch?v=pRZKyVVYPXM. Accessed on 10 June 2021.

'Sahaja Yoga' in *Thirumoolar Thirumandiram*. Madras, 1998.

Sahayog Ranjit, 'दुर्गा माता को मूर्ति बनाउन सर्लाही देखि काठमाडौं सम्म, मूर्ति बनाएर मधेश र पहाड जोड्दै' https://bizmandu.com/content/20191005124249.html. Accessed on 10 June 2021.

Sanjeev Chowdhary, director. 'Sanjhi Mata Ki Arti सांझी माता की आरती। पश्चिमी उत्तर प्रदेश की संस्कृति.' *YouTube*, 23 September 2019, www.youtube.com/watch?v=BUTWI7sZqds. Accessed on 10 June 2021.

Sanjeev Chaudhary, 'Important Tharu Festivals', https://tharuculture.blogspot.com/2012/03/10-important-tharu-festivals.html. Accessed on 10 June 2021.

'Sanjhi: Almost Forgotten Festival of North India.' https://idyllicweb.com/2020/06/26/sanjhi-almost-forgotten-festival-of-north-india/. Accessed on 10 June 2021.

'Sanjhi Mata Aarti, Budhlada Punjab.' *YouTube*, 17 October 2020, www.youtube.com/watch?v=w9rbVBv7h8M. Accessed on 10 June 2021.

'SANJHI MATA KI KATHA सांझी माता की कथा। सांझी/संजा माता की कहानी सुनें.' *YouTube*, 15 October 2020, www.youtube.com/watch?v=agNe0xtx-SA. Accessed on 10 June 2021.

'Sanjhi Mata Ki Katha सांझी माता की कथा। संतान प्राप्ति, धन और इच्छित फल

पाने के लिए सुनें।' *YouTube*, 18 September 2019, www.youtube.com/watch?v=RROb8JQSkHk. Accessed on 10 June 2021.

'Sanjhi सांझी-कैसे बनाएं और कैसे मनाएं।' *YouTube*, 18 October 2020, www.youtube.com/watch?v=I6yGAZlETzw. Accessed on 10 June 2021.

Saryu Prasad Dwivedi and Dr Sudhakar Malviya, *Agam Rahasya*. Chaukhamba Sanskrit Series Office.

'Sharada Mahotsav in Mangalore-Youth of GSB.' *YouTube*, https://www.youtube.com/watch?v=4c1WC6VTtxs. Accessed on 10 June 2021.

Shri Adinath, *Shri Mahakal Samhita—Guhya Kali Khand*. Chaukhamba Surbaharati Prakashan, 2014.

Shri Swami Ji, *Lekh Sangrah*. Shri Pitambara Peeth Datia, 2014.

S. Kak, 'Brahmavidya: The Great Goddess Lalita and the Sri Cakra.' *The Adyar Library Bulletin*, 72–73, 155–172, 2008–2009.

S. Kak, *The Wonder That Was Kashmir*. Oklahoma State University, Stillwater, 2021.

S. Lakshmanjoo, *The Pancastavi*. Srinagar, 1987.

Surya Kiran, 'दशैं भर्सेज मोहिनी', *Annapurna Post*, 2018.

Various Writers, *Mahaparva Navaratra Visesank*. Kalyan Mandir, Prayagraj, 2009.

Veda Vyas (2070 Vik.), *Shrimad Devi Bhagavat*, Gita Press, Gorakhpur.

'Vidyarambham.' *Prokerala*, https://www.prokerala.com/festivals/vidyarambham.html. Accessed on 10 June 2021.

'Village Lifestyle of Punjab: Sanjhi Mata Di Aart—Durga Mata Pooja Pind Punjab De.' *YouTube*, 23 October 2020, www.youtube.com/watch?v=cBJ3g2fWgRQ. Accessed on 10 June 2021.

Vinayak Pandit and Kamalakant Tripathi, *Navaratra Pradeep*. Chaukahmba Surbharati Prakashan, 2017.

V.M.Pai, et al. *Srimad Bhagavatham*, 7 March 2020, srimad.org/?p=507. Accessed on 10 June 2021.

About the Contributors

Subhash Kak is Regents Professor at Oklahoma State University, Stillwater. Born in Srinagar, Kashmir he obtained his PhD from the Indian Institute of Technology, Delhi and he has taught in the United States since 1979. He has published 20 books that include his autobiography titled *The Circle of Memory* and *Matter and Mind*, a translation of Kanada's *Vaisesika Sutra*.

Bibek Debroy is an economist, but has also translated (and is translating) unabridged versions of *Itihasa-Purana* from the Sanskrit to English. Translations of *Valmiki Ramayana*, *Mahabharata*, *Bhagavat Gita*, *Hari Vamsha*, *Bhagavata Purana* and *Markandeya Purana* have been published. *Brahma Purana*, *Vishnu Purana* and *Shiva Purana* translations will be published in the course of 2021 and 2022.

Lakshmi Anand grew up in Africa in a very traditional Tamil family and spent many years in India and the US. After a BA in English and an MBA from Pennsylvania State University, she worked in finance. Now, she writes as a freelancer on classical music, culture, food and the world-at-large. Her articles have appeared in *The Hindu*, *Sruti*, *The Times of India*, *The Indian Express* and more. Her writing can be found on www.lakshmianand.com

Divya Prasad is a writer, storyteller, travel blogger, sacred geometric artist and energy healer. A traveller of life; curating tales on spirituality, culture, Indology, folk, travel, people and the indigenous. Over years of living in Himalayas, she has penned down tales on Shakti for her series 'Goddesses of Himalayas'. And her journey towards Devi goes on...

Jaya Rao Dayal attempted pursuing psychology for close to a decade. She uses her training in Bharatanatyam and her interest in Indian Aesthetics to review performances. She has submitted a dissertation on an eighth-century temple complex in Andhra Pradesh, to Jnanapravaha, Mumbai, as part of a post graduate program in Indian Aesthetics. She lives in Gurugram, India.

Rupa Joshi is a grandmother of four and mother of three, living in Kathmandu, Nepal, with her husband and his centenarian grandmother. She pursued her master's in journalism from the University of Southern California as a Fulbright scholar. She worked with the United Nations for over 20 years as communications officer, 15 of those with UNICEF Nepal, and took early retirement from UNICEF in 2018. Rupa writes frequently in local magazines and portals about environmental, social and cultural issues, and spends her spare time delving into her multifarious hobbies—trying out new recipes, stitching or knitting/crocheting garments and reading stories to children.

Nivedita Panda Ganapathi is a personal coach, spiritual seeker and self-awareness teacher. She earned her master's in law from Harvard University and a master's in high tech law from Santa Clara University. She is passionate about learning the symbolism behind ancient Hindu philosophy, mythology and rituals and teaching its relevance from a modern lens. Nivedita has presented on her work at Stanford and UC Santa Cruz, and has taught Conscious Leadership programs at Oracle and LinkedIn. She holds spiritual workshops and gives talks on demystifying Hinduism.

Giriratna Mishra, born in Varanasi to Smt. Padma Mishra and Shri Raghavendra Mishra, is Grihastha Sadhak and an Indologist. He started his career in the IT&C sector. He practises under the guidance of masters like Avadhoot Bhagwan Ram Ji and Shri Swami Ji Maharaj of Datia, and has written books in the field of

ABOUT THE CONTRIBUTORS ॐ 229

Tantra, such as *Hatharattnavali* (2020), *Shri Tantraloka Vol. 1* (2018), *Shri Matrikacakra Viveka* (2016) and *Shri Uddish Tantra* (2015), among others.

Ramachandra Murthy Kondubhatla has master's in political science, PhD in journalism and was editor of the Telugu dailies *Udayam*, *Vaartha*, *Andhra Jyothy* and *Sakshi*, of the English daily *Hans India* and of HMTV news channel. He has worked in Delhi, Bengaluru, Vijayawada and Hyderabad, and until recently he was advisor on Public Policy to the Andhra Pradesh government. He has published a dozen books.

Anuradha Goyal studies the intersection of her three prime interests—business innovation, travel and books—by writing about them in books, blogs and columns. She is the founder of *IndiTales*, a leading bilingual travel media portal where she documents her global travels through written word, audio and video formats, with a focus on ancient India. She is also the author of *Lotus in The Stone: Sacred Geography in Eternal India* (2020), *Unusual Temples of India* (2020), *Bharat Ke Anokhe Mandir* (2020) and *The Mouse Charmers: Digital Pioneers of India* (2014), and translator of *Ayodhya Mahatmya* (2021) from the *Skanda Purana*.

Sajeesh Kumar N. is a career civil servant working with the Government of India. He has done his master's in public management from LKY School of Public Policy (NUS, Singapore) and Harvard Kennedy School (HKS). He was Lee Kuan Yew fellow at Harvard. He has co-authored many articles with Bibek Debroy on infrastructure and financing in leading dailies such as the *Economic Times*, *Financial Express* and *Mint*. He has also been a speaker at many domestic and international forums. His interest also lies in understanding Indian mythology and its relevance in the social context.

Pulak Trivedi is a well-known writer, currently serving as additional director of information, Government of Gujarat. A recipient of the Dr Bholabhai Patel Award, he is also a well-known motivational speaker and leading advisor, best known for his rapid-learning techniques. His well-acclaimed books—*Tunku ne Tach* (ટૂંકું ને ટચ) and *Sidhu ne Sat* (સીધું ને સટ)—have been published in Gujarati. His column 'Aatmnad' ("આત્મનાદ") in a leading daily newspaper is quite popular. He has edited more than 300 government and private publications while being the managing editor of the magazines, *Gujarat* in Gujarati, *The Gujarat* in English and *Gujarat Rojgar Samachar*. He has also been a guest faculty in the field of journalism at various renowned universities. His popular blog www.aatmnad.blogspot.com has over one lakh followers.

Manu Khajuria is a freelance writer/storyteller, activist from Jammu tracing her roots to Bumnal a small village in Bishnah Tehsil of Jammu. She is founder director of 'Voice of Dogras', a community organization which espouses the rights of the Jammu Region and aims to preserve and promote its unique history and cultural identity. She has presented many papers, curated seminars, and has also been a TV panelist on the legacy of the Dogras. She received the Maharaja Gulab Singh Memorial Annual Award 2019 and Web Wonder Women award 2019. She lives in London and is currently working on a book about Jammu.

Parthasarathi Mahanta is a police officer with an abiding interest in religious and spiritual matters. His devotion to Mahadev has taken him on many pilgrimages, many of them very tough ones, including the one to Kailash Mansarovar. He is a deeply spiritual person and among his many pursuits is the study and analysis of ancient Hindu religious texts. It is this knowledge and understanding that finds expression in the books *Kamakhya* and *Shiva* coauthored by him. Mahanta, a masters in Economics, is a poet of repute in Assamese

ABOUT THE CONTRIBUTORS 231

and editor of Assamese lifestyle magazine *Aaina*. He is also involved in cinema and conservation activities.

Radhika Prabhu earned her PhD in higher education administration from Penn State University and a master's of management studies from the University of Mumbai. She has worked in the media industry and has authored articles as a freelancer for national newspapers. Currently, she is working on a book set in modern and Portuguese Goa.

Diwakar Jhurani is a senior economic adviser at the Foreign, Commonwealth & Development Office, British High Commission, New Delhi. He has worked at the Economic Advisory Council to the Prime Minister of India (EAC-PM). He is a graduate of the Fletcher School of Law and Diplomacy at Tufts University and Pandit Deendayal Petroleum University. Diwakar has co-authored a book on India's policy reforms and has written book chapters, columns and op-eds for various publications.